John B. Cobb, Jr., is Ingraham P[...]
the School of Theology, Claremo[...]

Christopher Ives is Assistant Professor of
Theology at the University of Puget Sound.

The Emptying God

FAITH MEETS FAITH

An Orbis Series in Interreligious Dialogue

Paul F. Knitter, General Editor

In our contemporary world, the many religions and spiritualities stand in need of greater intercommunication and cooperation. More than ever before, they must speak to, learn from, and work with each other, in order to maintain their own identity and vitality and so to contribute to fashioning a better world.

FAITH MEETS FAITH seeks to promote interreligious dialogue by providing an open forum for the exchanges between and among followers of different religious paths. While the series wants to encourage creative and bold responses to the new questions of pluralism confronting religious persons today, it also recognizes the present plurality of perspectives concerning the methods and content of interreligious dialogue.

This series, therefore, does not want to endorse any one school of thought. By making available to both the scholarly community and the general public works that represent a variety of religious and methodological viewpoints, FAITH MEETS FAITH hopes to foster and focus the emerging encounter among the religions of the world.

Already published:

Toward a Universal Theology of Religion, Leonard Swidler, Editor
The Myth of Christian Uniqueness, John Hick and Paul F. Knitter, Editors
An Asian Theology of Liberation, Aloysius Pieris, S.J.
The Dialogical Imperative, David Lochhead
Love Meets Wisdom, Aloysius Pieris, S.J.
Many Paths, Eugene Hillman
The Silence of God, Raimundo Panikkar
The Challenge of the Scriptures, Groupe de Recherches
   Islamo-Chrétien
The Meaning of Christ, John P. Keenan
Hindu-Christian Dialogue, Harold Coward, Editor

FAITH MEETS FAITH SERIES

The Emptying God

A Buddhist-Jewish-Christian Conversation

Edited by
John B. Cobb, Jr., and Christopher Ives

ORBIS BOOKS

Maryknoll, New York 10545

BR
128
.B8
E578
1990

The Catholic Foreign Mission Society of America (Maryknoll) recruits and trains people for overseas missionary service. Through Orbis Books, Maryknoll aims to foster the international dialogue that is essential to mission. The books published, however, reflect the opinions of their authors and are not meant to represent the official position of the society.

Copyright © 1990 by Orbis Books
Published by Orbis Books, Maryknoll, New York 10545
Manuscript Editor: William E. Jerman

Library of Congress Cataloging-in-Publication Data

The Emptying God : a Buddhist-Jewish-Christian conversation / edited
   by John B. Cobb, Jr., and Christopher Ives.
      p.   cm. — (Faith meets faith series)
   Essays by Masao Abe, with responses by seven Jewish and Christian
writers.
   Includes bibliographical references.
   ISBN 0-88344-671-5. — ISBN 0-88344-670-7 (pbk.)
   1. Christianity and other religions — Buddhism.   2. Buddhism —
Relations — Christianity.   3. Judaism — Relations — Buddhism.
4. Buddhism — Relations — Judaism.   5. Sunyata.   6. Incarnation.
7. Holocaust (Christian theology)   8. Abe, Masao, 1915-   .
I. Cobb, John B., 1925   .   II. Ives, Christopher, 1954-   .   III. Abe, Masao,
1915-   .   IV. Series: Faith meets faith.
BR128.B8E578   1990
291.1'72 — dc20
                                                                    90-31442
                                                                    CIP

Contents

III
A REJOINDER

IV
MASAO ABE BIBLIOGRAPHY

Acknowledgments

The editors are grateful to Dr. Paul Knitter of Xavier University, Cincinnati, Ohio, who as general editor of the Orbis Faith Meets Faith Series took an interest in and supported this project from the start. *The Emptying God* is one of many projects he has promoted in the arena of interfaith dialogue.

This project also received support from the University of Puget Sound in the form of a typing grant during the final stages of preparation. At that time, Ms. Carol Avery typed major sections of the manuscript and offered valuable editorial suggestions.

A Note on Orthography

The problem of rendering non-Western systems of writing into Roman letters for English and other modern European languages is notoriously difficult. Joining many publishers who do not insert diacritical marks for words such as the Sanskrit *Śūnyatā*, this book also omits them.

Scholars and others who know languages such as Sanskrit, Pali, Arabic, or Japanese do not need the diacritical marks to identify words in their original written form. And persons who do not know these languages gain little from having the marks reproduced. We recognize that languages employing different orthographic systems have a richness and distinctiveness that are partially conveyed by the orthographics of diacritical marks. And while we do not wish to be part of flattening out the contours of our linguistically plural globe, the high cost of ensuring accuracy in using the diacritical remarks does not justify reproducing them here.

Preface

JOHN B. COBB, JR.

Beginning in the 1920s, dialectical theology or neo-orthodoxy brought to the Christian community a sense of excitement confirming the importance of the central ideas of the Christian tradition in the modern context. This mood continued through World War II and its immediate aftermath, but then it began to fade. The repetition of traditional doctrines and of the accents given them by dialectical theology or neo-orthodoxy still held center stage, but it ceased to elicit creative response.

In the mid-1960s excitement was renewed in theology but this time through radical criticism, by denial rather than by affirmation. Of course there were affirmations contained in the denials, but these tended to focus on what was felt to be different from traditional Christianity. The continued affirmation of central doctrines sounded somewhat hollow, and although important work was still being done by traditionalists, intellectual energy was to be found chiefly elsewhere.

The major exception to this redirection of attention has been found in interreligious dialogue. In conversation with those who see reality quite differently, elements of Christian tradition that had lost their interest through repetition came alive again. In general, dialogue partners wanted to deal with the mainstream of the tradition rather than with recent radical alternatives, rightly sensing that the great issues on which the traditions divide are to be found more clearly in this way. Often they saw the significance of traditional doctrines more clearly than those theologians who had adapted or softened them in the interest of credibility. And often adaptations that seemed to make Christian teaching more credible in the modern Western context appear in dialogue to remove it even further from the insights of those nurtured in other faiths.

In many ways the dialogue with Jews and the efforts to reformulate Christian teaching so that it will cease to generate anti-Jewish feelings, are the most important part of the interreligious development for Christians. The practical consequences of Christian teaching in this area over centuries of Christian history and culminating in the Holocaust are overwhelming. That discussion must go on.

But at other levels the dialogue with Buddhism has been equally important. Just because the practical problems are less acute, the theological discussion is freer. Christians can express their critical objections to the positions adopted by Buddhists without special fear that this will be heard as justification for continuing prejudice and persecution. Christians can also hear Buddhist criticisms of Christianity as challenges to our deepest beliefs based not on how these beliefs affect Buddhists politically but on the Buddhist perception that they are intellectually indefensible or spiritually limiting. There is danger, of course, from a Christian point of view, that the results may be too far removed from the political sphere, even the sphere of church politics. But in a context in which a primary danger is anti-intellectualism, the possibility of engaging in high-level discussion of the most fundamental assumptions of one's tradition and personal faith is refreshing and healing, and in the long run it cannot fail to have political implications as well.

In general the quest for dialogue with other religious traditions has come from the Christian side. Its motivations have been mixed. Sometimes the suspicion that it is an indirect effort at proselytizing have been warranted. Sometimes it has been in the interest of forging alliances to advance common causes. More often it has sprung from a hunger to understand and learn as well as to explain oneself in open discussion. On the whole, representatives of other traditions do not feel these needs as keenly, so that although they often respond to the Christian invitation, they rarely initiate the dialogue.

There are, however, exceptions. Some of the new religious movements in Japan aggressively promote interreligious dialogue and cooperation. The Unification Church, stemming from Korea, seeks to move toward religious and cultural understanding and unity through dialogue. But these movements do not touch the deep nerves of Christians as do the great traditional religions. And among them the relative passivity remains dominant.

Nevertheless, there are exceptions there, too. Of these one of the most important has been the Buddhism associated with the Kyoto School. D. T. Suzuki took as his vocation an evangelistic and dialogue mission to the West, especially to the United States. In the past few decades, Masao Abe has continued and deepened that work.

In 1963 Abe published an article on Buddhism and Christianity in *Japanese Religions* and solicited Western responses. These were published and Abe replied. A quarter of a century later he is repeating this process. The years between have been filled with vigorous and generally successful efforts on his part to communicate his perceptions to Christian theologians in a way that evokes serious attention to the Buddhist message.

The Kyoto School as a whole has represented a style of Buddhist thought deeply informed by the study of Western philosophy. More than any other member of this school, Abe has added to this a study of Christian theology. When he speaks of Christian teaching it is out of serious engagement with its classical and modern forms. Often he is able to instruct his Christian dialogue partners about the meaning of our own heritage. This adds a dimension to the dialogue that has been rare in the past.

Christians have been engaged in dialogue on many fronts. There is a tendency for the dialogues on these diverse fronts to bring to the fore different aspects of Christian faith. For example, the dialogue with Jews heightens sensitivity to the kinds of claims made for Jesus and for the New Testament, whereas dialogue with Buddhists often focuses on the nature of ultimate reality and the deepest religious experience. There is danger that in the process of one dialogue what is learned in another be forgotten. For example, while talking with Buddhists, Christians often lack sensitivity to the implications of what they are saying with regard to the problem of anti-Judaism. Indeed, there is danger that Judaism (and perhaps Hinduism as well) be pejoratively treated as Christians and Buddhists engage one another.

For this reason, we can be particularly glad that Abe has recently begun to extend his efforts at dialogue toward Jews. This has given an opening for including a Jewish voice in this volume. A Jewish presence will check the all-too-easy forgetfulness of Christians. It will also enrich the Buddhist conversation partners. We hope that in continuing dialogues the Jewish presence will grow.

Part of the strength of Abe's approach to Christianity is his uncompromising rejection of theism. Other members of the Kyoto School have used the word God in a positive sense. Abe has seen that this softens the challenge to Christianity in a misleading way. Furthermore, Abe himself grew up in a quasi-theistic form of Buddhism and was converted away from that to what he is convinced is the true and pure form. Hence he understands theism from within and hopes to liberate from it those who are still attached to it. The contrast with the biblical faiths thus becomes stark. The too-easy solution to our differences of identifying the true God with *Dharmakaya* or *Sunyata*, thus reaffirming a common referent beyond the differences, becomes much more difficult when confronted with the rigor and clarity of Abe's formulations.

This is one of the elements of Abe's thought that renders him a particularly effective teacher of Christians. He hammers home a few central features of the Buddhist vision with vivid images and strong negations—to say nothing of the characteristic negation of negations. His position, or his "positionless position," comes through with stark force, rendering problematic all the ideas and tools with which Christians are accustomed to work.

Dialogue does not always bring the discussants closer together. The reader of this volume will find that the Christian and Jewish participants are often quite sharp in our disagreement with Abe and even our disapproval of his position. This is itself healthy. Arguments between Christians and Buddhists have become as frank and blunt as those within the two communities have long been. We are becoming one community of discourse. To this achievement, no one has contributed more than Masao Abe. Readers of this book are invited to listen in on the current stage of the discussion.

Introduction

CHRISTOPHER IVES

Since the death of D.T. Suzuki in 1966, Masao Abe has served as the main representative of Zen Buddhism in Europe and North America. Through his teaching, writings, and participation in conferences, he has conveyed to a wide audience the worldview of Zen and the philosophy of the Kyoto School.[1] His expression of Buddhism has proved especially valuable for those involved in interreligious dialogue. We can best understand his unique role in this dialogue by considering his philosophical development and professional career up to the present.

The third of six children, Abe was born in 1915. His father was a doctor in Osaka, the major commercial center of western Japan. His mother was a devoted follower of Pure Land Shin Buddhism, the sect to which his family belonged. According to Abe, the family, with the exception of his mother, was not especially religious.

While in high school Abe begin to wrestle with issues in philosophy and religion. As he once said, "I came to realize that while I was living my life I was unconsciously hurting others' lives." Facing this dilemma, he experienced anguish for the first time. Eventually he turned to Shinran's *Tannisho*[2] for a solution to his dilemma. Impacted greatly by what he read, he began to study and practice Pure Land Shin Buddhism, which emphasizes a type of "sinfulness" and the impossibility of religious liberation through one's own efforts. More specifically, he started seeking to realize pure faith in the unconditional mercy and absolute "other power" of Amida.

After graduating from high school Abe entered Osaka Commercial University to study Economics and Law. While in college he continued to struggle with his dilemma. He spent more time studying Buddhism on his own and working for a Buddhist association—Ashiya Bukkyo Kaikan—than focusing on his major areas of study. Though he recognized the value of faith in Amida, he could not overcome his intellect, which stood in his way as a colossal barrier to embracing faith. In his words, "While I was keenly feeling my own sinfulness, I could not give up my reasoning power."

As graduation approached, Abe longed to enter Kyoto University, for he was convinced that he could solve his personal dilemma through the study of philosophy and Buddhism. Due to family circumstances, however, such study proved impossible. With his problem still unresolved, he started working for a company in Kobe. Over time, the more he attempted to devote himself to business, the more empty it felt. And the more this sense of emptiness deepened, the more urgent the desire to solve his dilemma became.

Although this inner problem pressed upon him, family circumstances still did not allow him to change course. Moreover, this process was unfolding in the 1930s, a time of tension in Japan: the country was at war with China and relations with the United States were steadily worsening. Through it all, his problem would not go away.

Several months before the Japanese attack on Pearl Harbor, Abe finally decided to jettison his career in business and enter Kyoto University to study Western philosophy. This was a radical move for a man of twenty-six in Japan at the time. Looking back on his decision he has said:

> To do this I was forced to abandon almost everything I had acquired, privately and publicly, because I was reproached for breaking family solidarity and for being an unpatriotic person who began to study philosophy in the midst of national crisis despite his ability to contribute to the nation.

Abe risked everything on this move because he felt he had no other choice than to confront his intellect—the barrier to faith—by pushing his rationality to the breaking point through intensive study of philosophy. He was convinced that this was the way to overcome the intellect and attain pure faith in Amida. It was thus out of desperate existential concern, not mere intellectual interest, that he began his formal study of philosophy and religion.

In the faculty of letters at Kyoto University Abe studied Western philosophy under Hajime Tanabe.[3] He took a keen interest in Plato, Augustine, Hegel, and Kierkegaard and felt drawn especially to Kant and his moral philosophy. What was most significant for him at Kyoto University, however, was his encounter with Shin'ichi Hisamatsu.[4]

Abe met Hisamatsu for the first time soon after he entered Kyoto University. He sensed immediately that Hisamatsu embodied a special sort of truth. He explained his predicament and his Pure Land approach to it, only to have Hisamatsu maintain from his Zen perspective that ultimately the realization of sinfulness is an illusion and the absolute "other power" of Amida is something to be overcome. Though deeply impressed by Hisamatsu's personality, Abe could not accept Hisamatsu's negative view of Pure Land faith, for to accept it would be to see as meaningless his critical decision to quit his job in order to study philosophy, thwart the intellect, and attain pure faith in Amida. This led Abe to what he has called an ongoing "battle" with him that extended outside the classroom and beyond graduation. Throughout this "battle" he tried to defend his Pure Land faith from Hisamatsu's severe criticism, and this forced him to deepen his faith.

While engaged in this "battle," Abe worked with Professor Hisamatsu and other students—many of whom are now professors and Zen masters in Kyoto—to revitalize the Buddhist Youth Organization at Kyoto University. They started a lay organization, "Gakudo-Dojo" (Place for the Study of the Way), for Zen meditation and study. (Later, after several developmental stages, the F.A.S. Society[5] emerged.)

Through his study of Buddhism and interaction with Hisamatsu in the "Gakudo-Dojo" organization, Pure Land faith opened up in him as a gift from Amida. When Hisamatsu heard about this conversion he celebrated it, and from then he never criticized Abe. Having gone through this change, Abe now believed he could "embrace" any person with his Pure Land faith, however different the person might be.

Gradually, however, he came to realize that there was one person he could not embrace with his faith: Shin'ichi Hisamatsu. Present there before him, Hisamatsu's silent existence posed a serious challenge to his faith, for it became increasingly clear to him that the truth embodied by Hisamatsu was essentially different from the truth found in Pure Land faith. Abe struggled to determine which was more authentic—the truth of Zen awakening embodied by Hisamatsu or the truth of Pure Land faith realized in himself. Confronting this question, he resumed his "battle" with Hisamatsu.

For several years the "battle" continued. Finally, during a winter retreat of the F.A.S. Society, Abe's Pure Land faith crumbled away. He realized that even the truth found in Pure Land faith was false, as was everything in this world and in the transcendent realm he had believed in to that point. This discernment of absolute falsehood came to him through the painful realization that even Amida and his unconditional mercy are sacred fictions. With this realization Abe found a close affinity with Nietzsche, who once declared, "God is a holy lie."

Nietzsche's positive nihilism provided Abe with a perspective from which he could see Hisamatsu's Zen differently than he had from his earlier Pure Land perspective. Yet as he gradually began to understand Hisamatsu's talk of "Absolute Nothingness" and the "Formless Self as the True Self," he became dissatisfied with Nietzsche. This plunged Abe into an inner struggle with Nietzsche's positive nihilism and Hisamatsu's Absolute Nothingness,[6] and it was from this, according to Abe, that he awakened to the "True Self" that is entirely without form and cannot be objectified. To him, this "Self" is truly formless and unobjectifiable because it is beyond any personal deity like Amida and any positive nihility in Nietzsche's sense.

Through his confrontation with Hisamatsu over the years, Abe came to regard him as a true teacher. For this reason, Hisamatsu's importance in Abe's work cannot be overestimated. In Abe's own words, "To me, Professor Hisamatsu is not only a lifelong teacher but also a life-changing and life-giving teacher. Without him I am not what I am."

Hisamatsu is not, however, the only influence on Abe's life and thought. Although he received the "bones" or basic structure of his standpoint from Hisamatsu, he received the "flesh and blood" from another teacher, Keiji Nishitani. He values Nishitani's philosophy as "rich and vivid" in nurturing his understanding of Buddhism and Western thought. Abe also refers to Kitaro Nishida as an indirect teacher, a grandfather of sorts, for Hisamatsu and Nishitani studied under him at Kyoto University and his philosophy of Absolute Nothingness and logic of place (*basho*) have exerted a strong influence on Abe's own thought. In addition, he regards D.T. Suzuki as a "grand uncle" whose personality and way of thinking impacted him greatly during the last twelve years of Suzuki's life, when Abe maintained a close personal acquaintance with him.

Abe added to his graduate studies of religion and philosophy in the 1950s. Though Japan was still struggling to recover from the devastation of World War II, he went to New York in 1955. At Columbia University he studied philosophy and assisted D.T. Suzuki, who was lecturing there at the time. He also studied Christian theology with Paul Tillich and Reinhold Niebuhr at nearby Union Theological Seminary.

Abe spent two years in New York, and his studies there had a great impact on his development. At Columbia his association with D.T. Suzuki became quite close. Because of his time at Union, much of his dialogue with Christianity has focused on Tillich, as evidenced by the title of one chapter in his recent book, *Zen and Western Thought*, "Tillich from a Buddhist Point of View." He has also participated in activities of the Tillich Society; at the 1988 annual meeting of the society he delivered a lecture, "A Buddhist View of 'The Significance of the History of Religions for the Systematic Theologian,'" which will be published in the *Journal of Religion*. Moreover, Niebuhr and his Christian realism played a role in stimulating Abe's interests in social issues. And in more general terms, Abe's time at Columbia and Union set the stage for over three decades of involvement in interfaith dialogue.

Abe's varied educational experiences in Japan and New York have borne fruit in his teaching. He began his teaching career at Kyoto Women's College (1946–48) and Otani University (1948–50). He then took a position at Nara University of Education (1952–80), which was his main affiliation throughout his professional career. During his tenure there he also taught at Kyoto University (1955–58) and Hanazono University (1964–80). His successes as a teacher have also extended to numerous institutions outside Japan. He taught at the Claremont Graduate School and the School of Theology at Claremont in the fall 1965 semester and at Columbia University the following semester. He took positions at the University of Chicago (spring 1969), Redlands University (January 1973), Carleton College (spring 1974), Claremont Graduate School and the School of Theology at Claremont (fall 1976), and Princeton University (fall 1977–spring 1979). In 1980 Abe moved to the United States to devote himself more intensively to what he calls "the East-West encounter," especially Buddhist-Christian dialogue. Once again he joined the faculty of the Claremont Graduate School and the School of Theology at Claremont (spring 1980–spring 1983). From there he moved to the University of Hawaii (fall 1983–spring 1985), Haverford College (fall 1985–spring 1987), University of Chicago Divinity School (fall 1987), and the Pacific School of Religion in Berkeley (spring 1988 and from fall 1989 to the present).

Throughout his teaching career Abe has participated in numerous conferences and organizations in North America and Europe. Although a mere listing of these conferences would encompass several pages, two of the more important arenas have been the ongoing East-West Philosophers' Conferences at the University of Hawaii and the North American Buddhist-Christian Theological Encounter, which he has been directing with John B. Cobb, Jr. As a further facet of his work in international academic circles, Abe has served as vice president of the executive board of the International Association for the History of Religions (1975–80) and as director of the International Society of Metaphysics (since 1973).

In addition to his teaching and participation in conferences, Abe has exerted a major impact through his writings. He has written extensively on Zen Buddhism, especially Dogen, the founder of Soto Zen in Japan and to many the greatest thinker in the history of Japanese Buddhism. He has authored a variety of articles on other facets of Buddhism and the philosophy of Kitaro Nishida. Much of his writing has been in dialogue with Western philosophy and religion, as reflected in his numerous articles on Kant, Kierkegaard, Marx, Nietzsche, Whitehead, Jung, Tillich, Heidegger, and others. In 1985 Abe published a collection of his articles in a book entitled *Zen and Western Thought*, which earned him an award from the American Academy of Religion in 1987 as the best recent work in the "constructive and reflective" field.

The essay in this present work, "Kenotic God and Dynamic Sunyata," has already contributed significantly to interfaith dialogue in numerous settings. It is one of a long line of essays Abe has written in the context of dialogue, each of which is academically oriented yet based on his personal existential struggle with Zen and Pure Land faith. As indicated by John Cobb in his Preface, certainly the first key essay in this line is "Buddhism and Christianity as a Problem of Today," published in *Japanese Religions* [vol. 3, nos. 3–4 (1963)].[7]

Abe's efforts in his studies, teaching, writing, and conference participation have not gone unnoticed. In recognition of his far-reaching academic achievements, Abe was decorated by the Japanese government in 1988.

Simply mentioning his teaching positions, publications, and awards, however, does not do justice to the way Abe has strived throughout his life to promote genuine understanding of Buddhism. Rooted in his own anguish and religious practice, he expresses the tradition from within. As a scholar based not only in the texts and philosophy of Buddhism but also in its spirit, he is especially well equipped to express the Buddhist standpoint, with its empirical orientation and its grounding in a type of religious experience that calls mere intellectual understanding into question. In short, he embodies what his teacher Hisamatsu called the "unity of study and practice," and it is this "living" approach that has impressed those who have met him or read his writings.

Although Abe sees his work in the West as a type of life vocation, a continuation of the efforts of D.T. Suzuki (albeit with more training in Christian theology and a more philosophical approach), Abe's goal is not simply to convey Buddhism and Japanese philosophy to others. He directs his efforts primarily toward the emergence of a unified world. The media, international trade, and cross-cultural exchange are currently linking people to an unprecedented degree and thereby calling into question the nation-state as a form of political organization.[8] But these linkages do not constitute a sufficient foundation for a peaceful, creative, and harmonious global community. To Abe, the world now requires a spiritual foundation — not a single global religion but a depth of spirituality from which all religious traditions can emerge anew as mutually supportive facets of cultural diversity in the context of a global community. It is toward this goal of opening up a new spiritual horizon that Abe has directed his efforts throughout his life.

NOTES

1. Founded by the foremost philosopher of modern Japan, Kitaro Nishida (1878–1945), the Kyoto School sets forth Mahayana Buddhist thought in dialogue with Western philosophy and religion.

2. The *Tannisho* (Statements Deploring Deviations from Faith) is a collection of talks by Shinran (1173–1262), compiled by his disciple Yuien after Shinran's death.

3. Hajime Tanabe (1885–1962) is the successor of Kitaro Nishida and the second leading philosopher in the Kyoto School.

4. For an introduction to Shin'ichi Hisamatsu (1889–1980), see his book, *Zen and the Fine Arts* (Kodansha International, 1975) and Masao Abe, "Hisamatsu's Philosophy of Awakening" and "Hisamatsu Shin'ichi, 1889–1980," *The Eastern Buddhist*, vol. 14, no. 1.

5. The F.A.S. Society is a lay study/practice group based to a large extent on Hisamatsu's critique of traditional Zen and his formulation of a new type of Zen that links religious practice with issues in human society and history, especially in the contemporary situation of humankind. This acronym, F.A.S., represents the central focus of Hisamatsu's standpoint and the Society:

> To awaken to the Formless Self,
> stand in the standpoint of all humankind,
> and create history supra-historically.

Through his leadership in this group over the years, Abe has influenced many, including foreign students of Buddhism living in Kyoto.

6. This inner struggle finds expression in Abe's essay, "Zen and Nietzsche," in *Zen and Western Thought* (London: Macmillan, 1985), pp. 135–51.

7. This essay and the responses it prompted from a variety of major theologians and philosophers will be published by the State University of New York Press in a book entitled *Searching for Common Ground: Buddhism and Christianity Challenged by Irreligion.*

8. See Abe's article, "Sovereignty Rests with Mankind," in *Zen and Western Thought*, pp. 249–60.

PART I

Kenotic God
and
Dynamic Sunyata

Kenotic God and Dynamic Sunyata

MASAO ABE

INTRODUCTION

Interfaith Dialogue and Antireligious Ideologies

Over the past few decades the dialogue between Buddhism and Christianity has evolved considerably. It has gone beyond the stage of promoting mutual understanding between the two religions, and is now entering a new stage in which the mutual transformation of Buddhism and Christianity is being seriously explored.[1] This development concerns not only theology or doctrinal understanding but also spirituality. This tendency, I hope, will continue to accelerate in the future.

The dialogue between Buddhism and Christianity should not, however, be regarded simply as an interfaith dialogue, for it must be engaged in with awareness of a wider socio-historical context. In particular, while interfaith dialogue presupposes the validity and significance of religion, many persons in our present secularized world do not. They ask, "Why is religion necessary?" and "What meaning does religion have for us today?" They think they can live without religion and thus are quite skeptical about or indifferent to religion. Moreover, ideologies that negate religion prevail in our society. Scientism, Marxism, traditional Freudian psychoanalytic thought, and nihilism in the Nietzschean sense all deny the raison d'être of religion, not merely on emotional grounds but on various rational or theoretical grounds. Not stopping with criticism of particular religions, these ideologies negate the very being of religion itself.

The most crucial task of any religion in our time is to respond to these antireligious forces by elucidating the authentic meaning of religious faith. This is why, as early as 1963, in a paper entitled "Buddhism and Christianity as a Problem of Today," I emphasized:

Apart from the context of the issue between religion and irreligion there wouldn't be much sense in taking up the problem of Buddhism

3

and Christianity. If a discussion of the theme should not throw any light on our search for the being of religion itself which can overpower all negation, then it would be indeed futile to engage in it. It is precisely at the meeting point of the two problems, namely, the interreligious problem of Buddhism and Christianity on the one hand, and the problem of religion and irreligion on the other, that the most serious question for modern man, the question of his self-estrangement should be asked; and it is precisely there that we may expect to find an answer to it.[2]

The necessity of considering Buddhist-Christian dialogue not merely as interfaith dialogue but as an inseparable part of the wider, socio-cultural problem of religion versus irreligion has become increasingly evident in the past few decades. To use the terminology of Thomas S. Kuhn and Hans Küng, both Buddhism and Christianity are now facing "a transitional period of uncertainty" or "crisis" in which continuous "organic development" or the usual cumulative process of "normal science" is no longer appropriate.[3] Both religions must fundamentally transform themselves such that their prevailing basic assumptions are drastically changed and a new paradigm or model of understanding can emerge. This might involve a revolutionary reinterpretation of the concept of God in Christianity and the concept of emptiness in Buddhism.

Insofar as Buddhist-Christian dialogue is undertaken as an interfaith dialogue in which the validity and significance of religion are taken for granted, it will fail to reach the core of the present crisis all religions are now facing, and will not lead to a much-needed search for a new paradigm. Only when Buddhist-Christian dialogue is pursued with an appreciation of the wider context of the contemporary confrontation of religion and irreligion will it be able to open up a deeper religious dimension in which Buddhist and Christian truth can be fully realized in a new paradigm beyond the religion-negating principles of scientism, Marxism, traditional Freudian psychoanalytic thought, and nihilism in the Nietzschean sense.

Scientism and Religion

In this paper I will confine my discussion of religion-negating ideologies to only scientism and nihilism in the Nietzschean sense.[4]

We should not confuse the basis of science with the basis of scientism. The standpoint of science does not necessarily contradict that of religion. Of course, science and religion exhibit points of essential difference, but they do not always mutually exclude each other, and are at least potentially compatible. The standpoint of scientism, however, can never be compatible with that of religion. By making the standpoint of science absolute, scientism claims that the "scientific" method constitutes the *one* and *only* criterion of truth. Anything nonscientific is false. Religion, being nonscientific, is thus considered false. Because science has made remarkable advances in modern times and scientific laws are subject to widely accepted forms of experimental demonstration, scientific truth has impressed many as the absolute truth, even though it is only one kind of truth. Although eminent scientists rarely espouse scientism, there are many scientists and nonscientists who judge everything in a scientistic way. And if "scientific" truth is taken as the only criterion of truth, the dismissal of religion inevitably follows.

Proponents of scientism maintain that religion still exists today only because the scientific way of thinking has not yet sufficiently permeated the masses. Scientism believes that religion will naturally disappear once science has progressed to the extent that the scientific way of thinking is embraced by all. For scientism, the continued existence of religion has nothing to do with the nature or essence of religion but merely reflects slowness in an inevitable demise in history. Thus, religion is dismissed in principle by scientism.

Given this situation, we must ask the question, "What is the 'scientific' method?" Classical physics was based on mathematical rationality and viewed humans and nature mechanistically. In contrast to this view, contemporary physics, with Einstein's theory of relativity and Heisenberg's uncertainty principle, does not consider its method and perceived truth absolute. As Hans Küng expresses it:

> Hence today, in physics, chemistry, biology and other natural sciences, it is customary to speak not of universally valid truths copying reality but of hypothetically valid "projects" and "patterns" that hold only in virtue of certain conditions and within certain limits, while fully permitting the coexistence of other projects and patterns.... An absolutely objective truth is not envisaged but only one that is relatively objective. In perspectivity and variability, any number of methods and aspects, projects and patterns, are possible in regard to the one reality, which itself always remains infinitely richer and more complex than all the statements—even the most exact—about it.[5]

The mechanistic and strictly objective view of nature in classical physics has been jettisoned by contemporary physics with its relativistic and more process-oriented paradigm of nature. Consequently, the "scientific" way of thinking and the "scientific" picture of the world now are certainly less mechanical and consequently less incompatible with religion than earlier in the history of modern science.

This does not mean, however, that contemporary science no longer challenges religion. However relativistic the contemporary scientific view may be, if its perspective is dogmatized, or is taken ideologically, it turns into a form of scientism. In this regard, I agree with Hans Küng when he says,

The idea of critical rationality must be entirely approved; but the ideology of a critical rationalism, absolutizing and mysticizing the rational factor, must be rejected. ... Rationalistic ideology is characterized by rationalistic dogmatism and rationalistic intolerance.[6]

Hans Küng also reminds us that in the sixteenth and seventeenth centuries, because of their failure to become allies with the new science and new philosophical and social-political development, Christian theology and the church contributed substantially to the rise of both scientific and political atheism. But Küng insists,

There was, however, no necessity in principle for autonomous reason, for modern natural science, increasingly so, to generalize their conclusions as to leave no place for a belief in God and in practice largely to substitute belief in science for belief in God.[7]

While I have no real objection to this statement, I am tempted to ask how belief in God can embrace autonomous reason without marring it. It is clear that, as Küng emphasizes, "the God of the Bible is not identical with the God of the ancient world picture or with the God of Greek philosophy."[8] God in the Bible is "one who faces me, whom I can address,"[9] and is "subject and not predicate: it is not that love is God, but that God is love."[10] Precisely in this sense, God in the Bible is "a thou who may be called person and personal or even suprapersonal and transpersonal."[11] If, as Küng rightly suggests, we must entirely approve the idea of critical rationality and autonomous reason,[12] what is the ground on which critical rationality, autonomous reason, and God as thou, are not only compatible but also work positively together without detracting from one another? To this serious challenge of contemporary science, Christianity must respond.

This challenge of modern science is much less serious for Buddhism, because its basis is not faith in a God who faces us and can be addressed as a thou, but awakening to the Dharma (truth) that is termed "suchness" or "emptiness." Even Pure Land Buddhism, which, like Christianity, emphasizes faith (though in Amida Buddha), takes suchness or emptiness as the basic Reality (*Dharmakaya*). Nevertheless, Buddhism must still address the issue of how the Buddhist notion of suchness or emptiness can embrace critical rationality while still allowing reason to function autonomously. An important task for contemporary Buddhist thinkers is to demonstrate the religious significance of Buddhist truth in relation to scientific truth.

Nihilism in the Nietzschean Sense and Religion[13]

The problem of nihilism *for us today* is neither an emotional problem masquerading as an intellectual one, nor a recurrence of the age-old issue of nihilistic feeling found in both the East and the West. Since the writings of Friedreich Nietzsche, nihilism is no longer an emotional and timeless theme universally seen in human history; it has become an acute issue that, through a discerning historical awareness of human destiny, demands the modern person to rethink the foundation of cultural and religious life. Indeed, Nietzsche's nihilism is an existential realization clearly based on a philosophy of history. This is, I understand, why Heidegger says, "Nietzsche thinks of nihilism as the 'inner logics' of occidental history."[14] Elucidating Nietzsche's phrase, "God is dead," Heidegger says, "The names of God and Christian God in Nietzsche's thought are used as the designation for the supersensible world in general,"[15] and "the phrase 'God is dead' means: the supersensible world is without active power. It dispenses no life."[16] Nietzsche's nihilism is an acute realization, through the history of European nations, that "the highest values are 'depreciated' (*sich entwerten*),[17] entirely deprived of meaning," the highest values here meaning the supersensible world established by Platonism and Christianity.

In his book *Beyond Good and Evil*, Nietzsche presents his unique idea of the three stages of human history:

> Once on a time men sacrificed human beings to their God, and per-
> haps just those they loved the best . . . Then, during the moral epoch
> of mankind, they sacrificed to their God the strongest instincts they
> possessed, their "nature"; *this* festal joy shines in the cruel glances of
> ascetics and "anti-natural" fanatics. Finally, what still remained to be
> sacrificed? . . . Was it not necessary to sacrifice God himself . . . ? To
> sacrifice God for nothingness—this paradoxical mystery of the ulti-
> mate cruelty has been reserved for the rising generation; we all know
> something thereof already.[18]

To the first stage of human history Nietzsche ascribes the sacrifice of all primitive religions and also the sacrifice of the Emperor Tiberius in the Mithra Grotto on the Island of Capri. It may be said that this first stage corresponds to the time of the Old Testament which relates the stories of this kind of sacrifice in such cases as Abraham and Isaac. The second stage of human history indicates the time of the New Testament and the Christian era following it, in which the death and sacrifice of Jesus has been seen as the redemption of original sin inherent in human nature. The third historic stage, in which one does "sacrifice God for nothingness," indicates nihilism in Nietzsche's sense.

Here we see how deeply and uniquely Nietzsche's nihilism is rooted in a historical awareness of human destiny. It is noteworthy, however, that Nietzsche regards Christian morality, at least hitherto, as a "support" that preserves the integrity of human existence and as a "great antidote"[19] for nihilism. For Christian morality, in Nietzsche's view, gave humans an abso-lute value to counteract the meaninglessness of life, and served as an advocate for God against suffering and evil in the world. Thus, for Nietzsche, Christianity (as well as metaphysics) has had biological utility in the sense that it was an invention useful for the preservation of human beings, an invention of the instinct for self-preservation inherent in us. Yet Nietzsche believed that in Christianity (and metaphysics) there was a latent fiction, indispensable to human life, which "deceives oneself in an effective way."[20] According to Nietzsche, though, the time when Christianity (and metaphysics) could have utility for human beings has ended. This implies the arrival of the third stage, in which one should "sacrifice God for nothingness." Upon realizing that faith in God is an unconscious fiction invented by the more basic will that is the "will to power," is it not being honest to one's life to return consciously to and ground oneself in the "will to power" as such? Nietzsche thus declares "God is dead" and thereby announces the advent of nihilism, in which one ought to endure meaninglessness—without God.

In this connection, we need to distinguish two forms of nihilism, "nihilism before religion" and "nihilism beyond religion."[21] Nihilism is often understood as a standpoint from which one recognizes the meaninglessness of human life, while denying everything, including the existence of God. It is in this naive nihilistic perception, and not through and after one's God-experience, that one opts for nihilism and insists "there is no God." This form of nihilism I call "nihilism before religion," for it is a realization of the meaninglessness of life before definitive religious experience, and it therefore may be overcome by religion when one comes to have a genuine religious experience. This "nihilism before religion" is found universally in human history and recurs as a theme in both Eastern and Western thought.

Though equally godless, Nietzsche's nihilism declares "God is dead" rather than "God is not." The statement, "God is dead," can be uttered only by those for whom God *was alive*—that is, by those who have lived religion. Nietzsche came to advocate nihilism through the clear realization of the "depreciation" (*Unwertung*) of the traditional religious values of the past, including those of Christianity. For him, nihilism is a realization of the nothingness or meaninglessness of human life, not before, but through and after, religion. Accordingly, his nihilism cannot be overcome by religion, at least in its traditional form. In this sense, I would call Nietzsche's nihilism "nihilism beyond religion," in contrast to "nihilism before religion."

Unlike "nihilism before religion," which simply maintains "God is not," Nietzsche's nihilism, declaring "God is dead," challenges the core of traditional religion. He negates religion not simply from the outside, but from within. This is why in my paper, "Buddhism and Christianity as a Problem of Today," I stated:

Nihilism, though it may not yet be a conspicuous historic power [as scientism and Marxism], should be regarded as a sharp dagger pointed at the very heart of religion, because it radically negates religion, threatening to destroy it in its innermost core.[22]

Although Nietzsche criticizes Christianity exclusively, all religions, including Buddhism, lie vulnerable to his attack. Now that Nietzsche's nihilism is so influential, it is perhaps meaningless for us, without confronting his nihilism, to speak of a religion as something self-evident—as a "religion." All religions, then, must now examine whether or not Nietzsche's nihilism is really "nihilism *beyond* religion," and assume the burden of demonstrating, practically and theoretically, the raison d'être of religion.

The problem of scientism and nihilism are thus a serious challenge to all religions today: we should not avoid the confrontation. To become truly significant and creative, inter-faith dialogue between Buddhism and Christianity must be set against the background of these two issues. Bearing this in mind, let me propose how Buddhism and Christianity can overcome these issues. And at the same time, let me also propose how the two religions can respectively open up a deeper religious dimension in which they can collectively share a much greater religiousness.

KENOTIC GOD

The Kenosis of Christ

As a starting point for exploring Christianity, I should like to quote the following passage of Paul from the Epistle to the Philippians:

> Have this mind in you, which was also in Christ Jesus, who, existing in the form of God, counted not the being on an equality with God ₎ a thing to be grasped, but emptied himself, taking the form of a servant, being made in the likeness of man; and being found in fashion as a man, he humbled himself, becoming obedient *even* unto death, yea, the death of the cross.[23]

To me, this is one of the most impressive and touching passages in the Bible.

I feel this way for two reasons. First, although Christ existed in the form of God—that is, was of the same divine nature as God—he refused to dwell in the glory which belonged to God: instead he abdicated his divine rank and assumed the form of a servant. Thus, while in the form of God, Christ emptied himself.[24] Further, according to the scripture, "he humbled himself, becoming obedient *even* unto death, yea, the death of the cross." This is a complete abnegation of Christ as the Son of God.

Second, this abnegation of Christ indicates the self-sacrificial love of Christ for humankind disobedient to and rebellious against the will of God. Through the incarnation (kenosis), death, and resurrection of the Son of

God, Christ, God reveals Godself in terms of unconditional love beyond discriminatory justice. The unfathomable depth of God's love is clearly realized when we come to know and believe that Christ as the Son of God emptied himself and became obedient to the point of death on the cross.

According to the exegesis of that passage in *The Interpreter's Bible*, at one time—as most readers well know—there was a theological debate "which turned largely on the question of how far Christ had ceased to be God when he became man. Did he strip himself entirely of the divine nature, or merely forgo certain attributes of majesty?"[25] In my view, however, such a theological debate misses the point. Christ's kenosis and his abnegation must be understood not as partial, but as complete and thoroughgoing. As *The Interpreter's Bible*, states, "He [Paul] says only that Christ *emptied himself*,"[26] and "emphasizes the full identity of Christ with the race of men."[27] Christ did not merely disguise himself as a servant, as Docetism suggests, but in fact became a servant. Inasmuch as the term "form" (*morphei*) in the above passage signifies not mere shape or appearance, but substance or reality,[28] so we can say that in Paul's understanding the Son of God abandoned his divine substance and took on human substance to the extreme point of becoming a servant crucified on the cross. Accordingly, Christ's kenosis signifies a transformation not only in appearance but in substance, and implies a radical and total self-negation of the Son of God.

Further again in my view, this doctrine of Christ's kenosis should not be understood to mean that Christ was *originally* the Son of God and *then* emptied himself and became identical with humans. Such a view in the temporal order, or the sequential order, is nothing but a conceptual and objectified understanding of the issue, not an experiential and religious understanding. Instead, we should understand the doctrine of Christ's kenosis to mean that Christ as the Son of God is *essentially* and *fundamentally* self-emptying or self-negating—because of this fundamental nature, the Son of God *is* Christ—that is, the Messiah. It is not that the Son of God *became* a person through the process of his self-emptying but that fundamentally he *is* true person and true God at one and the same time in his dynamic work and activity of self-emptying.

This signifies that traditional understandings of incarnation, especially based on John's prologue—that is, the preexisting Logos (the Son of God) "became flesh" for us—need a new interpretation. Does John's Gospel talk about the Logos and its preexistence simply *objectively* apart from the grace of God and thereby apart from us? Who can properly and legitimately talk about the Logos and its preexistence without its revelation to the person? Is it not that only a person who receives revelation can properly speak of the Logos and its preexistence? There can be no Son of God existing merely as "the Son of God" apart from us. Without encountering it, one can talk about the preexistence of Logos only theoretically or theologically. The "preexisting" Son of God must be realized right here, right now, at the depth of our present existence, as the self-emptying Son of God. The Son

of God becomes flesh simply because the Son of God is originally self-
emptying.

Consequently, we may reformulate the doctrine of Christ's kenosis as
follows:

> The Son of God is not the Son of God (for he is essentially and
> fundamentally self-emptying): precisely because he *is not* the Son of
> God he *is* truly the Son of God (for he originally and always works
> as Christ, the Messiah, in his salvational function of self-emptying).

If we speak of *homoousia* indicating an identity of the full divinity and
full humanity of Jesus Christ in one person, it must not simply signify
"consubstantiality" of two substances, divine and human, as understood
traditionally, but rather "one function" or "nondual function" of self-emptying or self-negation. Without the deeply dynamic nondual function of
self-emptying, the consubstantiality of the divinity and the humanity in
Jesus Christ cannot be properly understood.

All discussion of Christ as the Son of God will be religiously meaningless
if engaged in apart from the problem of human ego, our own existential
problem of the self. The notion of Christ's kenosis or his self-emptying can
be properly understood only through the realization of our own sinfulness
and our own existential self-denying. Jesus himself emphasizes, "he that
finds his life shall lose it; and he that loses his life for my sake shall find
it."[29] And Paul says, "even so reckon you also yourselves to be dead unto
sin, but alive unto God in Christ Jesus."[30] "We are . . . always bearing about
in the body the dying of Jesus, that the life of Jesus may also be manifested
in our body."[31] These words of Jesus and Paul clearly indicate that the
denial of our life, or the death of our ego-self, because of our sinfulness,
is necessary for our new life in Christ Jesus. This denial of our life, this
death of our ego-self, should not be partial but total. Without the total
negation of our life, or the complete death of our ego-self, our new life as
a manifestation of the life of Jesus is impossible. There can be no continuity
between the "old person" and the "new person" in the Pauline faith. If
one believes the self of Christianity is somewhat continuous between the
"old person" and the "new person" in terms of a responsible subject in
relation to God's calling, the religious significance of the self-emptying and
abnegation of Christ—that is, the death and resurrection of Jesus—is not
fully grasped.

Just as the self-emptying or abnegation of the Son of God must not be
partial but total and thoroughgoing for him to be Christ, the self-denial or
death of the human ego-self must not be partial, but also total and complete. Only then can the new person be realized as the true and authentic
self who confesses "it is no longer I that live, but Christ liveth in me; and
that *life* which I now live in the flesh I live in the faith, *the faith* which is in
the Son of God, who loved me, and gave himself up for me."[32]

*true
self*

Accordingly, can we not reformulate the notion of the new person as the true self who resurrects through the death of the old person in such a way that "self is not self (for self as the old person must die on account of its sin): and precisely because it is not, self is truly self (for self is now alive as the new person, together with Christ)." This is especially the case when we recall the following point made by Paul: "As in Adam all die, so also in Christ all shall be made alive,"[33] and "faithful is the saying: For if we died with him, we shall also live with him."[34] Or in our faith in Jesus as Christ, we die together with Christ day by day and are revived together with Christ day by day.[35] Everyday, here and now, we die as the old person and resurrect as the new person with Christ. In this absolute present, we can properly say "self is not self; precisely because it is not, self is truly self."

Now, we have two formulations. First, in relation to the Son of God, we can say:

> The Son of God is not the Son of God (for he is essentially and fundamentally self-emptying); precisely because he *is not* the Son of God he *is* truly the Son of God (for he originally and always works as Christ, the messiah, in his salvational function of self-emptying).

Second, in relation to the human self, we can say:

> Self is not self (for the old self must be crucified with Christ); precisely because it is not, self is truly self (for the new self resurrects with Christ).

The two formulations do not stand separately but signify respectively the two aspects of one and the same living reality—that is, one's faith in Jesus Christ.

The Humiliation and Exaltation of Christ

With regard to the kenosis of Christ, however, there is an important point for Christian faith that one should not overlook. Immediately after the above quotation from the Epistle to the Philippians (2:5-8), the following passage occurs:

> Wherefore also God highly exalted him, and gave unto him the name which is above every name; that in the name of Jesus every knee should bow, of *things* in heaven and *things* on earth and *things* under earth, and that every tongue should confess that Jesus Christ is Lord, to the glory of God the Father.[36]

This is the exaltation of Christ, whereas the kenosis in the previous passage signifies the humiliation of Christ. Precisely as a result of his humiliation,

Christ was raised to place a higher than before. "The way he took was that of self-denial and entire obedience, and by so acting he won his sovereignty."[37] In order to properly understand the kenosis of Christ we must clearly recognize the two states of Christ, that is, the state of humiliation and the state of exaltation. Criticizing a perceived one-sidedness in Martin Luther's *theologia crucis*, Karl Barth emphasizes that the theology of the cross is abstract without the theology of glory—that is, *theologia gloriae*; the state of humiliation and the state of exaltation must be grasped inseparably:

> We cannot properly magnify the passion and death of Jesus Christ unless this magnifying includes within itself the *theologia gloriae*—the magnifying of the one who in His resurrection is the recipient of our right and life, the One who has risen again from the dead for us.[38]

Given the inseparability of the state of humiliation and the state of exaltation, my formulation of the doctrine of Christ's kenosis, which reads: "The Son of God *is not* the Son of God; precisely because he is not the Son of God, he is truly the Son of God," may appear to unduly emphasize the state of humiliation or that of self-emptying in relation to the state of exaltation. This is so especially when I reject the notions of sheer "preexistence" of the Son of God and his "becoming flesh," and instead emphasize the complete self-emptying or negation of the Son of God in the absolute present.

As I suggested earlier, however, I believe that it is now necessary to take a new look at the notion of the preexistence of the Logos as the Son of God. Although this notion is essential to Christian faith, if we take current religion-negating ideologies into account, it must be reexamined or at least be demonstrated through confrontation with these ideologies. For the notion of preexistence of the Son of God is incompatible with the critical rationality and autonomous reason so important in the modern world. The notion of preexistence of the Son of God is also challenged by contemporary existentialistic atheism and active nihilism, which proclaim the death of God.

Another reason for a reexamination of the notion of the preexistence of the Son of God arises not merely from the necessity of responding to challenges posed by today's antireligious ideologies, but from within Christian faith itself. For in Christian faith, the problem of the kenosis of Christ inevitably leads us to face the problem of the kenosis of God. In other words, if Christ the Son of God empties himself, should we not consider the self-emptying of God—that is, the kenosis of the very God? We must now ask together with Jürgen Moltmann, "What does the cross of Jesus mean for God himself?"[39] This is not merely a theological question, but an existential and religious question deeply rooted in Christian faith.

The Kenosis of God

Christian theology generally states that the Son of God became a human without God ceasing to be God. In his book, *Does God Exist?* Hans Küng says:

> The distinction of the Son of God from God the Father, his obedience and subordination to the Father, is of course upheld everywhere in the New Testament. The Father is "greater" than he is and there are things that are known only to the Father and not to him. Neither is there any mention anywhere in the New Testament of the incarnation of God himself.[40]

Küng also clearly says, "We should not of course speak of a 'crucified God.' That would suggest that God the Father, and not the Son, had been crucified. . . . But we can and may certainly speak of a 'hidden God revealed in the Crucified.'"[41] As a Buddhist, however, who is concerned with promoting Buddhist-Christian dialogue to open up a new and deeper religious dimension in the contemporary context of religion versus antireligious ideologies, I realize that the kenosis of God is a crucial issue for our dialogue. Is it not that the kenosis of Christ—that is, the self-emptying of the Son of God—has its origin in God "the Father"— that is, the kenosis of God? Without the self-emptying of God "the Father," the self-emptying of the Son of God is inconceivable. In the case of Christ, kenosis is realized in the fact that one who was in the form of God emptied "himself" and assumed the form of a servant. It originated in the will of God and the love of God, which is willing to forgive even the sinner who has rebelled against God. It was a deed that was accomplished on the basis of God's *will*. On the other hand, in the case of God, kenosis is implied in the original *nature* of God, that is, love.[42] In this sense, the notion of "crucified God," as discussed by Moltmann, is essential.[43]

My emphasis on the kenosis of God seems to be supported by Karl Rahner, who says in *Foundations of Christian Faith*:

> The primary phenomenon given by faith is precisely the self-emptying of God, his becoming, the kenosis and genesis of God himself. . . . Insofar as in his abiding and infinite fullness he empties himself, the other comes to be as God's very own reality. The phrase is already found in Augustine that God "assumes by creating" and also "creates by assuming," that is, he creates by emptying himself, and therefore, of course, he himself is in the emptying.[44]

In *Sacramentum Mundi*, under the title, "Jesus' death as the death of God," Rahner emphasizes the death of Jesus as the death of God:

Christology at the present day must reflect more closely on Jesus' death, not only in its redemptive effect, but also in itself. . . . If it is said that the incarnate Logos died only in his human reality, and if this is tacitly understood to mean that this death therefore did not affect God, only half the truth has been stated. The really Christian truth has been omitted . . . Our "possessing" God must repeatedly pass through the deathly abandonment by God (Matt. 27:46; Mark 15:4) in which alone God ultimately comes to us, because God has given himself in love and as love, and thus is realized, and manifested in his death. Jesus' death belongs to God's self-utterance.[45]

Reading Karl Rahner more closely, however, I find an important point I cannot accept. Referring to the mystery of the incarnation, Rahner says:

God can become something. He who is not subject to change in himself, can *himself* be subject to change *in something else*.[46] . . . The absolute One [God] in the pure freedom of his infinite unrelatedness, which he always preserves, possesses the possibility of himself becoming the other, the finite. He possesses the possibility of *establishing* the other as his own reality by dispossessing *himself*, by giving *himself* away.[47] . . . God goes out of himself, he himself, he as the self-giving fullness. Because he can do this, because this is his free and primary possibility, for this reason he is defined in scripture as love.[48]

Although these statements emphasize the self-emptying of God, they still leave behind traces of dualism, a dualism of God and the other, the infinite and the finite, immutability and change, within and without, and so forth. Of course, this is not a simple dualism in the ordinary sense, because God as the absolute, infinite One is understood here to possess "the possibility of becoming the other, the finite . . . by dispossessing himself." This dynamic interpretation of God, however, implies two things. First, by virtue of love, God does not remain in infinite unrelatedness but goes out of "himself" and gives "himself" away to the other. Second, even so, as the absolute One, God "always preserves" this infinite unrelatedness. This implies that God's infinite unrelatedness has priority over this relatedness with the other. Again, God's infinite fullness, being abiding, has priority over God's self-emptying. This is clearly seen in Rahner's statement, "Insofar as in his abiding and infinite fullness he empties himself, the other comes to be as God's very own reality."[49]

This second point is what I referred to by speaking of "traces of dualism." Are these "traces of dualism" absolutely necessary for Christian faith in God? Do these "traces of dualism" have a positive rather than negative significance in Christianity? Rahner himself emphasizes, "the primary phenomenon given by faith is precisely the self-emptying of God, his becoming, the kenosis and genesis of God himself."[50] If this is the case, then the "traces of dualism" must be not only minimized, but also eliminated. God's self-emptying must be understood not as partial but as total to the extent that God's infinite unrelatedness has no priority over relatedness with the other and that God's self-emptying is dynamically identical with God's abiding and infinite fullness.

Inasmuch as we do not see this kind of *total* self-emptying of God In Rahner's interpretation, I cannot help but say that even for Karl Rahner, the kenosis of God, God's self-emptying, is still somewhat conceptualized or objectified. If God is really unconditional love, the self-emptying must be total, not partial. It must not be that God *becomes something else* by partial self-giving, but that in and through total self-emptying God *is* something — or more precisely, God *is* each and every thing. This emphasis, however, should not be taken to signify pantheism (see the following section). On the contrary, only through this total kenosis and God's self-sacrificial identification with everything in the world is God truly God. Here we fully realize the reality and actuality of God, which is entirely beyond conception and objectification. This kenotic God is the ground of the kenotic Christ. The God who does not cease to be God even in the self-emptying of the Son of God, that is, the kenosis of Christ, is not the true God.

Accordingly, concerning faith in God, it must be said:

God is not God (for God is love and completely self-emptying); precisely because God is not a self-affirmative God, God is truly a God of love (for through complete self-abnegation God is totally identical with everything including sinful humans).

This means that kenosis or emptying is not an *attribute* (however important it may be) of God, but the fundamental *nature* of God. God is God, not because God had the Son of God take a human form and be sacrificed while God remained God, but because God is a suffering God, a self-sacrificial God through total kenosis. The kenotic God who totally empties Godself and totally sacrifices Godself is, in my view, the true God. And it is precisely this kenotic God who thoroughly saves everything, including human beings and nature, through self-sacrificial, abnegating love.

I also believe that the notion of the kenotic God can overcome Nietzsche's nihilism, which insists upon the need to "sacrifice God for nothing," because instead of being sacrificed for nothingness by radical nihilists in the third stage of human history, the kenotic God sacrifices Godself not for relative nothingness but for *absolute* nothingness, which is at one and the same time absolute Being.

God's total kenosis is not God's self-sacrifice for something else or God's self-negation for nihilistic nothingness, but God's self-sacrifice for absolutely "nothing" other than God's own fulfillment. Only in God's total kenosis is everything, including the unjust and sinner, natural and moral evil, forgiven, redeemed, and satisfied, and the love of God completely fulfilled. The notion of the kenotic God thus goes beyond Nietzsche's radical nihilism by deepening the religious significance of the Christian notion of the love of God.

In addition, the notion of kenotic God opens up for Christianity a common ground with Buddhism by overcoming Christianity's monotheistic character, the absolute oneness of God, and by sharing with Buddhism the realization of absolute nothingness as the essential basis for the ultimate. This can be accomplished through the notion of the kenotic God—not through losing Christianity's self-identity, but rather through deepening its spirituality.

Furthermore, the notion of the kenotic God can also embrace the autonomous reason of modern science and the rationalistic subjectivity of the modern world because in the notion of the kenotic God, who is totally self-emptying, God's infinite unrelatedness and abiding fullness, which are incompatible with the autonomous reason and modern rationalistic subjectivity, are eliminated. And yet, through total self-emptying, God is believed to reveal love most profoundly to embrace even a person's ego-self, which with its autonomous reason stands against God.

However, insofar as a person's ego-self remains with itself, the kenotic God is not really understood. Only when the ego-self negates itself completely does it come to understand who the kenotic God is and what God's total self-emptying means to the self. Accordingly, the above statement, "God is not God, and precisely because God is not a self-affirmative God, God is truly God," can be properly grasped by the parallel existential realization that "self is not self, and precisely because it is not, self is truly self."

God: Each and Every Thing

In the previous section, I emphasized that in and through God's total self-emptying, God does not become something else, but *is* something or, more precisely, God *is* each and every thing. This emphasis may immediately give rise to the following two objections. First, such an emphasis leads to pantheism, which is rejected by authentic Christianity. Second, such an emphasis excludes the uniqueness of Jesus Christ as the only incarnation of the son of God in history.

As for the first objection, I argue that the above emphasis should not be confused with pantheism. Pantheism as exemplified by Spinoza's dictum, *deus sive natura*, signifies the identity between God and empirical things in the world without a realization of God's self-negation. I am, however, discussing God's *being* each and everything through God's total kenosis, through the complete abnegation or self-emptying of God. Accordingly, my understanding of the relationship between God and nature is essentially different from that of Spinozan pantheism. Although Spinoza conceives of God as impersonal and immanent in all finite things and the individual self,

God is still somewhat transcendent in that God's countless attributes remain inaccessible to us.[51]

In contrast, I am contending that through the kenosis of God, "God is truly God." This indicates a truly personal God who is identical with everything—including the sinful person—precisely because God is not a self-affirmative God (not one substance) but a completely self-emptying God. The completely kenotic God, in my view, is neither immanent nor transcendent, but thoroughly immanent and thoroughly transcendent at one and the same time. The completely kenotic God is not merely impersonal but deeply personal, in the sense that this God is self-emptying and fulfills God's unconditional love to save everything without exception, including the unjust and sinful. In the completely kenotic God, personality and impersonality are paradoxically identical.

The second possible objection concerning my emphasis that God *is* each and everything through total kenosis demands a more detailed exploration and response. My emphasis seems to exclude the uniqueness of Jesus Christ as the only incarnation of the son of God in history. That emphasis is, however, based on the notion that the kenotic Christ cannot be fully grasped without a realization of the total kenosis of God. Ultimately God incarnates Godself in the form of Jesus Christ not because God "can himself be subject to change in something else,"[52] but because through unconditional love God abnegates Godself so completely that God fully identifies with the crucified Christ on the cross. The resurrection of Christ should be understood precisely on this basis. If this total identity of God with the crucified Christ on the cross is a necessary premise for Christian faith, why is this total identity of God with Christ through God's kenosis not applicable to everything in the universe beyond Christ? Can we not legitimately say that each and every thing in the universe is also an incarnation of God together with Jesus Christ on the cross and his glorious resurrection?

But a further objection to this understanding might be raised by claiming that it eliminates the uniqueness of Jesus Christ in history, a concept essential to Christianity. To this objection, the following two points must be raised.

First, if Jesus Christ *is* uniquely Christ in the sense that the Son of God *became* a human through the process of self-emptying but *without a total abnegation of divinity*, his uniqueness as Christ will be destroyed or at least diminished by saying "each and every thing in the universe is equally an incarnation of God together with Jesus Christ and his glorious resurrection." However, if the uniqueness of Jesus Christ is understood in the sense that the Son of God is essentially self-emptying and the crucified Christ is nothing but the revelation of this completely self-emptying Son of God *through total abnegation of his divinity*, the situation is different.

In other words, if the uniqueness of Jesus Christ is understood in the sense that the Son of God is truly the Son of God precisely because the Son of God *is not* the Son of God, then that statement does not necessarily eliminate the uniqueness of Jesus Christ. Rather, due to his uniqueness of this kind, everything in the universe is understood to be incarnation of God as well, for the uniqueness of Jesus Christ is here grasped in and through / the total abnegation of the divinity of the Son of God.

Second, as discussed earlier, the kenosis of Christ has its origin in God, in the kenosis of God. Without the self-emptying of God, the self-emptying of the Son of God is inconceivable. In interpreting Paul, Moltmann states that just as the Son is delivered up to the death on the cross in order to become the Lord of both dead and living, "the Father delivers up his Son on the cross in order to be the Father of those who are delivered up."[53] It is worth noting that Cyril of Jerusalem said, "On the cross, God stretched out his hands to embrace the ends of the earth," and "O blessed tree on which God was outstretched."[54] On these words of Cyril, Moltmann comments:

He [God] invites the whole earth to understand his suffering and his hopes in the outstretched arms of the crucified Jesus and therefore in God . . . This symbol is an invitation to understand the Christ hanging on the cross as the outstretched God of the trinity.[55]

If this is the case, my understanding that each and every thing in the universe is also an incarnation of God together with Jesus on the cross and his glorious resurrection—because God is completely self-emptying—does not necessarily exclude the uniqueness of Jesus Christ, but broadens the Christian notion of an all-loving God.

Moltmann's Notion of the Crucified God

On the basis of the preceding understanding of the kenotic God, I find Jürgen Moltmann's notion of the "crucified God" extremely provocative and penetrating. In his book, *The Crucified God*, Moltmann takes the event of the cross as an event of God[56] and states that "[God] also suffers the death of his Fatherhood in the death of the Son."[57] For Moltmann, God is crucified in the crucified Christ. He emphasizes, however, that the trinitarian interpretation of the event of the cross rather than the traditional doctrine of the two natures in the person of Christ is necessary to properly understand the notion of the crucified God.

In the following I will: (1) clarify why the trinitarian interpretation of the Christ event on the cross is necessary to Moltmann, (2) try to summarize his discussion of the trinitarian interpretation of the event on the cross, and (3) offer a critique of Moltmann's interpretation and thereby conclude with my own view.

Moltmann appreciates Karl Barth's position because "Barth has consistently drawn the harshness of the cross into his concept of God."[58] After quoting Barth's words in *Church Dogmatics*, "In God's eternal purpose it is God Himself who is rejected in His Son," for "God wills to lose that man may win,"[59] Moltmann states,

> Because Barth thought consistently of "God in Christ," he could think historically of God's being, speak almost in theopaschite terms of God's suffering and being involved in the cross of the Son, and finally talk of the "death of God," *de facto*, if not in those very words.[60]

Moltmann, however, criticizes Barth because Barth's approach is still too *theo*-logically oriented and is not sufficiently trinitarian. "In stressing constantly and rightly that '*God* was in Christ,' *God* humbled himself, *God himself was on the cross,* he [Barth] uses a simple concept of God which is not sufficiently developed in a trinitarian direction."[61] For Moltmann, once one abandons the simple concept of God, there is a trinitarian solution to the paradox that God is "dead" on the cross and yet is not dead.[62]

Thus, Moltmann strongly emphasizes the necessity of the trinitarian understanding of God as the proper way to understand the significance of the death of Jesus for God:

> When one considers the significance of the death of Jesus for God himself, one must enter into the inner-trinitarian tensions and relationships of God and speak of the Father, the Son and the Spirit. But if that is the case, it is inappropriate to talk simply of "God" in connection with the Christ event. When one uses the phrase "God in Christ," does it refer only to the Father, who abandons him and gives him up, or does it also refer to the Son who is abandoned and forsaken? The more one understands the whole event of the cross as the event of God, the more any simple concept of God falls apart. In epistemological terms it takes so to speak trinitarian form. One moves from the exterior of the mystery which is called "God" to the interior, which is trinitarian. This is the "revolution in the concept of God" which is manifested by the crucified Christ.[63]

Thus Moltmann extensively discusses the trinitarian interpretation of the event of the crucified Christ in contrast to the traditional doctrine of two natures.

Moltmann's discussion may be summarized in the following three points:

First, the doctrine of two natures understands the event of the cross statically as a reciprocal relationship between two qualitatively different natures, the divine nature, which is incapable of suffering, and the human nature, which is capable of suffering.[64] The doctrine of kenosis, the self-emptying of God, was conceived within the framework of the distinction of the divine and the human. It has found few followers, because the framework of thought it has presented leads to difficult and impossible statements.[65]

In the trinitarian interpretation, by contrast, the event of the cross is grasped as an event concerned with a relationship among the three persons, the Father, the Son, and the Spirit. The death of Jesus is not interpreted as a divine-human event, but as a trinitarian event among the Son, the Father, and the Spirit:

> What is in question in the relationship of Christ to his Father is not his divinity and humanity and their relationship to each other but the total, personal aspect of the Sonship of Jesus.[66]

> Christian theology cannot develop any bipolar theology of the reciprocal relationship between the God who calls and the man who answers: it must develop a trinitarian theology, for only in and through Christ is that dialogical relationship with God opened up.[67]

This implies that the event of the cross in God's being must be understood in both trinitarian and personal terms.[68]

Second, within the framework of the doctrine of two natures:

> One would have to say: what happened on the cross was an event between God and God. It was a deep division in God himself, insofar as God abandoned God and contradicted himself and at the same time a unity in God, insofar as God was at one with God and corresponded to himself. In that case one would have to put the formula in a paradoxical way: God died the death of the godless on the cross and did not die. God is dead and yet is not dead. If one can only use the simple concept of God from the doctrine of two natures, one will always be inclined to restrict it to the person of the Father who abandons and accepts Jesus, delivers him and raises him up, and in so doing will "evacuate" the cross of deity.[69]

In contrast, to talk in trinitarian terms, Moltmann maintains:

> In the forsakenness of the Son the Father also forsakes himself. In the surrender of the Son the Father also surrenders himself, though not in the same way . . . The Son suffers dying, the Father suffers the death of the Son. The grief of the Father here is just as important as the death of the Son. The fatherlessness of the Son is matched by the Sonlessness of the Father, and if God has constituted himself as the Father of Jesus Christ, then he also suffers the death of his Fatherhood in the death of the Son. Unless this were so, the doctrine of the trinity would still have a monotheistic background.[70]

Furthermore, Moltmann emphasizes the deep community of will between Jesus and his God, which is expressed even in their deepest separation. Moltmann holds that it is through the Spirit that such community and separation between Jesus and his God can go together:

In the cross, Father and Son are most deeply separated in forsaken-ness and at the same time are most inwardly one in their surrender. What proceeds from this event between Father and Son is the Spirit which justifies the Godless, fills the forsaken with love and even brings the dead to life, since even the fact that they are dead cannot exclude them from this event of the cross; the death in God also includes them.[71]

Third, stating that the doctrine of the two natures in Christ began from the distinction between the immortal, unchangeable God and the mortal corruptible human, Moltmann insists:

The theistic concept of God according to which God cannot die, and the hope for salvation, according to which man is to be immortal, made it impossible to regard Jesus as really being God and at the same time as being forsaken by God.[72]

Moltmann maintains that the Godforsakenness of Christ is a historical event; his resurrection, however, is not a historical but an eschatological event.[73] If both historical Godforsakenness and eschatological surrender can be seen in Christ's death on the cross, then we can realize that this event contains community between Jesus and his Father in separation, and separation in community[74]:

Faith understands the historical event between the Father who for-sakes and the Son who is forsaken on the cross in eschatological terms as an event between the Father who loves and the Son who is loved in this present spirit of the love that creates life.[75]

Like Hegel, speaking of the life of God within the trinity as the "history of God," Moltmann states:

The concrete "history of God" in the death of Jesus on the cross on Golgotha therefore contains within itself all the depths and abysses of human history and therefore can be understood as the history of history. All human history, however much it may be determined by guilt and death, is taken up into this "history of God," i.e., into the trinity, and integrated into the future of the "history of God." There is no suffering which in this history of God is not God's suffering, no death which has not been God's death in the history of Golgotha. Therefore there is no life, no fortune and no joy which have not been integrated by his history into eternal life, the eternal joy of God.[76]

Precisely in this sense, Moltmann speaks of a "theology after Auschwitz" and maintains that "like the cross of Christ, even Auschwitz is in God himself. Even Auschwitz is taken up into the grief of the Father, the surrender of the Son and the power of the Spirit."[77]

The above three points are a synopsis of Moltmann's discussion of the event of Christ on the cross in trinitarian terms. To Moltmann, the doctrine of the trinity is not "an exorbitant and impractical speculation about God"[78]:

[But it] is nothing other than a shorter version of the passion narrative of Christ in its significance for the eschatological freedom of faith and the life of oppressed nature. It protects faith from both monotheism and theism because it keeps believers at the cross.[79]

Appreciation and Criticism of Moltmann

To me, Moltmann's interpretation of the event of Christ on the cross in trinitarian terms is quite discerning and stimulating. Moving from the traditional doctrine of two natures to the doctrine of trinity in the understanding of the significance of the death of Jesus for God, Moltmann then moves "from the exterior of the mystery which is called 'God' to the interior, which is trinitarian,"[80] from the simple concept of God (*esse simplex*) to the inter-trinitarian tensions of God.[81] I have a great sympathy and appreciation for Moltmann's approach. I have, however, two mutually related questions concerning the basic standpoint of Moltmann's trinitarian interpretation.

Moltmann presents a trinitarian interpretation of the significance of the crucified Christ for God as *the solution* to the paradox inevitable in the doctrine of two natures—that is "God is 'dead' on the cross and yet is not dead."[82] My first question is whether the trinitarian interpretation as illustrated by Moltmann is a *real* solution of that paradoxical statement of God. And my second question, closely related to the first, is whether in Moltmann's trinitarian theology the event of the cross in God's being is, as Moltmann claims, really understood in *both* trinitarian *and* personal terms, or in *both* christocentric *and* trinitarian terms?

It is clear that by adopting the trinitarian interpretation instead of the doctrine of two natures Moltmann moves from the exterior of the mystery of God and enters into the interior. Is not this movement, however, merely one step into the interior and not a complete penetration into the depth of God's mystery? Is it not a partial solution rather than a complete solution? In order to completely resolve the paradox involved in the traditional doctrine of two natures in the person of the Christ, must one not enter into still greater "interior" than the trinitarian position outlined by Moltmann? Can the mystery of God be found not in the interior as distinguished from the exterior, but only in the still greater interior of the interior? Cannot God's mystery and therefore the solution of the paradoxical statement

"God is dead on the cross and yet is not dead" be realized only in the absolute interior which, transcending the duality between the interior and the exterior is neither interior nor exterior in the relative sense?

These questions may be restated in the following manner:

Can the doctrine of Trinity, which may be "the unity of three persons in one God or Godhead," truly resolve the paradox involved in the doctrine of two natures? In the doctrine of the Trinity, it is clear that the one God is not the fourth person or the fourth being. One God is the common *substantia* or *essentia* whereas the three persons are three distinct *hypostases*. Although there are clear differences and mutual relationships among the three persons, the one God is the undivided essence, indicating the unity of God. The distinction between *essentia* (which is one and unity) and *hypostasis* (which is three and trinity) is indispensable and should not be confused in the doctrine of the Trinity. If this distinction is vital, however, the one God as *essentia*, though clearly not the fourth being, is not completely independent of or free from the character of the fourth being. In my view, in order to overcome the presence of the character of the fourth being, the oneness of this one God must possess the characteristic of zero. The one God in the Trinity must be the great zero that is free even from the oneness as distinguished from the threeness.

This means that only when one God is understood to have the characteristic of zero can the doctrine of Trinity be fully and dynamically realized. This is because three distinctive beings—Father, Son, and Spirit—are then clearly and thoroughly realized in their distinctiveness without any possibility of being reduced to one Godhead, and because at the same time the oneness of the one God is completely preserved from the haunting presence of the fourth being. Furthermore, only at this point (only when one God is understood in terms of the great zero) can the doctrine of Trinity be a real solution of the paradox involved in the traditional doctrine of two natures, that is, God is dead on the cross and yet God is not dead.

What, then, is the nature of zero which is indispensable to the one God of the trinity? It indicates *Nichts* or *Ungrund* as the Godhead as exemplified by Christian mystics such as Meister Eckhart and Jakob Böhme. And it is nothing other than "the still greater interior of the interior" mentioned earlier. In order for the trinitarian structure to be truly possible, that one God should not be *essentia* as distinguished from *hypostasis*, much less *substantia*, but *Nichts* or *Ungrund*. Only when the doctrine of Trinity is understood in this way are the unity and the trinity of God fully and harmoniously realized without conflict. And only then is the event of the cross in God's being, as Moltmann requires, understood in *both* trinitarian *and* personal terms,[83] or "simultaneously in both christocentric and trinitarian terms."[84]

This last point leads us to my second question and raises the following issue. When one moves from the traditional doctrine of two natures in Christ to the trinitarian understanding of the Christ event and thus moves from the exterior of the mystery of God to the interior, one may lose direct contact with the historical event of the cross. Even in entering into the inner trinitarian tensions in God, the human hope for salvation should not be neglected. This is precisely because Moltmann emphasizes the necessity of understanding the event of the cross in God's being simultaneously in both christocentric and trinitarian terms.

I do not see, however, that Moltmann's interpretation of Trinity sufficiently enables one to understand the event of the cross in God's being simultaneously in both christocentric and trinitarian terms. For by the relative movement from the exterior of God's mystery to the interior, one cannot reach the deepest depth of God's mystery, which is common ground (as *Ungrund*) for both the unity and the trinity of God. Only when one goes beyond the interior of God's mystery and enters into its still more fundamental interior, the absolute interior, can one understand the event of the cross in God's being simultaneously in christocentric and trinitarian terms. This is because the absolute interior is dynamically identical with the absolute exterior—the interior still more fundamental than the mere interior is nothing but the exterior still more fundamental than the mere exterior. In the deepest dimension of God's mystery, the absolute interior and the absolute exterior are paradoxically and dynamically identical and are beyond dualism. Right here, both the eschatological hope of salvation and the internal, undivided oneness of God are fully and thoroughly realized.

The simultaneous understanding of the event of the crucified Christ both in christocentric and trinitarian terms is possible only by penetrating into the absolute interior of God's mystery which is the absolute exterior at one and the same time. And this greatest depth of God's mystery is precisely the Godhead as *Nichts* or *Ungrund*, not one God as *essentia* or *substantia*. The real solution of the paradox inevitable in the doctrine of two natures— that "God is dead on the cross and yet is not dead"—is also fully realized in understanding Godhead as *Nichts*.

The death of Jesus on the cross is not a divine-human event, but is most certainly a trinitarian event of the Father, the Son, and the Spirit. What is important in this regard is the total, personal aspect of the sonship of Jesus. This sonship of Jesus, however, is ultimately rooted in *Nichts* or *Ungrund* as the Godhead in "the unity of three persons in one God." Only here, but not in a trinitarian interpretation according to which God is *una substantia* (one nature), can we say with full justification—as Moltmann states—that "in the cross, Father and Son are most deeply separated in forsakenness and at the same time are most inwardly one in their surrender."[85] Again, only here—when the sonship of Jesus is understood to be ultimately rooted in *Nichts* as Godhead—can the event of the cross of Jesus be understood truly as the event of an unconditioned and boundless love fully actualized for the Godless and the loveless in this law-oriented society.

In his book *Does God Exist?*, Hans Küng says: "God in the Bible is subject and not predicate: it is not that love is God, but that God is love—God is one who faces me, whom I can address."[86] Can I not address God, however, not from the outside of God, but from within God? Again, is it not that God faces me within God even if I turn my back on God? the God who faces me and whom I address is God as subject. However, the God within whom I address God and within whom God meets me is not God as subject but rather God as predicate. Or, more strictly speaking, that God is neither God as subject nor God as predicate but God as *Nichts*. In God as *Nichts*, God as subject meets me even if I turn my back on God and I can truly address the God as Thou. An I-Thou relationship between the self and God takes place precisely in God as *Nichts*. Since God as *Nichts* is the *Ungrund* ground of the I-Thou relationship between the self and God, God as *Nichts* is neither subject nor predicate but a "copula" that acts as a connecting or intermediating link between the subject and the predicate. This entails that God as *Nichts* is *Nichts* as God: God is *Nichts* and *Nichts* is God. And on this basis we may say that God is love and love is God because *Nichts* is the unconditional, self-negating love. This is the absolute interior of God's mystery which is its absolute exterior at one and the same time. We may thus say,

> God is love because God is *Nichts*:
> *Nichts* is God because *Nichts* is love.

Here, both human longing for salvation and the deepest mystery of God are thoroughly fulfilled. Here again, the event of the cross in God's being is understood in both trinitarian and personal terms most profoundly.

God as subject who meets one and whom one can address as Thou is incompatible with the autonomous reason peculiar to modern humanity, and is also nowadays challenged by Nietzschean nihilism and atheistic existentialism. The notion of God as *Nichts*, however, is not only compatible with but also can embrace autonomous reason because there is no conflict between the notion of God as *Nichts* (which is neither subject nor predicate) and autonomous reason, and because the autonomy of rational thinking, however much it may be emphasized, is not limited by the notion of God as *Nichts*. In the kenotic God who is *Nichts*, not only are modern human autonomous reason and rationalistic subjectivity overcome without being marred, but also the mystery of God is most profoundly perceived. God as love is fully and most radically grasped far beyond contemporary atheism and nihilism.

All this is implied when I stated earlier that God is not God; precisely because of this, God is truly God. And, as I also emphasized before, this statement of God cannot be properly understood without our own parallel existential realization that "Self is not self, and precisely because it is not, Self is truly Self."

DYNAMIC SUNYATA

Sunyata as the Buddhist Ultimate

Now I turn to Buddhism and discuss how Buddhism can overcome scientism and Nietzsche's nihilism, and can also open up a basis for dialogue with Christianity.

The ultimate reality for Buddhism is neither Being nor God, but Sunyata. Sunyata literally means "emptiness" or "voidness" and can imply "absolute nothingness." This is because Sunyata is entirely unobjectifiable, unconceptualizable, and unattainable by reason or will. As such it cannot be any "something" at all. Accordingly, if Sunyata is conceived as *somewhere outside of* or *beyond* one's self-existence, it is not true Sunyata, for Sunyata thus conceived outside of or beyond one's existence turns into *something* which one represents and calls "Sunyata." True Sunyata is not even that which is represented and conceived as "Sunyata." In Nagarjuna's *Mulamadhyamaka-karika*, Sunyata, which is dimly perceived, is likened to "a snake wrongly grasped or [magical] knowledge incorrectly applied."[87] Throughout its long history, Mahayana Buddhism has strongly rejected such a view of Sunyata—that is, Sunyata represented and thereby attached to as "Sunyata," as "Sunyata perversely clung to," as a "literal understanding of negativity," or as a "view of annihilatory nothing-ness." Instead, Mahayana Buddhism emphasizes that "Sunyata is non-Sunyata (*asunyata*): therefore it is ultimate Sunyata (*atyanta-Sunyata*)."[88] Sunyata not only is not Being or God, but also *not* emptiness as distinguished from somethingness or fullness. Just as the attachment to being must be overcome, the attachment to emptiness must also be surmounted. Accordingly, however important the notion of Sunyata may be in Buddhism, following Martin Heidegger, who put a cross mark "X" on the term *Sein*, thus rendering it as ~~Sein~~, in order to show the unobjectifiability of *Sein*, we should also put a cross mark "X" on Sunyata, and render it ~~Sunyata~~.

What has been said above indicates that Sunyata is not self-affirmative, but *thoroughly* self-negative. In other words, emptiness not only empties everything else but also empties itself. Sunyata should not be conceived of somewhere *outside* one's self-existence, nor somewhere *inside* one's self-existence. True Sunyata is neither outside nor inside, neither external nor internal, neither transcendent nor immanent. Sunyata completely empties everything, including itself. That is to say, the pure activity of absolute emptying is true Sunyata. Hence, the well know passage in the *Prajnaparamita-hrdaya-sutra*—the Heart Sutra:

> Form is emptiness and the very emptiness is form; emptiness does not differ from form; form does not differ from emptiness; whatever is form, that is emptiness; whatever is emptiness, that is form.[89]

As the Heart Sutra clearly indicates, the realization that "form is emptiness," however important and necessary it may be, is not sufficient; it must be immediately accompanied with the realization that "the very emptiness is form." And these two realizations are one, not two.

"Form" should not be grasped and attached to as something substantial but should be emptied as nonsubstantial or formless. We should not become attached to such discriminations as "mountains are mountains; water is water," but should awaken to the nonsubstantiality or emptiness of such discriminations by realizing that "mountains are not mountains; water is not water." At the same time, however, "emptiness" should not be grasped and attached to merely as something nonsubstantial or formless—formless emptiness must itself be emptied and grasped in terms of form. Thus, we must realize discrimination through non-discrimination—that is, "mountains are really mountains precisely because mountains are not mountains; water is really water precisely because water is not water."[90]

Accordingly, although the Heart Sutra states, "whatever is form, that is emptiness, whatever is emptiness, that is form," this does not indicate a static or immediate identity of form and emptiness. Nor does it signify an identity of form and emptiness, which are set forth and represented before one's eyes. It is a dynamic identity that is to be grasped only in an unobjectifiable and pre-representational manner—through the pure activity of emptying. In the realization of true Sunyata, form is ceaselessly emptied, turning into formless emptiness, and formless emptiness is ceaselessly emptied and forever freely taking form. This total *dynamic movement* of emptying, not a *static state* of emptiness, is the true meaning of Sunyata. If we conceive of this total dynamic movement of emptying as *somewhere outside* us or *some time beyond* our present self-existence, however, we fail to realize Sunyata. Sunyata is not outside us, nor are we outside Sunyata.

In one sense, we are right here, right now, *in* Sunyata. We are always involved in the ceaseless emptying movement of Sunyata, for there is nothing outside it. And yet, in another sense, we are always totally embracing this ceaseless movement of Sunyata within ourselves. We *are* Sunyata at each and every moment of our lives. For true Sunyata is not Sunyata thought by us, but Sunyata lived by us. In this living realization of true Sunyata, self and Sunyata are dynamically identical. That is to say, true Sunyata is nothing but the true self and the true self is nothing but true Sunyata. Apart from the absolute present—right here, right now—this dynamical identity of self and Sunyata cannot be fully realized. Again, apart from the nonobjectifiable and pre-representational standpoint, the absolute present, and the dynamical identity of self and Sunyata cannot be properly grasped. And this dynamic identity of self and Sunyata is equally true of everyone and everything throughout the universe. Consequently, although the term Sunyata or emptiness may sound negative, it has positive, soteriological meanings.

The Positive Meanings of Sunyata

The positive, soteriological meanings of Sunyata may be summarized in five points.

First, in Sunyata, regardless of the distinction between self and other, humans and nature, humans and the divine, everything without exception is realized *as it is* in its *suchness* (in Sanskrit, *tathata*, which may also be rendered as "is-ness"). The realization of the suchness of everything is an important characteristic of the dimension of Sunyata. This does not, however, indicate that in Sunyata the distinctiveness of everything is eliminated. On the contrary, in the locus of Sunyata the distinctiveness of everything is clearly and thoroughly realized without being reduced to any monistic principle such as Brahman, Substance, or God, and yet everything is *equally* realized in its as-it-is-ness or suchness.

In the realization of Sunyata in the light of suchness, both distinction and equality, distinctiveness and sameness, are fully realized. For example, in the locus of Sunyata you are thoroughly you as you are and I am thoroughly I as I am—with our distinctive individuality and without ending in a single ultimate principle—and yet you and I are equally sharing the sameness in that both you and I are equally realized in terms of being-as-we-are. This is true not only of you and me, but also of the self and any other, the self and nature, and self and the divine. The self is the self, nature is nature, and God is God, all with their distinctiveness, and yet they all are equal in terms of "each is as each is" or "as it is." Accordingly, in the realization of suchness, there is no difference between human beings and nonhuman beings (nature and supernatural entities).

This emphasis on there being no difference between human and nonhuman beings in the realization of "suchness" should not, as is often the case, be misunderstood as signifying a disregard of the particularity of human (and divine) personality.

Like Christianity, Buddhism is primarily concerned with human salvation—that is, the deliverance of human beings from suffering. Unlike Christianity, however, Buddhism does not take the personalistic divine-human relationship (I-thou relationship) as the *basis* of salvation, thereby regarding impersonal nature as something peripheral, but instead takes as the basis of salvation the transpersonal, universal dimension common to human beings and nature. This is why in Buddhism the clear realization of impermanency or transiency common to everything, including humans and nature, is the turning point from samsara to nirvana. In this transpersonal, universal dimension, everything, human and nonhuman, is equally and individually realized in its as-it-is-ness.[91]

Furthermore, unlike Christianity, which talks about God as the ruler and the savior, Buddhism does not accept the notions of a transcendent ruler of the universe or of a savior outside one's self. A Buddha is not a supernaturally existing being, but is none other than a person who awakens to the dharma, the truth, the suchness or as-it-is-ness of everything in the realization of Sunyata. This means that it is by a person—by an awakened one—that the suchness of everything is realized. But suchness thus realized by a person encompasses everything in the universe, including human beings, nature, and the divine—the secular and the sacred.

For the elucidation of the issue, we should make a distinction between salvation as such and the *basis* of salvation, that is, between the problem of what salvation is conceived to be in a particular religion and the problem of on what *basis* that salvation is understood to take place. The realization of the "such-ness" of everything as the basis of salvation entails the awakening of one's original nature together with the awakening of the original nature of everything else, and the emancipation from attachment to the self and others.

Second, Sunyata indicates *boundless openness* without any particular fixed center. Sunyata is free not only from egocentrism but also from anthropocentrism, cosmocentrism, and theocentrism. It is not oriented by any kind of centrism. Only in this way is "emptiness" possible. Accordingly, in Sunyata there is no fixed dominant-subordinate relationship among things in the universe. Humankind is not simply subordinate to Buddha, nor is nature simply subordinate to humankind. In this boundless openness everything without exception is dominant as subject over everything else, and *at the same time* is subordinate to everything else. Such a dynamic, mutual dominant-subordinate relationship is possible only in the locus of Sunyata, which is completely free from any centrism and is boundlessly open. This is a complete emancipation and freedom from any kind of bondage resulting from discrimination based on any kind of centrism.

We find an idea strikingly similar to this mutual dominant-subordinate relationship in Christianity where Martin Luther emphasizes the following two propositions in his treatise, *The Freedom of a Christian*[92]:

A Christian is a perfectly free lord of all,
    subject to none.
A Christian is a perfectly dutiful servant of all,
    subject to all.

The essential difference between Luther and Buddhism in this connection, however, lies in the following two points: (1) In Luther the mutual dominant-subordinate (lord of all and servant of all) relationship is realized only between human beings but not between human beings and nature. By contrast, in Buddhism the mutual dominant-subordinate relationship is realized not only among *each and every human being*, but also among *each and every thing* in the universe including human beings and nature. There is no anthropocentrism as occurs in Christianity. (2) In Luther, the mutual dominant-subordinate relationship is based on union with Christ, sharing with each other the things of God. Faith in Christ, the word of God alone, justifies, frees, and saves people. Without this christocentric and theocentric basis, the mutual dominant-subordinate relationship is not possible for Luther. On the other hand, the Buddhist idea of the mutual dominant-subordinate relationship occurs because there is no centrism whatsoever in the boundless openness of Sunyata.

While the freedom of the Christian is realized through faith in the gospel of Christ, the freedom of the Buddhist is found in the awakening to the nonsubstantiality and the interdependence of everything in the universe. If, in Christianity, as I suggested earlier, not only the kenosis of Christ, but also the kenosis of God is fully realized, and God completely empties God-self, the dynamic relationship of mutual domination-subordination or mutual immanence and mutual transcendence between human beings and God, and human beings and nature, can be fully realized. This is possible only by overcoming the theocentrism innate in Christianity.

Third, Sunyata translated by *jinen* in Japanese, or *svayambhu* in Sanskrit, which means "self-so," "so of itself," "things as they are," or "spontaneity." It also means "natural-ness," not as a counter concept to human agency, but as the primordial or fundamental naturalness underlying both human beings and nature. It is the most basic original "nature" of things prior to the separation between human beings and nature, between the divine and the human. Accordingly, *jinen* is beyond any kind of will, including human will, God's will, and the will to power in Nietzsche's sense. *Jinen* is, however, not a motionless, static, fixed state, but rather a pure activity of the most dynamic spontaneity, because it signifies unconstrained spontaneity realized in Sunyata without any will, whether it be will of self or other, human or divine. God's complete self-emptying (the kenosis of God) as the absolute self-negation of the will of God must be based on this spontaneity in terms of *jinen*. Indeed, *jinen* is the dynamic open abode to which everything returns for its final rest, and from which everything and its activity come forth spontaneously.

Fourth, in Sunyata, not only the interdependence and interpenetration but also the mutual reversibility of things is fully realized. This is a natural consequence of the previously mentioned mutual dominant-subordinate relationships among things. Even the unity of opposites is fully realized in Sunyata because Sunyata is the locus of the boundless openness without any center and circumferential limitation. Accordingly, not only can this and that, here and there, up and down, right and left, East and West (in terms of spatiality) be realized to be interpenetrating and reciprocal, but also beginning and end, before and after, past and future (in terms of temporality) can be grasped as interpenetrating and reciprocal. Accordingly, time and history are not simply understood to be linear and unidirectionally moving toward a particular end, but are understood to be reciprocal and even reversible. (See the section below, "Time and History in Buddhism".) In this way, each and every moment of time and history can be realized as the beginning and the end at once. Furthermore, in the locus of Sunyata, good and evil, right and wrong, beauty and ugliness, and all value judgments, without being fixed in their orders, but without losing their differences, can be realized to be interpenetrating and reciprocal. Hence, there is no supreme good or eternal punishment. Nirvana is realized amid samsara, and samsara, when its nonsubstantiality is realized, immediately transforms into nirvana.

Fifth, and most importantly, Sunyata contains the two characteristics of wisdom (prajna) and compassion (karuna). Positively speaking, Sunyata is wisdom in the light of which the suchness of everything is clearly realized in terms of its distinctiveness and sameness. And, in the light of wisdom, the aforementioned *jinen* is also clearly realized. Accordingly, in the locus of Sunyata, by virtue of wisdom, all things including the natural, the human and the divine, regardless of their differences, are each equally affirmed in their suchness and *jinen*. This is, however, not an uncritical affirmation of the given situation. On the contrary, it is a great and absolute affirmation beyond – and thus not excluding – any critical, objective, and analytical distinction. This is because the absolute affirmation realized in Sunyata is established through the negation of negation; this is the negation of nondistinction, which is in turn the negation of distinction in the ordinary sense.

This wisdom aspect of Sunyata is inseparably and dynamically connected with the compassion aspect of Sunyata. Sunyata is compassion in the light of which the dominant-subordinate relationship among things in the ordinary and relative sense is freely turned over, and moral and ethical judgments in terms of good and evil, right and wrong on the human, historical dimension, are transcended in the ultimate dimension. Through compassion realized in Sunyata even an atrocious villain is ultimately saved, even evil passions are transformed into enlightenment. In contrast to the ordinary statement – "Even an evil person is born in the Pure Land, that is, can be saved, how much more so a good person" – Shinran, the founder of Pure Land True Buddhism, declares: "Even a good person is born in the Pure Land, how much more so is an evil person."[93]

Zen, too, emphasizes the same reversal of moral order in the deeper religious dimension by saying that: "The immaculate practitioner takes three kalpas (aeons) to enter nirvana, whereas the apostate bhikku (monk) does not fall into hell."[94] Such transmoral compassionate activities and universal salvation are possible because they come spontaneously out of the unfathomable depth of Sunyata and because they are based on the great affirmation of all things realized through wisdom.

In the above five points, I described the positive meanings of the Buddhist notion of Sunyata. In our times, however, because of these characteristics of the Buddhist principle of Sunyata, the Buddhist cannot escape at least the following three criticisms often raised by Western and Christian friends.

First, if the realization of the suchness and *jinen* of everything, a realization which is beyond the critical, objective, and analytical distinctions, is essential to Sunyata, how can human reason and intellect, so important in the modern world, work in the context of Sunyata? Are they merely to be disregarded? What is the relationship between Buddhism and science, Sunyata and rational thinking?

Second, if value judgments, including the distinction between good and evil, right and wrong, are completely reciprocal or reversible, how can human ethics be established? In particular, how is the problem of evil to be understood in the realization of suchness and *jinen*?

Third, if past and future are completely interpenetrating and reciprocal, how can history be understood to take place? How can we talk about the novelty of things in history and the direction and end or outcome of human history? In addition to this criticism, Christian friends often make the following point:

> Christianity also, to some extent, talks about the interpenetration of past and future, for example, in terms of the eternal creation and the realized eschatology, and talks about the reversibility of value judgment, for example, as we see in Jesus' words "I come not to call the righteous, but the sinner." In Christianity, however, Jesus Christ as the Messiah and God as the ruler of history provide a criterion of ethical judgment and the aim of history along with the sense of novelty. How does the Buddhist principle provide a criterion of ethical judgment and the aim and direction of human history?[95]

My response to these criticisms requires both some further basic considerations about Sunyata and some critical reflections. First, there are two basic considerations about Sunyata that need to be elaborated. (1) Sunyata should not be understood as a goal or end to be attained in Buddhist life, but as the ground or the point of departure from which Buddhist life and activity can properly begin. Sunyata as the goal or end of the Buddhist life is Sunyata conceived outside one's self-existence, which, as I mentioned earlier, is not true Sunyata. True Sunyata is only realized in and through the self here and now and is always the ground or the point of departure for Buddhist life.

(2) Sunyata is fundamentally non-Sunyata—that is, Sunyata with an "X" through it, (~~Sunyata~~). That is the true and ultimate Sunyata. This means that true Sunyata empties not only everything else, but also empties itself. Through its self-emptying it makes everything exist as it is and work as it does. In other words, through its self-emptying the realization of Sunyata reestablishes a dualistic view and value judgment clearly, without being limited by them. Sunyata should not be understood in its noun form but in its verbal form, for it is a dynamic and creative function of emptying everything and making alive everything.

The Role of Human Reason in Buddhism

On the basis of these two basic considerations, I should also like to make three critical remarks concerning the Buddhist notion of Sunyata. Let us examine the role of human reason in Buddhism, the meaning of free will in Buddhism, and time and history in Buddhism.

First, the role of human reason in Buddhism. Throughout the long history of Buddhism, human reason or intellect has not been grasped positively. Human reason or intellect as a mental ability to think, to measure and discriminate objects, is called *vikalpa* or *parikalpa*, and has been regarded as something to be overcome in order to attain awakening or wisdom—that is, *jnana*.

This is significantly different from the Western tradition, in which, from ancient Greece to today, human reason has generally been regarded as something essential to attaining true knowledge. This is especially the case when *nous* or *intellectus*, which is distinguished from *logos* or *ratio* as the power of conceptual and discursive thinking, connotes higher activities of the human mind which can intuitively realize ultimate reality and strive for positive unity in thought and action.

In Kant, pure theoretical reason can provide synthetic a priori knowledge that makes pure mathematics and pure natural science possible. With his theory of pure theoretical reason, Kant gives a firm philosophical foundation to empirical knowledge of the phenomenal world. Although Kant clearly realized the limitation of pure theoretical reason in that the "thing itself" cannot be known, though it is "thinkable" by theoretical reason, he philosophically demonstrates the possibility of knowledge of metaphysical entities such as freedom, the immortality of the soul, and God, by pure practical reason. In Kant, ultimate reality is knowable not theoretically but only practically in ethics. And to him, ethics is to be based on pure practical *reason*.

Arguing "what is rational, that is actual; and what is actual, that is rational,"[96] Hegel emphasizes the dynamic identity of the rational and the actual. To Hegel, philosophy is nothing but the reconciliation with actuality. He advances the notion of "absolute knowledge" in which the opposition between subjectivity and objectivity, between rationality and actuality, is completely overcome. But, because Hegel's philosophy was later criticized as a panlogism, it is not completely free from the superiority of rationality over actuality, subjectivity over objectivity, form over matter. This can be seen in the fact that Hegel himself calls his logic "Subjective Logic."[97] Through this brief excursion into the history of Western philosophy, one can see how strong and persistent the reliance on speculative reason is in that intellectual tradition.

In marked contrast, the Buddhist tradition espouses persistent distrust of human reason. Buddhism did not find in human reason an intuitive ability to grasp ultimate reality. Buddhism thus has not developed human reason in the direction of transcendental pure reason as Kant did, or in Hegel's direction of dialectical, speculative mind. As a result, pure science and pure theoretical philosophy did not emerge in the long tradition of Buddhism. This is because the primary concern of Buddhism is not to study the laws of nature or to comprehend reality through speculation, but pragmatically to emancipate people from the suffering caused by the fundamental ignorance innate in human existence, ignorance of the ultimate reality, due to the conceptual, dualistic way of thinking peculiar to human reason. Buddhism insists that only by completely overcoming rational and conceptual thinking can one awaken to suchness, as-it-is-ness, or the original "nature" of everything in the universe, which is fundamentally unanalyzable, unconceptualizable, and unobjectifiable.

Inasmuch as this awakening to suchness is beyond discrimination, it is called in Buddhism *nirvikalpa-jnana*[98] — that is, nondiscriminating Wisdom. This, however, does not signify the absence of discrimination or the absence of thinking—that is, "not-thinking"— because "not-thinking" is a mere negation of thinking and is still discriminated from thinking. Wisdom that is truly nondiscriminating is free even from the discrimination between "thinking" and "not-thinking," between discrimination and nondiscrimination. Accordingly, nondiscriminating Wisdom is called *hishiryo*[99], that is, non-thinking thinking, beyond both *shiryo*, thinking, and *fushiryo*, not-thinking. Unlike not-thinking *(fushiryo)*, non-thinking thinking *(hishiryo)* is not an absence of thinking, but rather primordial thinking prior to the distinction and opposition between thinking and not-thinking. It is also primordial thinking prior to the bifurcation between the thinking subject and object of thinking. This is why Dogen, a Zen master in thirteenth-century Japan, said, "Non-thinking Thinking itself is Right Thinking."[100] In nonthinking thinking there is neither subject nor object, neither self nor no-self. It indicates the realization of the True Self which, being entirely unobjectifiable, is to be realized even more on the near side than self and no-self.

Nondiscriminating Wisdom, another term for nonthinking Thinking, signifies *satori*, the awakening to the true self. It is only in this nondiscrimination wisdom that the suchness or as-it-is-ness of everything in the universe is fully realized. Thinking and being in nondiscriminating wisdom are identical. And this identity is inseparably connected with the awakening to true self. This dynamic identity of thinking, being and the true self is possible because nondiscriminating Wisdom is a characteristic of Sunyata. Accordingly, although nondiscriminating wisdom is subjectless and objectless, it is not a special psychological state, but can be realized only by completely turning over all possible rational thinking, and by breaking through even what is called *nous* or *intellectus*.

Due to its dynamic character, nondiscriminating wisdom does not exclude thinking. Instead, being beyond both thinking and not-thinking, it includes both. It can include rational, discursive thinking and even pure theoretical reason. This is, however, only *potentially* so, for historically Buddhism has been hasty to go beyond human reason to arrive at the nondiscriminating wisdom because of the stance that human reason is merely discriminative. Thus Buddhism has not known the creative possibility of human reason developed in the modern West in terms of science.

Buddhism also failed to realize that transcendental pure reason as opened up by Kant and dialectical self-negating reason as advocated by Hegel can be developed and realized out of human reason. As a result, the traditional form of Buddhism contributes little to the problems of rationality and science. In my view, this historical fact derives from overlooking the dynamic character of the Buddhist notion of Sunyata. Unless the dynamic character of Sunyata is fully realized, nonthinking thinking is apt to turn into mere "not-thinking." But, as I suggested, the Buddhist notion of non-discriminating Wisdom can *potentially* include and operate human reason and thinking within itself. It is an urgent task for Buddhism to *actualize* this potentiality experientially and existentially in contemporary terms.[101]

In order to pursue this task, the dynamic structure of the Buddhist notion of Sunyata must be fully realized to the extent that it can legitimately recognize and embrace all possible rational thinking, including the transcendental pure reason in Kant and dialectical self-negating reason in Hegel, which are hitherto unknown to Buddhism. If transcendental pure reason and dialectical self-negating reason are fully embraced by the notion of Sunyata through its dynamism, however, then they are not maintained just as they stand, but *regrasped* radically as a part of nonthinking thinking in the light of wisdom. This means that the limitation of rational thinking— that is, the conceptual and speculative nature of rational thinking from which even transcendental pure reason and dialectical self-negating reason cannot be completely freed, must be clearly realized in the light of nondiscriminating Wisdom, must be turned over from its ground and *revived* as thinking on the basis of "suchness" through the realization of nonthinking.

In Christianity, which is based on God's revelation, the conflict between divine revelation and human reason has been a persistent problem. In Buddhism, which is based on the realization of Sunyata, there is no issue equivalent to that conflict. But to properly embrace reason in its pure and transcendental or dialectical form, and to make it alive and useful, Sunyata must be grasped most dynamically through the clear realization of self-emptying.

Free Will in Buddhism

Second, like the issue of human reason, the notion of free will has never been grasped positively in Buddhism. In the modern intellectual history of the West, the importance of human free will has been strongly emphasized. It has been generally recognized that humans have a capacity to make free decisions over and against external necessity. Only through free decision, through the exercise of free will, can one's subjectivity and personality be legitimately established. In this regard, Kant is more radical in rejecting all previous moral philosophies based on moral sense or moral reason as heteronomous ethical theory on the one hand, and, on the other hand, dispensing with the theonomous command and love of the Judaeo-Christian tradition. Kant thus opens up an entirely new and transcendental realm of noumena in which the autonomy of pure practical reason is grasped as authentic freedom. Kant's notion of "causality through freedom"—that is, categorical imperatives of morality as the autonomy of the pure will—gives a firm philosophical foundation to the modern view of human free will.

Unlike most of Western philosophy, Christianity regards human free will negatively as the root of original sin, while taking God's free will and God's word positively as the principle of creation, redemption, and last judgment. Although human beings are creatures, they alone were created in the image of God and are endowed with the Godlike faculty of free decision and speech. And thus, God's omnipotence, including foreknowledge and divine free will versus human free will, has constantly been an important theological issue. This, however, indicates Christianity's strong affirmation of God's will as the fundamental principle of the divine-human and the divine-nature relationship. Even Nietzsche, who rejects Platonism, Christianity, and modern humanism, including Kantian transcendental ethics, emphasizes the will to power as the basic principle of his radical nihilism. Though viewed in different senses in humanistic, Christian, and Nietzschean standpoints, the notion of "will" has thus always been viewed positively in the West.

In sharp contrast, Buddhism has never taken the notion of will positively. Buddhism grasps will negatively, in that the problem of human free will is grappled with in terms of karma which must be overcome to attain enlightenment or awakening and thereby to achieve real freedom. Emancipation from karma does not lead us to a realization of the autonomous pure practical reason as in Kant, to the omnipotent will of God as in Christianity, or to the will to power as in Nietzsche, but rather to the awakening to Sunyata, which is entirely beyond any kind of will. It is a realization of suchness of *jinen*, primordial naturalness or spontaneity without will.

In view of the problem of free will, the Buddhist notion of Sunyata as suchness or *jinen* has both positive and negative aspects. As for the positive aspect in Sunyata: (1) the distinction and opposition between humans and nature, which is caused by anthropocentrism based on the emphasis on the free will peculiar to human existence, is fundamentally overcome; (2) the struggle between flesh and reason in making decisions based upon free will, which is inevitable in human existence as the subject of free will, is also overcome; (3) original sin as the disobedience of human free will against God's will involved in theocentrism does not emerge in Sunyata as suchness or *jinen*.

The Buddhist notion of Sunyata as suchness or *jinen*, however, also has negative aspects in view of the problem of free will. The notion of Sunyata inescapably leads us to at least the following three questions: (1) How can the notion of free will, peculiar to human existence, be positively established in the locus of Sunyata, which is primordial naturalness without will? (2) How can the problem of evil be understood to take place in the locus of Sunyata, which is beyond any kind of will, and how can the problem be resolved there? (3) How can Sunyata, as agentless spontaneity in its boundless openness, incorporate a personal deity as the ultimate criterion of value judgment?

Unless these questions are adequately resolved, Buddhism cannot properly provide a ground for human ethics and modern rationality, nor can it overcome the problems raised by Nietzsche's principle of the will to power. To cope with these questions and to overcome the negative aspect of the Buddhist notion of Sunyata, Christianity may provide some helpful suggestions.

The Buddhist Notion of Karma

In order to deal with the above questions properly, it may be helpful to first discuss the Buddhist notion of karma. Karma means act or deed. An act here is not mere physical movement, but physical or mental activity oriented by volition, which is based on free will. As the Buddha himself said, "O bhikkhus, it is volition (*cetana*) that I call karma. Having willed, one acts through body, speech and mind."[102] Karma is primarily equated with volition, that is, mental or spiritual acts (*manasa*) and, being mentals volition, karma leaves traces in the series of consciousness (*vijnana*).

As volition connected with free will and consciousness, such mental acts are a basic element in karma, but what one does after having willed is more important than the willing.[103] Hence the importance of bodily and vocal acts is emphasized:

Once produced by a conscious and voluntary vocal or bodily act, it exists and develops of its own accord, without the agency of thought, unconsciously, whether a man is sleeping, waking, or absorbed in contemplation. It is part of the series that takes the place of the soul in Buddhism.[104]

As a "series" composed of thoughts, sensation, volition and material elements, the soul or ego is nothing but a collection of various elements constantly renewed. In reality there is no agent but the act and its consequences. Thus, karma is a causally efficient phenomenon but the effect (*vipaka, phala*) of an act is not determined solely by the act itself, but also by many other factors, such as the nature of the person who commits the act and the circumstances in which it is committed. Accordingly, even when two people commit similar, if not identical, evil acts, they may reap different consequences and in different ways. For the circumstances or factors surrounding the actions are very different.[105]

> Unlike the traditional Hindu view of karma the Buddhist doctrine of karma is not deterministic, but conditional and generative. Karma is not a mechanical but organic power. It grows, expands and even gives birth to a new karma. Our present life is the result of the karma accumulated in our previous existence, and yet in our practical life the doctrine of karma allows in us all kinds of possibilities and all chances of development.[106]

The Buddhist view of karma outlined above entails at least the following three points: First, being volitional action based on free will, karma is essentially action that can be morally characterized. Although the circumstances and external stimuli are recognized as factors of karmic causality, conscious motives rooted in volition play the most important role in the determination of karmic causality. Also good and bad actions are characterized by whether or not they are performed by such conscious motives as greed, hatred, and delusion. In such cases the responsibility of the individual is evident. Accordingly, it is in one's moral life that the law of karma operates most clearly.[107]

Second, that the Buddhist notion of karma is morally qualified, does not entail an individualistic view of karma. In other words, although karma is closely related to the problem of an individual's responsibility, this does not imply an exclusively individualistic view of karma in that such acts, good or evil, committed by a person determine only his or her own fate without affecting the lives of others. Instead, the karmic effect of one's own actions clearly determines one's own future and that of others as well. In the Buddhist cosmology, the whole universe, with all its variety, is the outcome of acts, and these acts constitute the collective mass of the acts of all beings.

In his book, *Outlines of Mahayana Buddhism*, D. T. Suzuki describes this sympathetic solidarity or contagious characteristic of karma:

> It [the universe] belongs to all sentient beings, each forming a psychic unit; and these units are so intimately knitted together in blood and soul that the effects of even apparently trifling deeds committed by an individual are felt by others just as much and just as surely as the doer himself. Throw an insignificant piece of stone into a vast expanse of water, and it will certainly create an almost endless series of ripples, however imperceptible, that never stop till they reach the furthest shore. The tremulation thus caused is felt by the sinking stone as much as the water disturbed. The universe that may seem to crude observers merely as a system of crass physical forces is in reality a great spiritual community and every single sentient being forms its component part.[108]

This sympathetic and generative character of karma is effective not only throughout the vast expanse of the present universe, but also throughout all human history. Again, as D. T. Suzuki says:

[The] history of mankind in all its manifold aspects of existence is nothing but a grand drama visualizing the Buddhist doctrine of karmic immortality. It is like an immense ocean whose boundaries nobody knows, and the waves of events now swelling and surging, now ebbing, now whirling, now refluxing, in all times, day and night, illustrate how the laws of karma are at work in this actual life. One act provokes another and that a third and so on to eternity without ever losing the chain of karmic causation.[109]

Third, the moral and individually self-responsible character of karma and the sympathetic and collective character of karma are not contradictory but rather complementary to one another. For the Buddhist view of karma is ultimately rooted in *avidya*—that is, the fundamental ignorance that "begins" without beginning and is unfathomably deep. *Avidya* is the ignorance of the true nature of things—that is, of emptiness and suchness, resulting in not recognizing the impermanency of worldly things and tenaciously clinging to them as final realities. Thus *avidya*, as the root of karma, is identical with *bhava-tanha*, the will or thirst to be, to exist, to continue, to become more and more, to grow more and more, to accumulate more and more.[110]

It is an unconscious, endless impulse which Schopenhauer called *blinder Wille zum Leben* (blind will to live). Since *avidya* as the blind will to live is the deepest root of one's karma, it is thoroughly individual and self-responsible and yet trans-individual by going beyond the realm of one's consciousness; and thus it is sympathetically leaving an ineffable, reverberating mark in the life of the universe.

Briefly put, in the unfathomable depth of *avidya* (ignorance)—that is, the blind will to live—the individual aspect and the collective aspect of karma are dynamically united. And karma, particularly one's free will involved in karma thus grasped in the unfathomable depth of *avidya*, is understood by oneself to be a center of the network of karma extending throughout the universe.

In the individual aspect of karma—that is, in terms of individual karma—we are responsible for everything caused by *our own avidya* realized in the innermost depth of our existence—that is for everything, including consequences affecting us by innumerable factors, known and unknown to us, in the universe. Our individual karma is not exclusively individualistic but also reflects effects made by the acts of other beings through the sympathetic character of karma. On the other hand, in the collective aspect of karma—that is, in terms of collective karma—we are responsible for everything caused by *human avidya* universally rooted in human nature—that is, for everything including what is apparently unrelated to us in the ordinary sense.

In our collective karma nothing happens in the universe entirely unrelated to us insofar as we realize that everything human is ultimately rooted in the fundamental ignorance, *avidya*, innate in human nature. In this fundamental ignorance innate in human nature, the individual karma and the collective karma inseparably merge with one another. When Buddhism talks about *jigo-jitoku*, that is, self-karma-self-obtaining — it must be understood to include not only the depth of individual karma, but also the breadth of collective karma. Only when this fundamental ignorance is overcome and the self-centeredness involved in karma is broken through, can one awaken to the true nature of things — that is, to emptiness and suchness.

The Problem of Evil in Buddhism

Now we must turn to the question of how the problem of evil takes place in the locus of Sunyata and suchness, and how the problem can be resolved there. According to the Buddhist doctrine of karma, one is free to act for better or for worse within the circumstances in which the action is committed. Acts motivated by greed, hatred, and delusion are evil acts producing unmeritorious karma while acts motivated by opposite qualities are good acts producing meritorious karma. The consequences of karma may be experienced in this life or in future lives. However, both good acts and evil acts are regarded, in Buddhism, equally as *evil acts* in the deeper and fundamental sense because both of them are determined not only by external stimuli and internal conscious motives but also by a deeply inner unconscious blind will, and thus bind one to the world of endless life-and-death-transmigration. As we see in the word, quoted below, of the Chinese Zen masters Lin-chi I-hsuan (d. 866) and Tai-chu Hui-hai (d. 788), even to seek Buddha and dharma, to try to attain nirvana, is regarded as evil karma. In his discourse Lin-chi said:

> Make no mistake! Even if there were something to be obtained by practice, it would be nothing but birth-and-death karma. You are saying, "The six paramitas and the ten thousand [virtuous] actions are equally to be practiced." As I see it, all this is just making karma. Seeking Buddha and seeking Dharma is only making hell-karma. Seeking bodhisattvahood is also making karma; reading the sutras and studying the teachings is also making karma.[111]

The following is an exchange between a monk-scholar and Tai-chu Hui-hai:

> Scholar: How can one attain Great Nirvana?
> Master: Have no karma that works for transmigration.

Scholar: What is the karma for transmigration?

Master: To seek after Great Nirvana is precisely the karma for transmigration. To abandon the defiled and take to the undefiled, to
assert that there is something attainable and something realizable,
not to be free from the practice of getting rid of evil passions—
this is precisely the karma that works for transmigrations.[112]

It is essential for Buddhists to seek Buddha and Dharma, to seek after
nirvana by getting rid of evil passions. Even so, however, Lin-chi and Tai-
chu mean that insofar as such religious practice is motivated by human
volition, it is the karma of life-and-death-transmigration and is karma making hell. One should not take these words to simply indicate a radicalism
peculiar to Zen. These words are nothing but an explicit expression of the
basic Mahayana view of karma.

Suchness or *jinen* (primordial naturalness) in the realization of Sunyata
is fully realized right here and right now when one is freed from all karmas
(volitional acts), good and evil, religious and secular. The following words
of Lin-chi and Tai-chu make this point in their own expressive ways.

When your seeking mind comes to rest, you are at ease—a noble man.
If you seek him [a Buddha], he retreats farther and farther away; if
you don't seek him, then he's right there before your eyes, his wondrous voice resounding in your ears.[113]

Scholar: How can one be emancipated?

Master: No bondage from the very first, and what is the use of seeking
emancipation? Act as you will, go on as you feel—without second
thought. This is the incomparable way.[114]

This is not an animallike instinctive spontaneity but a spontaneity deeply
based on the primordial naturalness (*jinen*) that can be realized only by
getting rid of karmic blind thirst.

How does evil take place in the realization of Sunyata? This question
can be properly restated by another question: How does karma take place
in the realization of Sunyata? For karma, with *avidya* as its root, is nothing
but the source of all evil. As already repeatedly stated, true Sunyata is not
a static state of emptiness but a dynamic movement of emptying everything,
including itself. This emphasis on the dynamic character of Sunyata, however, always leaves open the possibility for the realization of Sunyata to
remain in "emptiness," to dwell in "emptiness," and lead to an attachment
to "emptiness." Precisely because the realization of Sunyata is so essential
to Buddhists, Sunyata is often reified through conception as *something*
called "Sunyata." As stated before, however, the Mahayana tradition has
always warned against such a conceptualized and reified view of Sunyata
as "Sunyata perversely clung to." For as soon as Sunyata is conceptually

grasped, substantialized, and attached to as "Sunyata," it turns into karma. Substantialization of Sunyata is no less than a denial of true Sunyata, and an obstacle on the path to the realization of authentic Sunyata. While a realization of true Sunyata indicates enlightenment, attachment to Sunyata signifies unenlightened ignorance, *avidya*.

How does the ignorant conceptualization of Sunyata take place in the locus of Sunyata? *The Awakening of Faith in the Mahayana*, one of the most important classic treatises of Mahayana Buddhism states: "Suddenly a conception arises. This is called avidya."[115]

"Suddenly" (Chinese, *hu-jan*) in this context does not indicate "suddenness" in the temporal sense, but rather "without why" in terms of causality, because the reason for the arising of conception in the locus of Sunyata cannot be rationally analyzed and explained. And yet, it happens.

In this regard, it may be interesting to consider here the Genesis account of the Garden of Eden. According to the account, it is by means of the temptation of a serpent that Adam and Eve, originally innocent, committed sin by disregarding the words of God and partook of the fruit of the tree of knowledge. Without the serpent's temptation, Adam and Eve might not have committed sin. Where, then, did that serpent come from? One may say that the serpent appears "suddenly" in the Garden of Eden created by God. The very serpent in the Garden of Eden may be regarded as a mythological analogy to the statement in *The Awakening of Faith in the Mahayana* that "suddenly a conception arises." In the Genesis account, however, the serpent is not the cause of sin but merely an opportunity or occasion for Adam and Eve to sin. It is true that without the serpent's temptation, Adam and Eve might not have committed sin.

But it is exclusively by means of Adam and Eve's free will that they accepted the seduction of the serpent and made its temptation possible as "temptation." Wherever the serpent came from, it is not more than an occasion for the committing of sin by Adam and Eve. It is within Adam and Eve that the cause or ground of their commitment of sin is realized.

Here we see the profound meaning and profound problematic character of free will. Why does the cause or ground of committing sin lie in the innocent Adam and Eve created by God? It is a fact that is beyond sheer rational analysis, deeply rooted in the unfathomable depth of free will. This is the reality of human free will. Despite a serpent's temptation, it is Adam and Eve's responsibility that they were disobedient to God's will. And as Paul states, "as through one man sin entered into the world, and death through sin; and so death passed unto all men, for that all sinned."[116] That is, all of us sinned in and through Adam and death passed unto all as the "wages of sin."[117]

Likewise, for Buddhism, however suddenly a conception and *avidya* may arise "without why" within ourselves, we are not free from responsibility for its arising. Despite its suddenness we are thoroughly responsible for the arising of *avidya* because, though unconsciously deep and endless, *avidya* is a will or thirst to be and to live. And the arising of *avidya* is possible at each and every moment of our life. As soon as we attach to Sunyata in the process of its incessant movement of emptying, we are involved in *avidya* and thereby in karma. Because of our attachment and abiding at any moment, Sunyata turns into karma: *vidya* (enlightenment) turns into *avidya* (unenlightenment, ignorance). If we continuously attach to and abide in karma thus arisen, that karma creates more karma, and we become further involved in the endless process of the development of karma, in samsara, transmigration of life-and-death. If we, however, completely abandon our attachment and abiding, and empty our conception and its objects — that is, if we do not substantialize the self and its objects any longer and awaken to their nonsubstantiality — karma ceases and *avidya* is overcome.

Although this extermination of attachment must be deep enough to overcome the attachment to the unconscious blind will to be, the cessation of attachment can take place at each and every moment of our life. In other words, as soon as we become completely nonattached to the self and the world in the process of samsara, karma ceases and Sunyata and nirvana are fully realized. This is because just as "suddenly" conception arises and *avidya* emerges, "suddenly" conception ceases and enlightenment (*vidya*) takes place. As a result of our detachment and self-emptying, karma turns into Sunyata; *avidya* (unenlightenment) turns into *vidya* (enlightenment). Thus, we must say: "Suddenly conception perishes: this is called enlightenment."

True enlightenment is always sudden enlightenment which takes place "without why," beyond rational analysis. Both *avidya* and *vidya* take place suddenly. It is always suddenly that *vidya* turns into *avidya*, *avidya* turns into *vidya*, Sunyata turns into karma, and karma turns into Sunyata. We are originally and fundamentally standing in the "suddenness." We stand neither in sheer *vidya* nor in sheer *avidya*. Nor is it that at the outset there is *vidya* and then it turns into *avidya*. Nor that at the outset there is *avidya*, and then it turns into *vidya*, for this very understanding itself is again a conceptualization. In reality, we are standing in the "as-it-is-ness" of *"vidya-as-it-is-is-avidya: avidya-as-it-is-is-vidya."* And this "as-it-is-ness"is nothing but "suddenness." It is an instantaneous pivot from which incessant mutual conversion from *vidya* to *avidya* and from *avidya* to *vidya* is taking place.

It may be called "dazzling darkness." It is not half dark and half-dazzling. It is thoroughly dark, and yet, as darkness, it thoroughly dazzling at one and the same time; it is thoroughly dazzling, and yet, as it is dazzling, it is thoroughly dark at one and the same time. That we are fundamentally standing in this dazzling darkness indicates that we are thoroughly unenlightened and ignorant, and yet simultaneously we are thoroughly enlightened. This is why Mahayana Buddhism emphasizes "samsara as it is, is nirvana; nirvana as it is, is samsara" and "bodhi (enlightenment) and klesa (defilement) are one and non-dual — non-differentiated and equal."[118] Such a paradoxical situation is possible because (1) it takes place in the locus of

Sunyata, which is entirely nonsubstantial and unobjectifiable, being bottom-lessly deep, and because (2) it takes place right here, right now at each moment—that is, in the absolute present.

In short, evil and karma take place when one becomes attached to and dwells in Sunyata without emptying oneself and the objects of the self. The root of such an attachment is *avidya*, the endless, unconscious thirst to be. On the other hand, evil and karma can be overcome when one completely empties oneself and the objects of the self through the realization of Sun-yata in its dynamism. With this awakening, *avidya* turns into *vidya* and emancipation is realized. Suchness and *jinen* are nothing but terms that indicate Sunyata in its dynamism.

Suchness, Jinen, and Evil

The problem of ethics in Buddhism, however, is not resolved by what I have said thus far. The above discussion only clarifies the *fundamental* rea-son—in terms of "without why"—for the arising and ceasing of evil in human existence, whereas the problem of ethics is involved in a more *rel-ative* human situation, which is conditioned by society and history. Tradi-tionally, when Mahayana Buddhism seeks to explicate "suchness" and *jinen* (primordial naturalness or spontaneity), it often refers to natural phenom-ena as examples:

> Mountains and rivers and great earth:
> everything reveals the Body of Dharma.[119]

> From the start blue mountains never move;
> white clouds come and go.[120]

> Bamboo shadows sweep the stairs,
> Yet not a mote of dust is stirred;
> Moonbeams pierce to the bottom of the pool
> Yet in the water not a trace remains.[121]

This last phrase from the *Futoroku* (The Record of Universal Lamp) is highly appreciated and often quoted in Zen to indicate "suchness" and *jinen* as exemplified by the will-free, unconscious, spontaneous movements of bamboo shadow and moonbeam, which, however much sweeping the stairs or piercing to the bottom of the pool, do not disturb or injure others. However, natural evil such as earthquakes and tornadoes, which are also will-free, unconscious, and spontaneous activities, and the struggle for exis-tence in the animal world in which the weak become the victim of the strong, have scarcely been mentioned as examples of suchness.

Although human moral evils such as lying, stealing, killing, adultery, and so forth have been a deep concern throughout Buddhist history, clear discussion concerning how these human moral evils are to be understood in terms of the realization of suchness and *jinen* has not been explicit enough. Furthermore, a question arises about whether or not immense historical evil such as the Holocaust in Auschwitz and Hiroshima is an exception to suchness and *jinen*, and, if not, how such historical evil is to be grasped in terms of suchness and *jinen*. Though inevitably to be grappled with by religious thinkers, such a question is scarcely discussed by Buddhists. If suchness and *jinen* are the essential dimensions of Sunyata as Buddhist reality, these notions must be equally applied to natural evil, physical and biological, and human moral evil, individual and collective, and to whatever degree of evil. In other words, earthquakes, one species devouring another in the animal kingdom, individual murder, and the Holocaust in Auschwitz all must be grasped in light of suchness and *jinen*. How is this possible and how is this justifiable?

In order to properly answer these questions I must clarify that the issues include the following three different dimensions and that all issues are properly and legitimately understood *ultimately from the vantage point of the third dimension:*

1. A nonhuman, natural dimension represented by pure natural science.
2. A transnatural human dimension represented by individual morality, and collective social and historical ethics.
3. A transhuman fundamental dimension represented by religious faith or awakening.

Natural Evil, Human Evil, and Religion

From the vantage point of pure natural science — that is, in a non-human natural dimension, both earthquakes and sunshine are equally natural phenomena caused by natural law and entirely indifferent to human interest. An earthquake happens as an earthquake due to its natural necessity; the sun shines brightly as it does due to its natural law. In nature, both earthquakes and sunshine simply occur in their "suchness," purely objectively, without human subjectivity. Accordingly, we most note that the "suchness" or "as-it-is-ness" of natural phenomena reflected in natural science is an abstraction from which the concrete, living context in which we human beings are involved, is absent. The same is essentially true of the struggle for existence in the animal world. When a lion attacks a rabbit, and a snake swallows a frog, they engage in these "cruel" acts from their instinctive impulse to survive. In the purely nonhuman, natural dimension, their acts are as natural as a flower's blooming and the wind's blowing. If we do not project human feeling and human interest upon natural phenomena, both physical and biological phenomena in the natural world take place entirely naturally and spontaneously in their "suchness."

In the human dimension, however, earthquakes are often unfavorable disasters causing suffering and damage to individuals and society at large, whereas sunshine is usually regarded as a favorable benevolent blessing offered to human beings. Relatively speaking, in the human context, an earthquake is evil, whereas sunshine is good, although both of them equally are products of natural law. Likewise, while we humans feel pleasure and appreciation about a flower's blooming and a bird's singing, we may feel "cruelty" in a lion's attacking a rabbit or a snake's swallowing a frog. Our usual judgment of the flower and bird is "good," whereas that of the lion and snake is "bad" or "evil."

Such good and evil judgments are clearer and more definite in the case of human acts, individual and collective. In the human ethical dimension, honesty, kindness, integrity, courage, responsibility, and so forth are regarded as good, whereas lying, stealing, betrayal, killing, and so forth are regarded as evil. In broader, societal terms, peace and harmony are esteemed as good, while war and discord are depreciated as evil. And what is important in the human ethical dimension is not necessarily an outcome of one's act but an inner motivation. It is imperative in human ethical behavior to be good and right in one's motivation regardless of whether or not one's given physical, psychological, and social conditions are favorable to that motivation.

Human beings, however, are not so simple as to be ruled completely by ethical and moral principles. On the contrary, a painful confession, "for the good which I would I do not: but the evil which I would not, that I practice.[122] ... Wretched man that I am! Who shall deliver me out of the body of this death?"[123] is not peculiar to St. Paul, but is inevitable to all seriously reflective persons. However important ethics may be to human beings, ethics cannot stand by itself, because when carried out to its final conclusion it falls into a dilemma, as Paul's words show, and finally collapses. One must therefore go beyond the ethical dimension and enter into the religious dimension. Ultimately, the distinction between good and evil in the ethical dimension is relative, not absolute.

When we go beyond the human ethical dimension to a more fundamental religious dimension, however, the situation is quite different. In the religious dimension, even natural phenomena are grasped, no longer objectively, but deeply subjectively and experientially, not merely in the human context, but from a much deeper, most fundamental point of view. For example, in the faith of theistic religion, an earthquake may be believed to be a divine punishment upon us and the sunshine a divine grace upon us. They are no longer relatively evil or relatively good to our interest, but may be equally accepted by a believer of the divine will as a manifestation of divine providence. In theistic religion, human ethical good and evil are also grasped essentially in a different way from mere ethics. In Christianity, for instance, unlike Greek philosophy, good and evil are not grasped in terms of human-human relationships, but fundamentally in terms of the divine-human relationship. And in this divine-human relationship, as Paul said in the Epistle to the Romans: "We before laid to the charge both of Jews and Greeks, that they are all under sin; as it is written, there is none righteous, no, not one.[124] And as Jesus said: "Why do you call me good? Only God is Good."[125]

In the New Testament, sin is not a separate evil act or the total of such individual evil acts, but human disobedience and rebellion against the law of God and particularly the lack of faith in Jesus.[126] Sin is universal and common to all humankind. Jesus Christ, however, was sent into the world not to judge the world, but that the world should be saved through him[127]:

> For as through the one man's disobedience the many were made sinners, even so through the obedience of the one shall the many be made righteous. And the law came in besides, that the trespass might abound: but where sin abounded, grace did abound more exceedingly.[128]

Furthermore, in Paul, corruption and deliverance from its bondage are not limited to humankind but include the whole creation, as seen from the following words of his:

> For the creation was subjected to vanity, not of its own will, but by reason of him who subjected it, in hope that the creation itself also shall be delivered from the bondage of corruption into the liberty of the glory of the children of God. For we know that the whole creation groaneth and travaileth in pain together until now. And not only so, but ourselves also, who have the first-fruits of the Spirit, even we ourselves groan within ourselves, waiting for our adoption, to wit, the redemption of our body.[129]

Here we clearly see in Christianity, at least as confessed by Paul, the whole creation, including mountains, rivers, trees and animals viewed as groaning and travailing in pain together with us by being subjected to vanity and corruption, but now hopeful for deliverance through the salvific work of Jesus Christ.

Just like Christianity, Buddhism stands in the transhuman fundamental dimension of religion. Unlike Christianity, however, Buddhism is *fundamentally* not theistic and does not accept one personal God as the ultimate reality but Sunyata. Therefore, the term "transhuman" mentioned above has a different connotation. As discussed before, in Christianity only God is good and there is none that does good. All human beings have sinned in Adam, and the whole creation is subject to vanity. By contrast, in Buddhism, there is nothing permanent, self-existing and absolutely good, for everything without exception is co-arising and co-ceasing, impermanent, without "own-being," empty. The doctrine of dependent co-origination, one of the most basic teachings of Buddhism, clearly emphasizes that everything

without exception is interdependent with every other thing; nothing whatsoever is independent and self-existing. Accordingly one God as absolute
good cannot be accepted in Buddhism because, speaking from the perspective of dependent co-origination, a notion such as the one God as the
absolute good who must be independent is nothing but a reification and
substantialization of something ultimate as the only entity that has its own
being.

Of course, the Christian notion of one God as the absolute good is not
a theoretical or metaphysical one, but a deeply practical, devotional one,
which is considered crucial to one's salvation from sin and death. Yet, from
the standpoint of Mahayana Buddhism which emphasizes "Do not abide
in Nirvana" to attain true emancipation and cautions us about "Buddha-
bondage"[130] by saying, "the Buddha way and the Devil way are both evil."[131]
One God as the absolute good appears as a special form of attachment in
the religious and transcendent dimension. For Buddhism, the ultimate reality is neither secular nor sacred, neither samsara nor nirvana, neither sentient beings nor Buddha, neither emptiness nor fullness: It is true emptiness
dynamically identical with true fullness.

Accordingly, the "transhuman" religious dimension does not, in Buddhism, indicate the divine or the sacred that is believed to have sovereignty,
however immanent it may be, over the world, nor does it signify the absolute
good that is beyond the relativity of good and evil. Instead, the transhuman
religious dimension signifies that which is neither the divine nor the human,
neither the sacred nor the secular, neither the supernatural nor the natural,
and that which is neither absolutely good nor absolutely evil—Sunyata.

Accordingly, in Buddhism, though relatively in the human dimension,
an earthquake is evil and sunshine is good; absolutely speaking, in a transhuman religious dimension, the two events have no own-being or substance
as evil or as good, or as divine punishment or divine grace. Both earthquake
and sunshine, with their clear value distinction in the relative dimension,
are, in an absolute ultimate dimension, equally grasped as the appearance
of Sunyata in their suchness. There is absolutely *no thing*, including divine
providence, behind or beyond them. They happen just in their suchness.
This "suchness," however, is not abstract suchness as seen in pure natural
science, which is realized objectively excluding human subjectivity and indifferent to human interest. On the contrary, it is the most concrete
"suchness" that is only subjectively and experientially grasped at the unfathomable depth of our existence through the realization of the interrelationship (dependent co-origination) between all natural phenomena and us,
and the realization of emptiness (nonsubstantiality) of both nature and
human beings.

In other words, even such natural phenomena as earthquakes and sunshine are not excluded from the sympathetic universality of karma, but are
realized as a unitary dimension of karma pervading the entire universe,
this cosmic unity of karma being now realized at the depth of one's reali-

zation of individual karma. The law of dependent co-origination throughout the universe and the emptiness of everything can be existentially realized through the clear realization of the sympathetic universality and the cosmic solidarity of karma. Only here at this juncture is suchness in its most concrete sense realized.

It is precisely in terms of this most concrete "suchness" that Mahayana Buddhism states, "Mountains and rivers and the great earth: everything reveals the Body of Dharma," and "from the start blue mountains never move; white clouds come and go." This should not be confused with natural mysticism, which lacks the realization of dependent co-origination between humans, and nature and the realization of the emptiness of everything. And such biological phenomena as a lion's attack of a rabbit and a snake's swallowing a frog are not exceptions to this concrete "suchness," in that these biological phenomena are grasped as a part of collective karma in which we are also involved and as a manifestation of Sunyata without an unchangeable substance.

At this point, however, we should not forget that natural phenomena thus accepted at this present moment in terms of suchness as a part of collective and sympathetic karma and as an appearance of Sunyata *in the light of wisdom*, are also realized simultaneously *in the light of compassion*, which works for a better future from the unfathomable depth of Sunyata without attachment to individual interest. Here I find an echo in St. Paul when he says, "the whole creation groaneth and travaileth in pain together until now," and talks about "hope that the creation itself also shall be delivered from the bondage of corruption into the liberty of the glory of the children of God." In Buddhism, in terms of the universal compassion inseparably connected with universal wisdom, one can work toward bettering both humans and nature most effectively and appropriately when unattached to human self-interest.

A Buddhist View of the Holocaust

I should like to address now the specific evil situation of the Holocaust as centered in such concentration camps as Auschwitz during the Second World War. Speaking in terms of society and history, as a Japanese who was neither a German nor a Jew and who lived at that time on the opposite side of the world, I could be said to have had nothing to with that terrible event. And it is easy for me to condemn the Holocaust as a diabolical, inhuman, atrocious event. But, however serious I may be in this attack and in attempting to change the given social and historical situation, insofar as I stand outside of the event, my total approach is entirely wrong. From the perspective of the Buddhist doctrine of karma, I am not free from responsibility for the Holocaust in Auschwitz. I must accept that "Auschwitz is a problem of my own karma. In the deepest sense I myself participated as well in the Holocaust." It is indeed the problem of my own karma, not in terms of my individual karma in the narrow sense, but in terms of collective karma in that the Holocaust is *ultimately* rooted in the fundamental ignorance (*avidya*) and the endless blind thirst to live inherent in human existence in which I am also deeply involved through my own individual karma. I am sharing the blame of the Holocaust because at the depth of my existence I am participating in the fundamental ignorance together with the overt assailants in the Holocaust.

I believe that only through the realization of the collective karma and fundamental ignorance inherent in human beings which is realized at the depth of each one's existence, and through fundamental enlightenment as the realization of fundamental ignorance, can one properly and legitimately cope with such a historical evil as the Holocaust.

This, however, does not signify a joint responsibility of the victims in terms of the humanistic sense of justice, which is realized in the second human ethical dimension but in terms of solidarity realized in the third, most fundamental religious dimension. Furthermore, even within the third, religious dimension, what I have said above does not signify our solidarity with the case of Auschwitz equally through the realization of guilt and forgiveness under the sovereignty of one God, whether God is coercive (as some traditional theologies insist) or persuasive (as process theology maintains). Here, in this regard, the religious dimension is based on a God who is loving and just. Instead, what I am saying in terms of the religious dimension signifies the boundless openness or emptiness that is neither God, human, or nature, and in which all things, including the divine, the human, and the natural, are all interrelated with and interpenetrated by each other. Accordingly, even such an atrocious event as the Holocaust in Auschwitz, which is relatively unrelated to me, must be grasped as a matter of my own responsibility in terms of sympathetic and collective karma that reverberates endlessly and is unfathomably deep.

Not as an outsider humanist who attacks the Holocaust from the vantage point of social and international justice, nor as a religious subject who judges and acknowledges the Holocaust through dynamic interpretation of the divine justice and the all-loving God, but as one who painfully realizes the collective karma deeply rooted in human ignorance as the ultimate cause of the event in Auschwitz am I aware of and accept joint responsibility for the Holocaust and find in this realization the *basis* from which I can properly cope with the case of the Holocaust.

The standpoint of justice, humanistic or divine, cannot be a proper basis for our coming to terms with the Holocaust, because the notion of justice is a double-edged sword. On the one hand, it sharply judges which is right and which is wrong. On the other hand, the judgment based on justice will naturally cause a counter-judgment as a reaction from the side thus judged. Accordingly, we may fall into endless conflict and struggle between the judge and the judged. All judgment, "just" or otherwise, may perpetrate further karma. Instead, the standpoint of wisdom and compassion, which is realized through the realization of collective karma and the realization of the nonsubstantiality of everything in the universe, in my view, can provide a more proper basis to cope with the Holocaust without getting involved in an endless conflict. In this regard, a key point lies in recognizing that although the Holocaust was indeed a brutal, atrocious historical evil, we should not substantialize and cling to it as a fixed separate entity unrelated to the rest of the vast and endless network of human history. That is to say, we should realize the relationality and the nonsubstantiality or lack of self-being in that event.

By saying this, my intention here is not to diminish the reality of the evil of the Holocaust and to disengage it from the specific agony of the victims. No, not at all! As I said before, in the depth of my own being, I painfully realize the universal or collective karma innate in human existence in which the Holocaust is also ultimately rooted. This is a realization that inevitably emerges from the Buddhist doctrine of karma.

Obviously, the Holocaust constituted unimaginable sufferings for the Jewish people under Hitler and the manifestation of unprecedented moral evil. It may even be said to be an historical event qualitatively different from all other historical events. In the ethical and relative dimension, responsibility for the Holocaust clearly resides in Nazi, not in Jewish, individuals. But the same Buddhist doctrine of karma teaches us that however extraordinary and unique an event the Holocaust may be, it is not an isolated, independent event unrelated to the vast and boundless network of human history. In an immeasurable way, even the uttermost evil of the Holocaust is related to the innumerable events in the past and present of human history in which all of us, assailants and victims alike, are involved.

When we are victims of a horrible suffering such as what occurred in Auschwitz or Hiroshima, we tend to absolutize the evil involved as if it happened to us passively, unrelated to our own karma. However, insofar as we return to the deepest depth of our existence, we unavoidably realize the root of human karma which is common to all human beings and in which all good and evil are interrelated in one way or another. Accordingly, in absolutizing a particular evil or a particular good, however conspicuous it may be, a *real* view of the event is lost by substantializing it.

This absolutization entails a serious problem, because in practice it always is accompanied by an emotional attachment to the event and the people involved in it in terms of hatred or love. Such emotional attachment based on substantialization of the event creates further karma and thus we are more and more deeply enmeshed in the endless process of karma. To overcome this endless process of karma, it is necessary not to absolutize the event but rather to realize its relationality and nonsubstantiality.

This may be a Buddhist version of the kind of "reorientation" Irving Greenberg implies when, in his essay "Judaism and Christianity after the Holocaust," he states: "the Holocaust cannot be overcome without some basic reorientation in light of it by the surviving Jewish community."[132] I agree completely with Irving Greenberg when he further observes:

> Just as refusal to encounter the Holocaust brings a nemesis of moral and religious ineffectiveness, openness and willingness to undergo the ordeal or reorienting by the event could well save or illuminate the treasure that is still in each tradition.[133]

While in a human, moral dimension the Holocaust should be condemned as an unpardonable, absolute evil, from the ultimate religious point of view even it should not be taken as an absolute but a relative evil.

It is perhaps Emil L. Fackenheim who most accurately clarifies the uniqueness of the Nazi Holocaust in the human history. By employing a series of negations Fackenheim discusses the uniqueness of the Holocaust from seven points of view. For instance, he emphasizes that "the Holocaust was not a war, because while war is waged between parties endowed, however unequally, with power, the victims of the Holocaust had no power."[134]

What seems to me most important in this regard, however, is his following emphasis:

> The Holocaust was not a case of genocide . . . The genocides of modern history spring from motives, human, if evil, such as greed, hatred, or simply blind xenophobic passion. This is true even when they masquerade under high-flown ideologies. The Nazi genocide of the Jewish people did not masquerade under an ideology . . . The ideal was to rid the world of Jews as one rids oneself of lice. It was also, however, to punish the Jews for their "crime" and the crime in question was existence itself.[135]

This emphasis becomes clearer: "In all other societies [than Nazi Germany], however brutal, people are *punished for doing*. In the Third Reich "non-Aryans were *punished for being*."[136]

With these emphases Fackenheim clarifies that the uniqueness of the Holocaust lies in the fact that not for the "crime" of Jews, but for the "existence" of Jews, not for their "doing" but for their "being," did the Nazis intend the Holocaust of Jewish people. In this regard I recognize the essential difference between Auschwitz and Hiroshima. By the analysis of Fackenheim I fully realize how unique and terrible the Nazis' Holocaust was. However, I also realize that Fackenheim's discussion about the uniqueness of the Holocaust refers to only the second dimension I mentioned earlier, that is, a human dimension represented by individual morality and collective social and historical ethics, and does not refer to a more fundamental religious dimension.

Then, how does Fackenheim understand the problem of the Holocaust in the religious dimension? If I am not mistaken, *Tikkun* is a key term for

Fackenheim in this regard. *Tikkun* means a mending of what is broken or ruptured.[137] Referring to such philosophers and theologians as Martin Heidegger, Karl Barth, Paul Tillich, and Rudolf Bultmann and their views of the Holocaust, Fackenheim states:

> For the first time in this work, we are faced with the possibility that the Holocaust may be a radical rupture in history—and that among things ruptured may be not just this or that way of philosophical or theological thinking, but thought itself.[138]

Furthermore Fackenheim emphasizes that the dilemma in the post-Holocaust *Tikkun* "in which we are placed is so extreme, so unprecedented, so full of anguish as to seem to tear us in two."[139] This dilemma is clearly seen in the fact that "Holocaust theology" has been moving toward two extremes—a "God-is-dead" kind of despair, and a faith for which, having been "with God in hell," either nothing has happened or all has been mended. To this dilemma Fackenheim makes a significant comment: "However, post-Holocaust thought . . . must dwell, however painful and precariously, between the extremes, and seek a *Tikkun* as it endures the tension."[140]

He then discusses three elements which compose the *Tikkun* emerging from this tension: a recovery of Jewish tradition; a recovery in the quite different sense of recuperation from an illness; a fragmentariness attached to those two recoveries that makes them both ever-incomplete and ever-laden with risk. Referring to these elements, Fackenheim emphasizes:

> Without a recovered Jewish tradition . . . there is no Jewish future. Without a recuperation from the illness, the tradition must either flee from the Holocaust or be destroyed by it. And without the stern acceptance of both the fragmentariness and the risk, in both aspects of the recovery, our Jewish *Tikkun* lapses into unauthenticity by letting theirs, having "done its job," lapse into the irrelevant past.[141]

Finally he states:

> We remember the Holocaust; we are inspired by the martyrdom and the resistance; and then the inspiration quickly degenerates into this, that every dogma, religious or secular, is restored as if nothing had happened. However, the unredeemed anguish of Auschwitz must be ever-present with us, even as it is past for us.[142]

In the preceding, I have tried to follow Fackenheim's discussion on the Holocaust and to understand it as much as possible. I strongly feel how radically and painfully the Nazi Holocaust terrified the Jewish mind and how seriously and distressfully Jewish thinkers have been struggling concerning the problem of the Holocaust.

To me as a Buddhist, however, three question still remain. First, I fully understand the uniqueness of the Nazi Holocaust and its unprecedented evil in all human history. However, does this uniqueness mean to Jewish people that the Holocaust is an isolated event entirely unrelated to other events in the world and history, and thereby has a fixed, enduring absolute evil nature? If it has a fixed, enduring absolute evil nature, how can Jewish people come to terms with the Holocaust and with God, who ultimately allowed the Holocaust to occur?

Second, if the rupture caused by the Holocaust is not a rupture of this or that way of philosophical or theological thinking, but of thought itself, how is *Tikkun*—that is, a mending of the rupture—possible?

Third, if the Holocaust means a complete rupture in Jewish history how is a recovery of Jewish tradition possible? When Fackenheim emphasizes the "return to revelation," what revelation and what God does he maintain in his mind?

Free Will and the Ultimate Criterion of Value Judgment in Sunyata

Earlier, I mentioned three issues that the Buddhist notion of Sunyata must confront: How can the notion of free will, peculiar to human existence, be positively established in the locus of Sunyata which is primordial naturalness without will? How can the problem of evil be understood to take place in the locus of Sunyata, which is beyond any kind of will, and how can the problem be resolved there? How can Sunyata, as agentless spontaneity, incorporate a personal deity as the ultimate criterion of value judgment in its boundless openness?

In preceding sections, I have dealt with the second question in detail and treated the first question indirectly. In this section I will discuss the questions concerning free will and the ultimate criterion of value judgment in the locus of Sunyata. This issue may be restated, "How can Sunyata, which is free from any centrism, focus itself upon a particular center?" Unless this question is sufficiently resolved, Buddhism cannot properly ground human ethics or overcome Nietzsche's principle of the will to power.

As I have already tried to clarify, in Buddhism the problem of human free will is grappled with in terms of karma, which is ultimately rooted in *avidya*, fundamental ignorance, and *bhava tanha*, blind impulse or thirst to live, both deeply rooted in human existence. This means that in Buddhism, human free will is grasped as an endlessly self-determining, self-attaching, and self-binding blind power—which is the ultimate source of human suffering and which inevitably leads us to the final dilemma—that is, death in the absolute sense. However, when this endlessly self-binding blind power (karma) is realized as it is, through the practice of *dhyana*, meditation, one can be emancipated from it and awaken to boundless openness, Sunyata.

It is good to note here that *dhyana* in this connection is not a psychological process but a religious practice or discipline through which one experiences death (Great Death) and resurrection (Great Life). In this awakening to Sunyata, human free will is realized entirely anew in its pure form by eradicating its self-attaching and self-binding character. Instead of producing a chain of causation and transmigration, free will, which is now based on the awakening to Sunyata, freely works in this phenomenal world without attachment, delusion, or bondage. It is just as Lin-chi describes the "non-dependent Man of Tao" — that is, an awakened person:

> Entering the world of form, not suffering from form-delusion; entering the world of sound, not suffering from sound-delusion; entering the world of smell, not suffering from smell-delusion; entering the world of taste, not suffering from taste-delusion; entering the world of touch, not suffering from touch delusion; entering the world of cognition, not suffering from cognition-delusion. Thus realizing the six worlds of form, sound, smell, taste, touch, and cognition to be all Empty-Forms, nothing, can constrict this non-dependent Man of Tao.[143]

Like Buddhism, in which human free will is usually understood to be bound by the chain of causality and karma, in Christianity, human free will is under divine law and is dominated by sin. But Christians who believe in the grace of God in Jesus Christ are freed from the law itself and so from sin and its wages, death. "There is therefore now no condemnation to them that are in Christ Jesus. For the law of the Spirit of life in Christ Jesus made me free from the law of sin and of death."[144] "Where the Spirit of the Lord is, there is liberty."[145] "Now being made free from sin and become servants to God, ye have your fruit unto sanctification, and the end eternal life."[146]

Thus, both Christianity and Buddhism talk about freedom, or liberation from sin, death, or karma. In Christianity, however, this freedom is the gift of God and is based on the will of God. Liberation from sin and death is the divine work of God. On the other hand, liberation from karma in Buddhism is not based on any kind of will, divine or human. It is realized through the Great Death of human ego and is based on nothing whatsoever. It is *jinen*, primordial naturalness, and agentless spontaneity which springs from the bottomless depth of Sunyata. As the *Vimalakirti Nirdesa Sutra* states: "From the Non-abiding origin is produced all things."[147] It is a spontaneous action without a particular agent, human or divine. It is an action without agent and, in this naturalness or spontaneity, action as it is non-action and nonaction as it is action.

In this respect, Buddhism's notion of freedom is more akin to that of Nietzsche than that of Christianity. For Nietzsche's notion of freedom is based on *Unschuld des Werdens* — that is, the "innocence of becoming,"[148] which is without subject and object, and in which there is no "doer." Although Nietzsche clearly rejects the psychology of will which creates a right to take revenge, his philosophy is ultimately based on the will to power which is faithful to "life" in the deepest sense. His notion of "will to power" is clearly different from human free will in the ordinary sense, and the will of God in the Christian sense. It is the most fundamental will to live, which is functioning at the depth of the universe and regards the notion of human free will and even that of the will of God as self-deception—as human fabrication created by a human's preservation instinct.

When we return to the most fundamental will to power through the realization of the self-deceptive nature of human will and God's will, Nietzsche insists, we enjoy the "innocence of becoming," and intuitively realize eternity—eternal recurrence. Despite its great similarity with the Buddhist notion of *jinen*—that is, primordial naturalness or spontaneity—Nietzsche's notion of the "innocence of becoming" lacks the realization of Great Death without which *jinen* cannot be properly realized. The realization of Great Death is needed to overcome even the will to power, the basic principle of Nietzsche. Only when the will to power is broken through to the boundless openness Sunyata are Sunyata and its accompanying notion of *jinen* fully realized.

As I mentioned before, in the awakening to Sunyata, human free will is realized entirely anew in its pure form by getting rid of its self-attaching and self-binding character. This pure free will is "pure" and "free" not in terms of transcendental pure practical reason as in Kant, or in terms of divine will of an all-loving God as in Christianity, or in terms of innocence of becoming as in Nietzsche. It is pure and free because that will is always self-emptying and self-negating, not self-assertive or self-affirmative—it is absolute "willing" without the subject of will and the object of will, cheerful, intentionless, even playful, and yet most serious and untiring. It is pure and free without clinging to either the secular or the sacred, the self or others, cause or effect. In short, it is free will revived and working in the locus of Sunyata.

Just as one's free will, deeply involved in both individual and collective karma, was the center of the network of karma extending throughout the universe, pure and free will now revived in the locus of Sunyata permeates a center or locus of boundlessly open Sunyata. It is a center realized by Sunyata in its self-emptying nature. In other words, in and through the self-emptying of Sunyata, Sunyata concentrates itself into a particular center as the pure and free will.

This pure and free will is thoroughly one's free will and yet, at the same time, it is not one's free will, but the free will of Sunyata. This pure and free will is thoroughly Sunyata's free will and yet, at the same time, it is not Sunyata's free will, but one's free will. This dynamic identity of one's free will and Sunyata's free will is true with anyone's free will in the locus of Sunyata. The implication is that unlike one's self-centered free will involved in karma, pure and free will revived in the locus of Sunyata is self-emptying and self-negating.

This pure and free will revived in, and realized as the center of, Sunyata functions in terms of a "vow" that is traditionally called *pranidhana*. It is a vow to save others, however innumerable they may be, as well as one's self, a vow in which the mind to seek enlightenment and the desire to save all sentient beings are dynamically one. This is because in Sunyata the wisdom aspect and the compassion aspect are always working together through Sunyata's self-emptying. Sunyata remaining with itself, without turning itself into a vow, is not true Sunyata. However, Sunyata that remains only at the level of vow still cannot be true Sunyata either. Just as Sunyata must empty itself and turn itself into vow, it must empty even vow and turn itself into "act" or "deed" which is traditionally called *carita* or *carya*. For a vow that does not turn itself into act cannot be a true vow. In this way, in and through self-emptying, Sunyata always ceaselessly turns itself into vow and into act, and then dynamically centers itself in a focal point of this dynamism.

This development of Sunyata into vow and act, however, does not signify that Sunyata goes externally out of itself. This development takes place within the locus of Sunyata. For being boundless openness, Sunyata has nothing outside of itself. Rather, the development of Sunyata into vow and act signifies Sunyata's going internally into its own depth. More strictly and sufficiently speaking, in the development of Sunyata into vow and act, the outward movement and the inward movement, the centrifugal approach and the centripetal approach, are not two but dynamically one. This is true precisely because Sunyata is boundlessly open; in it, everything is interdependent and interpenetrating. This is the dynamism of Sunyata, and the focal point of this dynamism—which can be realized at each and every point of dynamism—is the "vow" to save one's self and all others and "act" to actually pursue the vow. Traditionally, Amida Buddha in Pure Land Buddhism is one of the personifications of such a vow and action.

The vow and act realized through the self-emptying of Sunyata provide not only the center of boundlessly open Sunyata but also the ultimate criterion of value judgment. This judgment is to be made in terms of whether or not a thing or action in question does accord with the vow and act to make one's self and all others awakened. If the thing or action accords with the vow and act realized in the dynamism of Sunyata it is regarded as valuable, whereas, if it does not, as "antivaluable." Valuable things will be naturally encouraged and promoted, but even "antivaluable" things will not be simply rejected or punished. Clearly recognizing the "antivaluable" nature of a thing in question in the light of wisdom, one will transform it from within itself in the light of compassion. Both promoting "valuable" things and transforming "antivaluable" things are the work of vow and act as the self-emptying of Sunyata. Vow and act, as the center of Sunyata and as the ultimate criterion of value judgment, are clearly realized only when Sunyata is fully realized dynamically in its self-emptying nature.

Time and History in Buddhism

Buddhism has a unique view of time. Time is understood to be entirely without beginning and without end. Inasmuch as time is beginningless and endless, it is not considered to be linear as in Christianity or circular as in non-Buddhist Vedantic philosophy. Being neither linear nor circular, time is understood to be not irreversible but reversible, and yet time moves from moment to moment, each moment embracing the whole process of time.

This view of time is inseparably linked with the Buddhist view of life and death. Buddhism does not regard life and death as two different entities, but one indivisible reality—that is, living-dying. For if we grasp our life not objectively from the outside, but subjectively from within, we are fully living and fully dying at each and every moment. There is no living without dying, and no dying without living. According to Buddhism, we are not moving from life to death, but in the process of living-dying. This must be clearly realized.

We must also realize that the process of our living-dying is without beginning and without end. The process extends itself beyond our present life both into the direction of the remote past and into the direction of the distant future. (This is the reason, for example, Zen raises the traditional question: "What is your original face before your parents were born?" as well as the question: "If you are free from life and death, you know where you will go. When the four elements [a physical human body] are decomposed, where do you go?") Due to the absence of God as the creator and the ruler of the universe, in Buddhism there is no beginning in terms of creation and no end in terms of last judgment. Accordingly, we must realize the beginninglessness and the endlessness of samsara—that is, the transmigration of living-dying. This realization is essential because it provides a way to overcome samsara and to turn it into nirvana. For if we clearly realize the beginning*less* and endless*ness* of the process of living-dying *at this moment*, the whole process of living-dying is concentrated *in this moment*. In other words, this moment embraces the whole process of living-dying by virtue of the clear realization of the beginninglessness and endlessness of the process of living-dying. Here, in this point, we can overcome samsara and realize nirvana right in the midst of samsara.

In this view of living-dying, time is understood to be beginningless and endless. And, as I mentioned above, in the clear realization of the beginninglessness and endlessness of the process of living-dying at this moment, the whole process of time is concentrated in this moment and, with this moment as a pivot, past and future can be reversed. (Otherwise an emancipation from karma is inconceivable.)

Because of this unique view of time, however, Buddhism is relatively weak in its view of history. Time is not directly history. Time becomes "history" when the factor of spatiality (worldhood, *Weltlichkeit*) is added to it. History comes to have meaning when time is understood to be irreversible and each moment has an unrepeatable uniqueness or once-and-for-all nature (*Einmaligkeit*). But since time is understood to be entirely beginningless and endless and thus reversible, the unidirectionality of time and the uniqueness of each moment essential to the notion of history are not clearly expressed in Buddhism.

Buddhism, however, can develop its own view of history if we take seriously the compassionate aspect of Sunyata—that is, the self-emptying of Sunyata. In the wisdom aspect of Sunyata, everything is realized in its suchness, in its interpenetration and reciprocity with everything else. Time is not an exception. Accordingly, in the light of wisdom realized in Sunyata, past and future are interpenetrating and reciprocal. Furthermore, the beginningless and endless process of time is totally concentrated in each moment. This is why in Buddhism each "now" moment is realized as the eternal Now in the sense of the absolute present. However, in the light of compassion, also realized in Sunyata, another aspect of time comes to be realized. Although all things and all persons are realized in their suchness and interpenetration in the light of wisdom *for an awakened one*, those *"unawakened" from their own side* have not yet awakened to this basic reality. Many beings still consider themselves unenlightened and deluded. Such persons are innumerable at present and will appear endlessly in the future. The task for an awakened one is to help these persons as well "awaken" to their suchness and interpenetration with all other things. This is the compassionate aspect of Sunyata that can be actualized only by emptying the wisdom aspect of Sunyata. As the generation of "unawakened" beings will never cease, this process of actualizing the compassionate aspect of Sunyata is endless. Here the progress of history toward the future is necessary and comes to have a positive signficance.

In the light of wisdom realized in Sunyata, everything and everyone is realized in its suchness and time is overcome. In the light of compassion also realized in Sunyata, however, time is religiously significant and essential. And the endless process of the compassionate work of an awakened person trying to awaken others is no less that the aforementioned process of Sunyata turning itself into vow and into act through its self-emptying. At this point, history is no longer a "history of karma" in which persons are transmigrating beginninglessly and endlessly. It becomes a "history of vow and act" in which wisdom and compassion are operating to emancipate innumerable sentient beings from transmigration. Here we do have a Buddhist view of history.

It is not, however, an eschatological or teleological view of history in the Christian or Western sense. If we use the term "eschatology," the Buddhist view of history is a completely realized eschatology, because in the light of wisdom everything and everyone without exception is realized in its suchness, and time is thereby overcome. If we use the term "teleology," the Buddhist view of history is an open teleology because in the light of compassion the process of awakening others in history is endless. And the completely realized eschatology and the entirely open teleology are dynamically united in this present moment, now. This is a Buddhist view of history as I understand it.

All that I have said about Sunyata can be summarized by saying that true Sunyata is not static but dynamic — it is a pure and unceasing function of self-emptying, making self and others manifest their suchness. It is urgently necessary to grasp the notion of Sunyata dynamically to give new life to Buddhism in the contemporary world.

In this paper I have suggested that in Christianity, the notion of the kenotic God is essential as the root-source of the kenotic Christ, if God is truly the God of love. I also suggested that in Buddhism, Sunyata must be grasped dynamically not statically, since Sunyata indicates not only wisdom but also compassion. And when we clearly realize the notion of the kenotic God in Christianity and the notion of the dynamic Sunyata in Buddhism — then without eliminating the distinctiveness of each religion but rather by deepening their respective unique characters — we find a significant common basis at a deeper dimension. In this way, I believe, Christianity and Buddhism can enter into a much more profound and creative dialogue and overcome antireligious ideologies prevailing in our contemporary society.

NOTES

This essay was originally delivered at the second conference on East-West Religious Encounter, "Paradigm Shifts in Buddhism and Christianity," held in Honolulu, Hawaii, January 3-11, 1984. The author is grateful to Professors S. I. Shapiro and Joseph S. O'Leary, as well as to Steve Antinoff and Christopher Ives, for their revisions and valuable suggestions.

1. A good example of this development is John Cobb's book, *Beyond Dialogue: Toward a Mutual Transformation of Christianity and Buddhism* (Philadelphia: Fortress, 1982). See also Masao Abe, "John Cobb's *Beyond Dialogue*," *The Eastern Buddhist*, vol. 18, no. 1 (1985) 131–137.

2. Masao Abe, "Buddhism and Christianity as a Problem of Today," *Japanese Religions*, vol. 3, No. 2 (1963) 15.

3. Thomas F. Kuhn, *The Structure of Scientific Revolutions* (Chicago: University of Chicago Press, 2nd ed., 1970) pp. 66–76. Hans Küng, "Paradigm Change in Theology," unpublished paper, pp. 7–8.

4. For the author's view of Marxism and Freudian Psychoanalysis, see Masao Abe, *Zen and Western Thought* (London and Honolulu: Macmillan and University of Hawaii Press, 1985), pp. 231–48.

5. Hans Küng, *Does God Exist? An Answer for Today* (New York: Random House, 1981), pp. 109–10.

6. Ibid., p. 124.

7. Ibid., pp. 123–24.

8. Ibid., p. 124.

9. Ibid., p. 634.

10. Ibid.

11. Ibid., p. 635.

12. Ibid., p. 124

13. This section on nihilism is largely taken from my essay "Christianity and Buddhism—Centering Around Science and Nihilism," *Japanese Religions*, vol. 5, no. 3 (1968) 36–62.

14. Martin Heidegger, *Holzwege* (Frankfurt am Main: Klostermann, 1950), p. 206.

15. Ibid., p. 199.

16. Ibid., p. 200.

17. Friedrich Nietzsche, *Wille zur Macht* (Stuttgart: Kröner Tachenausgabe, Band 78), p. 10.

18. *The Complete Works of Friedrich Nietzsche*, ed. Oscar Levy, vol. 12, p. 73.

19. Nietzsche, *Willie zur Macht*, p. 11.

20. Ibid.

21. My notions of "nihilism before religion" and "nihilism beyond religion" may roughly correspond to Nietzsche's notion of "passive nihilism" and "active nihilism."

22. Masao Abe, "Buddhism and Christianity as a Problem of Today," p. 17.

23. Philippians 2:5–8.

24. *Interpreter's Bible*, vol. 5, p. 49.

25. Ibid.

26. Ibid.

27. Ibid., p. 50.

28. Ibid., pp. 48–49.

29. Matthew 10:3–9.

30. Romans 6:11.

31. 2 Corinthians 4:10.

32. Galatians 2:20.

33. 1 Corinthians 15:22.

34. 2 Timothy 2:11.

35. 1 Corinthians 15:1; 2 Corinthians 4:16.

36. Philippians 2:9–11.

37. *Interpreter's Bible*, vol. 5, p. 50.

38. Karl Barth, *Church Dogmatics* IV/1, pp. 557f.

39. Jürgen Moltmann, *The Crucified God* (New York: Harper & Row, 1974) p. 201.

40. Küng, *Does God Exist?*, pp. 684–85.

41. Ibid., p. 690–691. In his notes, Küng calls the reader's attention to how Moltmann puts quotation marks in the title of the important chapter 6 of his *The Crucified God*.

42. Keiji Nishitani, *Religion and Nothingness* (Los Angeles: University of California Press, 1982), p. 59.

43. Moltmann, *The Crucified God*.

44. Karl Rahner, *Foundations of Christian Faith: An Introduction to the Idea of Christianity* (New York: Seabury Press, 1978), p. 222.

45. Karl Rahner, *Sacramentum Mundi*, vol 2 (London: Burns and Oates, 1969), pp. 207f.

46. Rahner, *Foundations of Christian Faith*, p. 220.

47. Ibid., p. 222.

48. Ibid.

49. Ibid.

50. Ibid.

51. Küng, *Does God Exist?*, p. 133.

52. Rahner, *Foundations of Christian Faith*, p. 220.

53. Moltmann, *The Crucified God*, p. 24.

54. Ibid., p. 207.

55. Ibid.

56. Ibid., p. 204.

57. Ibid., p. 243.

58. Ibid., p. 203.

59. Barth, *Church Dogmatics*, II/2, pp. 167, 162.

60. Moltmann, *The Crucified God*, p. 20.

61. Ibid.

62. Ibid.

63. Ibid., p. 204.

64. Ibid., p. 245.

65. Ibid.

66. Ibid.

67. Ibid., p. 274.

68. Ibid., p. 205.

69. Ibid., pp. 244–45.

70. Ibid., p. 243.

71. Ibid., p. 244.

72. Ibid., p. 228.

73. Ibid., p. 204.

74. Ibid., p. 244.

75. Ibid., p. 246.

76. Ibid.

77. Ibid., p. 278.

78. Ibid., p. 246.

79. Ibid.

80. Ibid., p. 204.

81. Ibid., p. 244.

82. Ibid.

83. Ibid., p. 205.

84. Ibid., p. 275.

85. Ibid., p. 244.

86. Küng, *Does God Exist?* p. 64.

87. Mulamadhyamakakarika, 24. See Frederick J. Streng, *Emptiness, A Study in Religious Meaning* (Nashville: Abingdon, 1967), p. 213.

88. *Prajnaparamita-sutra. Taisho* 8:250b.

89. *Prajnaparamita-hrdaya-sutra. Taisho* 8:848.

90. Masao Abe, *Zen and Western Thought*, pp. 4–24.

91. Ibid. pp. 31f.

92. *Martin Luther: Selections from his Writings*, edited and with an Introduction by John Dillenberger p. 53.

93. *The Tannisho*, translated by Ryukoku Translation Center, Ryoto, 1966, p. 22.

94. *Zenmon neniushu*, copied by Seizan Yanagida, vol. 2, p. 120.

95. Taken from conversations with several theologians.

96. G. W. F. Hegel, *Grundlinien der Philosophie des Rechts* (Hamburg: Felix Meiner Verlag, 1955), p. 14.

97. G. W. F. Hegel, *Science of Logic* (New York: Humanities Press, 1966), vol. 2, pp. 209ff.

98. *Mahayana-sutralamkara*, ed. Sylvain Levi (Paris, 1907), vol. 1. Index to the *Mahayana sutralamakara*, by Gadjin M. Nagao (Tokyo: Nippon Gakujutsu Shinkokai, 1958), Bodhis, p. 344.

99. Shobogenzo, "Zazenshin," in *Dogen, Nihon shiso taikei* (The Outline of Japanese Thought) (Tokyo: Iwanami, 1970), vol. 1, p 127.

100. Ibid., "Sanjushichibon-bodaibunpo," *Dogen*, vol. 2, p. 190.

101. Masao Abe, *Zen and Western Thought*, pp. 112, 119–20.

102. *Anguttara-nikaya*, ed. Devamitta Thera. Columbia, 1919, p. 590.

103. *Encyclopedia of Religion and Ethics*, vol. 7, p. 674.

104. Ibid.

105. David J. Kalupahana, *Buddhist Philosophy: A Historical Analysis* (Honolulu: University of Hawaii Press, 1976), pp. 48–49.

106. D. T. Suzuki, *Outlines of Mahayana Buddhism* (New York: Schocken Books, 1963), p. 198.

107. Kalupahana, *Buddhist Philosophy*, p. 47.

108. Suzuki, *Outlines of Mahayana Buddhism*, p. 193.

109. Ibid., pp. 207–208.

110. Walpala Rahula, *What the Buddha Taught* (New York: Grove Press, 1959), p. 31.

111. *The Record of Lin-chi* (Tokyo: Institute for Zen Studies, 1975), pp. 18–19.

112. Suzuki, *Essays in Zen Buddhism*, 3rd Series (London: Luzac, 1934), p. 26.

113. *The Record of Lin-chi*, p. 19.

114. Suzuki, *Essays in Zen Buddhism*, p. 26.

115. *The Awakening of Faith.*

116. Romans 5:12.

117. Ibid.

118. *Shohomugyo-kyo, Taisho*, vol. 15, No. 650, p. 759c.

119. *A Zen Forest: Sayings of the Masters* (Tokyo, 1981), p. 64.

120. Ibid., p. 81.

121. Ibid., p. 89.

122. Romans 7:19.

123. Romans 7:24

124. Romans 3:9–10, 12.

125. Mark 10:18.

126. John 8:24.

127. John 3:17.

128. Romans 5:19–20.

129. Romans 8:20–23.

130. *Lin-chi Record* (Rinzairoku), *Taisho*, vol. 47, 1985.

131. *Denshinhoyo, Taisho.* vol. 49, no. 1012A.

132. Irving Greenberg, "Judaism and Christianity after the Holocaust" in *Jews and Christians in Dialogue* ed. by Leonard Swidler, *Journal of Ecumenical Studies,* vol. 12, no. 4, p. 52.

133. Ibid., p. 51–52.

134. Emil L. Fackenheim, Foreword by Yehudah Bauer, *The Jewish Emergence from Powerlessness,* 1979.

135. Ibid.

136. Ibid.

137. Emil L. Fackenheim, *To Mend the World* (New York: Schocken Books, 1982), p. 252.

138. Ibid., pp. 192–93.

139. Ibid., p. 309.

140. Ibid., p. 310.

141. Ibid.

142. Ibid.

143. *The Lin-chi Record, Taisho,* vol. 47, no. 1985, p. 500c.

144. Romans 8:1–2.

145. 2 Corinthians 3:17.

146. Romans 6:22.

147. *Vimalakirti-Nirdesa Sutra, Taisho,* vol. 14, no. 475.

148. Friedrich Nietzsche, *The Will to Power,* ed. Walter Kaufmann (New York, Random House, 1968), p. 297.

PART II

Responses to Masao Abe

1

Buddhist Emptiness and the Crucifixion of God

THOMAS J. J. ALTIZER

Masao Abe has long since been established among us as one of our most important and fascinating theological thinkers, which he is above all in the deep challenge he continually brings to Christianity. That challenge is to the Christian doctrine of God, and to the Christian faith in God, a faith that can only appear as bad faith in the light of the Buddhist perspective.

Again and again Abe has unveiled the contradiction between established Christian doctrines of God and Christian faith in Christ, between the glory and transcendence of God and the humiliation and servanthood of Christ, between the eternal life of God and the eternal death of Christ. If kenosis or self-emptying is his most decisive symbol and key, and key to Christianity and Buddhism alike, that key is illusory and unreal if it unveils only the true identity of Christ and his sacrifice, and not the true and inner identity of Godhead itself. Thus the kenosis of the Son of God is inconceivable without the kenosis of God the Father, and the finality and totality of the love of God is inconceivable apart from the kenosis of Godhead itself. For even as the Buddhist notion of Sunyata signifies the dynamic of emptying everything, including itself, a genuine Christian notion of God must comprehend a Godhead which truly and actually empties itself.

David A. Dilworth has identified Kitaro Nishida's "The Logic of the Place of Nothingness" (1945) as the *fons et origo* of the Kyoto School.[1] Here Nishida claims forthrightly that the Mahayana schools have taken the paradox of God to its ultimate conclusion, a conclusion not reached by Hegel or any Christian thinker, and a conclusion which alone understands the paradoxical identity of the transcendence and the immanence of God. This identity arises from a self-contradiction in the absolute itself:

In what sense then is the absolute the true absolute? It is truly absolute by being opposed to nothing. It is absolute being only if it is opposed to absolutely nothing. Since there can be nothing at all that objectively opposes the absolute, the absolute must relate to itself as a form of self-contradiction. It must express itself by negating itself. Mere nonentity cannot stand in relation to itself. That which stands in relation to itself must negate itself. But by negating itself it is paradoxically one with itself. What is entirely unrelated to itself cannot even be said to negate itself.[2]

So it is that the true God or the true absolute possesses or realizes absolute self-negation within itself, and in this respect the absolute must be absolutely nothing.

Or, in Christian language, the absolute is truly itself by absolutely emptying itself. Nishida is the primary source of the kenotic thinking of Nishitani and Abe, and in the last writings of Nishida we can clearly see this thinking as Buddhist and Christian at once, and so much so that here there appears to be little difference between Buddha and God, except for the claim that in the bottomless depths of our own self we must refer either to God who is Father or to Buddha who is Mother.[3]

Nevertheless, Christianity is here understood to have brought the objective identity of transcendent transcendence to its ultimate conclusion, whereas the history of Buddhism reflects an experience of transcendence that is the reverse of this, for Buddhism has encountered the absolute in the direction of the absolute's subjectivity, and the special characteristic of Buddhism lies in this immanent transcendence.[4] Thus Christianity encounters the absolute's own self-expression as an objective transcendence, and Buddhism encounters it as an immanent transcendence. Now even if the absolute's own self-expression is identical with itself, that identity becomes difference in the histories of Buddhism and Christianity, a difference that our historical moment calls upon us to transcend. Such a movement of transcendence is more fully present in the Kyoto School than in any contemporary Christian thinking, and thereby it is the Kyoto School that is now providing a primary site of theological reflection itself.

If Buddhist history has never truly known an objective transcendence, and thus is innocent of what our Western history has known as God, it has nevertheless known a genuine transcendence, and a transcendence that is transcendent in its own absolute negation of itself. That self-negation is a universal self-negation, a self-negation realizing itself in consciousness and history alike, wherein absolute self-negation is the absolute presence of the absolute itself. Such absolute presence is absolute absence of all objective presence or manifestation, hence it is a wholly immanent transcendence, and an immanent transcendence which is the absolute's own subjectivity. That subjectivity or immanent transcendence is largely if not wholly absent from the historical expressions of Christianity, just as an absolute objectivity or absolutely objective presence or manifestation is absent from the historical expressions of Buddhism. Nonetheless it is the claim of the Kyoto School that in itself the absolute is identical with itself, and is so most fully and most truly in its own absolute self-negation. That self-negation is absolute presence itself, and it is present in all consciousness and history, present as their deepest and truest ground. But must that ground be objectively groundless, and thus historically and empirically invisible and absent?

Apparently Buddhism has never been beset by the Western problem of theodicy, and the truth is that this did not become a genuine Christian problem until the advent of modernity. Above all it is the objective or manifest absence of God from a distinctively modern history and consciousness that is the true ground of the problem of theodicy. Is this not a crucial point at which a Buddhist understanding of absence as presence could enlighten our Christian understanding of God? Is the absolute presence of God by necessity the absolute absence of all objective divine presence and manifestation? Or could one even say that transcendent transcendence must become objectively manifest as nothingness in the absolute presence of transcendence itself? If Buddhism has always known such presence, is it possible that Christianity is only historically encountering absolute presence in the absolute absence of God from our history and consciousness?

These possibilities might become actualities in the context and perspective of a Buddhist paradoxical identification of "is" and "is not." If true deity "is" in its "is notness" and its true "isness" is a consequence of its "is notness," then God is most truly God in the emptying and death of Godhead, in God's own full and final self-negation. Abe has been suggesting this for many years, and as the only Kyoto philosopher with a Christian theological training, he has again and again presented such an identity as a resolution of the contemporary Christian problem of God.

It is truly remarkable that contemporary Buddhist thinkers are able to think critically and sensitively about the contemporary Christian problem of God, and not the least reason for this is that they themselves have been so deeply open to modern radical thinking. Moreover, they are Buddhist and modern at once, and there is no such parallel in any group or body of Christian thinkers. Christian theologians are now profoundly alienated and estranged from the actual consequences of their own Christian history, whereas Buddhist thinkers have been reborn in response to this historical situation, and reborn as Buddhist thinkers. Thereby Buddhist thinking has become Eastern and Western at once, and Christian and Buddhist at once, and above all so by way of their understanding of absolute self-negation. If an absolute self-emptying or self-negation is the kenosis of the Godhead, and of the center or essence of the Godhead itself, then that kenosis cannot be absent in a real and actual disappearance of God, a disappearance that here could be known as an epiphany of the absolute ubiquity of God. Historical Christianity has never envisioned the full or total ubiquity of God, not even in Dante's *Paradiso*, and this is surely because historical

Christianity has been so deeply bound to the pure transcendence of God, or to the transcendence of transcendence itself.

That transcendence disappears in Buddhist thinking, and it is just such thinking that can now apprehend the kenosis of Godhead itself, and a kenosis that is the source and ground of an absolute presence of the Godhead in the absolute absence or death of God. Abe, Nishitani, and Nishida can know the death of God in the Incarnation itself, and thereby know the death of God as the compassion of God, a compassion that is the very embodiment of the absolute emptying of the Godhead. That very emptying is the fullness of Godhead itself, a fullness which is emptiness, and a fullness that is the emptiness or self-negation of God. Can such an emptiness or self-negation be present or manifest upon a historical horizon determined by the transcendence of transcendence? Perhaps only so if the transcendence of transcendence has disappeared in that horizon, and disappeared in the real and actual absence of God. Then Christian and Buddhist thinking would be homologous in their mutual ground in the absence of an objective or manifest transcendence, and each would be open to a wholly immanent transcendence, an immanent transcendence that Buddhism can know as the absolute's own subjectivity.

But as the Kyoto philosophers continually remind their Christian readers, Christianity has always known the absolute's own subjectivity as Christ, and from its very beginning Christianity has been initiated into Christ as the kenosis of God. So likewise Christianity has known an immanent transcendence in Christ, and even known it as the Kingdom of God. And perhaps not so paradoxically the modern historical discovery of the eschatological Jesus, or the discovery of Jesus as the proclaimer and parabolic enactor of an eschatological or apocalyptic Kingdom of God, occurred in the wake of the death of God. Only a historical and cultural world that was a consequence of the absence or death of God made possible the modern critical and historical understanding of the Bible, as Neo-orthodox theology realizes so deeply. And absent from a modern critical understanding of the New Testament is that very transcendence of transcendence which so dominated historical Christianity. Thus only the absence of God opened Christianity itself to a critical understanding of its original ground, and so, too, it was only in this historical situation that Christianity became open to the challenge of Buddhism. What could Buddhism mean to a Christianity that truly and fully knows the transcendence of God? And could Buddhist thinkers absorb a Christianity that is fully and finally grounded in the transcendence of transcendence?

So it is that the transcendence of transcendence is disappearing in modern Christian thinking even as it has always been absent in Buddhist thinking. But that disappearance could be a response to an epiphany of Godhead itself, and most particularly so if that were an epiphany of the kenosis of God, and a kenosis in which God's "isness" is identical with "is notness." Not even Buddhism has given us so fully a kenotic symbol as the Crucifixion of God, and if Christian orthodoxy has always refused this symbol as a symbol of Godhead itself, this is nevertheless the most overwhelmingly powerful symbol in both New Testament and modern Christianity, and it is also the symbol that since the Middle Ages has dominated the Christian imagination.

Now it is fascinating that the Kyoto philosophers have placed such a deep emphasis upon the Buddhist symbol of the Great Death, and have given themselves so fully to a quest for understanding eternal death, and eternal death as the eternal emptying of everything whatsoever. Only that emptying is true life, and only a full realization of the self's own nothingness is compassion and bliss. Quite naturally these thinkers have chosen Eckhart, Kierkegaard, and Nietzsche as the closest Western analogues to their own world, and thus they have unearthed deeply Western images of self-annihilation as their way into the very center of Christianity. And they have succeeded in finding a way into that center, and a Buddhist way at that.

Is this not decisive evidence of a Christian ground in their thinking, and a Christian ground in their very understanding of absolute self-negation? No doubt there are distinctively Buddhist and Christian ways of apprehending absolute self-negation, and clearly these have enormously differed from each other historically. But is there a deep or ultimate difference between them in their understanding and realization of the very center or essence of absolute emptying? Letting stand the common statement, and one made by Nishida himself, that the West has known being (u) as the ground of reality, whereas the East has taken nothingness (mu) as its ground, is there a full or final difference between the self-negation or self-emptying lying at the very center of both Buddhism and Christianity? Or would a Christian affirmation of the kenosis of God be at bottom a capitulation to Buddhism, and perhaps thereby a deep regression to the ultimate center of a primordial pagan world that both Israel and Christianity originally negated? Many critics have long identified both atheism and nihilism as such a regression, and a regression that from their point of view is fully embodied in modern totalitarianism. Is therefore the challenge of Buddhism a true temptation to Christianity, and a temptation threatening to dissolve both the center and the ground of Christianity and the Western world alike?

Yet it is scarcely deniable that both Christianity and the Western world have long since been passing through a dissolution of their center and ground, and this wholly independently of Buddhism. Indeed, it was the thinking and the consciousness that was a product of this self-dissolution that initially captured Nishida, and subsequently became a fundamental ground of the Kyoto School. Moreover, it was the genius of the Kyoto School that made possible their apprehension of this very ground as a way into the genuine center of Buddhism. While nothing is more deeply ambivalent in the Kyoto School as a whole than their relationship to Hegel, it is Hegel who was the first modern thinker to ground all thinking and consciousness in a universal movement of self-negation, and for Hegel himself that very movement is a consequence of the Incarnation and of the self-negation of God. That self-negation undergoes a modern epiphany with the advent of the Unhappy Consciousness, a form of consciousness that realizes itself by losing all the essence and substance of itself, and consciousness that actualizes itself by interiorly realizing that *God is dead.* Thus Hegel could apprehend the modern event of the death of God as a consequence of the self-negation of God, of a Calvary of absolute Spirit, a Calvary that is nothing less than the Crucifixion of God.

In this perspective, it would appear that the Kyoto School is calling upon the contemporary Christian world to recover our own Christian ground, a ground that was lost or forgotten in our common Christian world, and yet a ground that is paradoxically present in the deepest expressions of modernity. Nowhere is this challenge more fully present than in the modern theological problem of history, a problem resulting from the disappearance of God in all that truly modern history following the French Revolution, a disappearance that is manifest in the very advent of a post-Christian world. Now it is all too significant that Hegel himself created the philosophy of history, and created it by understanding the totality of history as a theodicy, as the self-embodiment of an absolutely providential God. True, the actuality of history is a world of violence and horror; nonetheless that horror is finally a redemptive horror, and a redemptive horror because it is the "labor" or actuality of absolute Spirit. At no other point has a deeper revulsion from Hegel occurred in our world, and a revulsion as fully present in twentieth century theology as elsewhere, and this despite the fact that Hegel's understanding of history is clearly grounded in the absolute providence of God. For it is the providence of God that has become unreal in the twentieth century, and above all unreal to Christian theologians who have attempted to speak in response to modern and contemporary history.

While Hegel's lectures on the philosophy of history were not intended for publication, and would seem again and again to be accommodations to the ruling powers of his day, they nevertheless remain before us as both the fullest expression of the modern idea of progress and as the most radical and comprehensive expression of Christian faith in the providence of God. Nothing is further from Buddhism itself, and seemingly nothing could be more alien to our contemporary world as a whole. Yet the question must be posed as to whether it is possible for a modern as opposed to an ancient Christian not to believe in the forward movement of history.

At no point was medieval Christianity more revolutionary than in its apocalyptic expressions, and those from Joachim of Flora through the Franciscan Spirituals and Dante were deeply grounded in a radically forward movement of history, a movement which itself became the center of the political and social revolutions of the modern world. This is the very movement that Christian conservative ecclesiastics from Augustine through Luther and Pius IX have denied and opposed. Yet this is the movement that was first conceptually understood by Hegel, an understanding giving birth to Marxism, and not only Marxism but a wide variety of powerful expressions throughout the world. Indeed, it was the very victory of such movements that marks the French Revolution as the great dividing line of world history.

Must not this or any other such dividing line be refused and erased if one denies the truly forward movement of history? Is Christianity by necessity, as virtually all its critics agree, a reactionary refusal and opponent of modernity? And is it not all too clear that it was the very victory of modernity that ushered in a post-Christian world? Nor should the Christian forget that Buddhism itself faces comparable opposition in Asia and elsewhere from its seeming identity as a reactionary and even primordial presence.

Are Buddhism and Christianity united on the basis of such an apparent identity, and does the destiny of each depend upon the erasure and dissolution of the forward movement of time and history? The genuine futurity of time and history was not truly born until the prophetic revolution of Israel, and then it arose in the context of the end of ancient Israel, an ending issuing in the birth of Judaism in the Exile. So likewise the modern idea of progress was born in the European Enlightenment, an Enlightenment that finally ended Christendom, an ending that may or may not have made possible the advent of a truly new or modern Christianity. So likewise the advent of the modern world may or may not have made possible the advent of a truly new or modern Buddhism. Many Buddhist critics oppose the Kyoto School because of their persuasion that it embodies a new Buddhism, a Buddhism just as Western as it is Eastern, and just as modern as it is ancient.

Perhaps nothing is more important in the Kyoto School than the balance that it apparently has achieved between its Eastern and its Western, its ancient and its modern, poles. Who could imagine such a new Christianity? Or is it even now being born in a new Catholicism? And is not some such birth the goal of all of our genuine theological labors? Nothing could more aptly or more fruitfully be the center of such labor than the idea and the symbol of the kenosis of God or the absolute, an idea lying at the center of both Hegelianism and the Kyoto School, and thus perhaps at the center of a new Christianity and a new Buddhism alike. Already these all two different movements share a common theological motif: the absence of any objective manifestation of God or the absolute from our history and consciousness, an absence that is nevertheless a possible sign of the full or total presence of absolute Spirit or Sunyata. To a Christian who accepts such a sign as a mark of total presence, ancient Buddhism is manifest as a wondrous world, for here, and here alone in the world of religion, Nirvana, or the pure sacred, is absolutely signless, invisible, and unheard. Thus here there is a full and integral conjunction of presence and absence that is unique in the history of religions, or unique unless its full parallel has been born in the advent of a truly new or truly reborn Christianity.

Nothing could be more alien to what the Christian knows as paganism than the full absence of the sacred, and if this occurs in ancient Buddhism, then who could imagine a Christian opening to Buddhism as a regression to paganism? But might it nevertheless be a regression to a primordial world or to an ahistorical or nontemporal consciousness? If Buddhism knows the pure simultaneity of time, or a time that is present, past, and future at once, does this preclude the possibility of a truly new or future time? Does such a simultaneity of time foreclose the possibility of a truly forward historical movement, and foreclose it by its envisionment of a time that is forward and backward at once? Does nothing whatsoever distinguish the time of the Buddha and the time of our present? Or is a Buddhist contemporaneity with the Buddha indistinguishable from a Christian contemporaneity with Christ? But if the Christian knows the Incarnation as a once and for all and final event, then surely this does distinguish Christian time from Buddhist time, just as what the modern historical consciousness knows as the irreversibility and finality of historical events decisively distinguishes that consciousness from any form of Buddhist consciousness that knows the full reversibility and repeatability of temporal events.

Nevertheless, both the Christian apprehension of the Incarnation as a once-and-for-all final event and what the modern historical consciousness knows as the uniqueness and irreversibility of historical events are radical expressions of demythologizing. That is to say, they are radical negations of the primordial world, and of the primordial mythical world, a world or worlds closed to the irreversibility and finality of historical or temporal events. So likewise ancient Buddhism is a radical expression of demythologizing, and this is one of the major motifs of the Kyoto School. Thus we might surmise that what Buddhism knows as the simultaneity of time is not to be confused with a mythical reversibility of time, just as a Buddhist vision of history should not be identified with the primordial myth of eternal return. Is it not rather that Buddhism divests time of all positive identity, therein and thereby negating every possible positive or definite image of time, including the images of past and future? Here is a demythologizing as radical or more radical than that of Christianity, and a demythologizing dissolving every possible image or sign. Consequently, it is not that Buddhism is closed to the possibility of a forward-moving and irreversible historical time, but rather that Buddhism transcends and negates every possible identity of history and time.

From this point of view, the pure simultaneity of Buddhist time is a purely negative simultaneity because rather than conjoining present, past, and future it knows a pure and empty time with no possible concrete temporal dimension or dimensions. Perhaps the only Western analogue to such a purely and totally empty time is Nietzsche's vision of eternal recurrence, and now that we have finally learned that this radically modern or postmodern vision is infinitely removed from the primordial myth of eternal return, it should not surprise us that Nietzsche has so deeply fascinated the Kyoto philosophers. Nietzsche is the Western thinker who finally and despite himself became most open to Buddhism, and nowhere more so than in his vision of eternal recurrence, a vision in which beginning and ending are one and the same. Therein and thereby a pure present dawns before us, but a present devoid of all positive or definite identity, even if it is nevertheless a once and for all final event, for it is an event or a present made possible only by the death of God. If the death of God is the ultimate historical event for Nietzsche, it is the absolute dividing line between our historical past and our historical future, and therefore is the very axis of historical time itself.

And this is an event that is open to Buddhism, and has even made possible for Buddhism a full entry into the modern world, a world from which Christianity is seemingly excluded. But that exclusion is an illusion if Hegel is accepted as a Christian thinker, for Hegel knew the death of God as a Christian event, and as that decisive modern historical event which is most deeply and most fully a repetition and renewal of the Incarnation.

Here, the death of God is the kenosis of God, the self-negation and Calvary of Spirit. Only that event made possible a full and actual vision of the ubiquity of God, a ubiquity present not only in the totality of history, but also in the deepest depths of a self-estranged and self-alienated consciousness. These were depths which a Blake, a Kierkegaard, and a Dostoevsky explored, and explored as Christian visionaries, and as Christian visionaries liberated from the objective or manifest presence and existence of God. Moreover, these purely negative visions of the depths of self-consciousness fully parallel Buddhist visions of the absolute emptiness of consciousness. If modern Christian visionaries have realized an opening to the kenosis of God, thereby they have realized an opening to absolute emptiness itself, an emptiness that is the very center of what the radical modern Christian has known as the Crucifixion of God.

Now that it is ever increasingly becoming apparent that the modern Christian will fully know that center only by becoming open to Buddhism, Christian theology itself will inevitably be partial and incomplete if it fails to realize for itself a Buddhist ground, and a Buddhist ground that is not only inseparable from a Christian ground, but a Buddhist ground that in this perspective will inevitably be known as a Christian ground. The Kyoto School discovered a Christianity that it could know as a Buddhist ground, and discovered it by way of the Christian symbol of the death or kenosis of God, a symbol it was able to understand as a symbol of an absolute and total self-emptying. Mahayana Buddhism has always known that self-emptying as total compassion, just as Christianity at bottom has always known the Crucifixion as the full embodiment and ultimate actualization of the love of God. Yet if the love of God is a self-emptying and self-negating compassion, then it is surely present in a Buddhist Emptiness or Sunyata, and present there more purely than it has ever been in the Christian tradition, and more purely because it is empty of every definite and actual image and form, and therefore by necessity is empty of "God."

NOTES

1. Nishida Kitaro, *Last Writings: Nothingness and the Religious Worldview*. Translated with an introduction by David A. Dilworth (Honolulu: University of Hawaii Press, 1977), p. 6.
2. Ibid., p. 68.
3. Ibid., p. 77.
4. Ibid., p. 99.

2

Dynamic Sunyata and the God Whose Glory Fills the Universe

EUGENE B. BOROWITZ

My response is divided into two disparate yet related sections. The first, though lengthier and theologically more substantive, is intimately, perhaps decisively, related to the second, which is shorter and more practical.

I

Having long puzzled about how to explain Judaism adequately in English terms—the language being so substantially shaped by Christianity—I greatly admire Masao Abe's accomplishment in conveying his Buddhist understanding of ultimate reality. The problems facing him are far more daunting than those confronting Jewish theologians, for he does not share a common Scripture and God with Christians as Jews do. Decreasing the linguistic barriers to greater understanding, as Masao Abe has so well done here, seems to me one of the most realistic and important aims of interfaith dialogue.

He also shows commendable openness to his dialogue partners' thought, not only seeking to learn from them but then integrating these insights into his statement of his distinctive Zen philosophy. Moreover, while not repressing the issues that Christianity and Judaism raise for his own thought and belief, he can firmly indicate his considerable questions concerning them. He thus admirably demonstrates the potentially transformative moral power of interfaith dialogue.

Though his primary discussion is with Christianity, Abe also seeks to understand how Jewish thinkers have come to terms with the Holocaust, hoping in this way to initiate Buddhist-Jewish dialogue. It is, to the best of my knowledge, the first step in direct academic exchange between these faiths, though Leo Baeck and Martin Buber had written about Buddhism many decades ago.[1] I feel privileged to be invited to enter into dialogue with Professor Abe.

There are many matters on which I can find Jewish points of agreement with him: individual responsibility is substantially corporate; an exaggerated thirst for life and attachment to things is a major source of evil; people need insight into a reality that is beyond the everyday and it is as much dependent upon "grace" (my discomfort with the Christian overtones of this term is so great that I had to signal it) as upon will and act; "salvation" might come at any moment, thus the present can be heavy with significance; "thingification" easily bars the way to true understanding; and much more. Yet, since holistic context radically shapes the distinctive significance of a specific theme in a given faith, all these points of agreement point us toward a more fundamental disagreement. Thus, if I may make a disinterested academic observation, Abe's reinterpretation of Christ's kenosis seems to me quite utterly to transform it from what I have understood contemporary Christian theologians to be saying; I therefore look forward to seeing how they respond to him.

The heart of the Jewish-Buddhist discussion may be approached most easily by beginning with the second of the two questions Abe asks of Jewish thinkers at the conclusion of his discussion of the Holocaust. He inquires: "If the rupture caused by the Holocaust is not a rupture of this or that way of philosophical or theological thinking, but of thought itself, how is *Tikkun*, that is, a mending of the rupture, possible?" To Abe as a Buddhist, "mending," *Tikkun*, has to do with thought or understanding, in a Mahayana sense, to be sure. That follows logically from his insight into the human situation and its remedy. *Avidya*, ignorance, is the fundamental evil, and thus enlightenment, *vidya*, true understanding, is its "mending." If, then, thought itself has been ruptured, the indispensable remedy is no longer available and all appears lost. How, then, can Jews still speak meaningfully of *Tikkun* after the Holocaust?

Abe's question is based on a citation from the writings of Emil Fackenheim and it will help to read it again. Fackenheim writes, "For the first time in this work [*To Mend the World*], we are faced with the possibility that the Holocaust may be a radical rupture in history—and that among things ruptured may be not just this or that way of philosophical or theological thinking, but thought itself." I understand Fackenheim to be saying that the Holocaust may be "a radical rupture in history," one so comprehensive that "among things ruptured" is thought—which is to say that the meaning of the Holocaust, *among other things*, exceeds the capacities of the intellectual activities the West calls philosophy or theology.

What, besides cognitive construction, does Fackenheim feel is now decisively challenged? More significantly than philosophizing, this qualitatively unique evil radically throws into doubt the Jewish people's very Covenant with God and the way of life it authorizes—and by extension it also threatens the covenant between God and all humankind, the children of Noah. The ultimate issue is not how we can now think, though that is important to *homo sapiens*. Rather, it is how we might now mend our covenant relationship with God so that the essential *Tikkun*, the mending of human history, can take place. In its Jewish context, *Tikkun* is attained by how one (everyone) lives, not primarily by what understanding they achieve. Thus, as Fackenheim has emphasized, Jews have "coped" (to use Abe's verb) with the radical rupture of the Holocaust by rededicating themselves to living in Covenant. Not the least significant part of this *Tikkun* has been their insistence on not merely continuing their inherited religious way of life but on creating various new-old ways to live in Covenant. Thus, Fackenheim's own hope for *Tikkun* is not based on an elevation of insight but by our building our lives, as best we can, on the example of those Jews and gentiles whose deeds demonstrated that the death camps could not destroy their spirit.

It should be emphasized that neither philosophy nor theology is the basis for identifying the critical Jewish response to the Holocaust. Instead, the surprisingly positive activity of the Jewish community in the post-Holocaust period finally forced Jewish thinkers to reflect on its meaning. They did not lead or even significantly direct the Jewish people's response to the horror. In fact, it took them about two decades to confront directly the questions raised by the Holocaust. Only then, after the living responses were well established, did the thinkers' ideas begin to have a significant impact upon our community.

It is still not clear to me whether the Christian death-of-God movement and, probably more importantly, its underlying cultural ferment were more responsible for bringing Holocaust theology into being than any indigenous demand by Jews for a fresh statement of their faith.[2] Jewish thinkers did confront this challenge. At their best, they sought to understand, learn from and interpret what the Jewish community had been going through—and it is on this secondary level that they have had their influence in reshaping Jewish life. In these observations I am, of course, reflecting my own understanding of Judaism as the enduring Covenant between God and the Jewish people, hence a religion as much of the group as of, at least to liberals, individuals. Unlike the Descartean bent of Western philosophy, I believe Jewish thinkers must constantly seek to think out of communal Jewish experience, seeking as best they can to understand its significance, though they must also do so out of their specific individuality.

Some comparative considerations may be helpful at this point. For Judaism the fundamental human concern is not redemption from sin. The God we stand in Covenant with "knows our frame and remembers that we are dust" and thus, as the prior verses say, directly has compassion upon us and forgives our sins (Ps. 103:8-14). This God can be heard by Ezekiel calling the people of Israel to repentance by saying climactically, "I have no pleasure in the death of him that dieth, says *Adonai*, God, therefore turn yourselves and live" (Ezekiel 18:32). Having no doctrine of original sin, Jews believe that the responsibility and the capacity to turn from evil is given not only to Jews but to all humankind, as the example of the Ninevites in the book of Jonah demonstrates. We further believe that people, Noachites or Israelites alike, are not fundamentally ignorant of how they ought to live because God has given us instruction (Torah) to that end and, in various ways, continues to do so. One requires no unusual intellectual or spiritual gift to know in the usual case how one ought to live. One learns it as much if not more from one's family and community as from one's formal religious training and from the great teachers of each generation. Thus, believing Jews are not surprised to discover genuine religion and morality, in quite diverse forms to be sure, among many peoples and faiths.

For Judaism, the primary human task is creating holiness through righteous living. The responsible deed, the one that simultaneously acknowledges God, others, time, place, nature, and self in Covenantal fulfillment, not only mends the torn but fulfills the promise inherent in existence.

What is at stake here is precisely the level of seriousness with which one should take this ethical/spiritual human capacity. For Masao Abe it is a deeply felt and humanly quite significant matter, one whose importance may certainly not be trivialized. But it is only the second level of the three dimensions of his thought. Thus he knows that all issues are properly and legitimately understood *ultimately* from the vantage point of the third dimension, which is that of a transhuman fundamental dimension represented by religious faith or awakening—that is, dynamic Sunyata. In it, all such dualities as good and evil, holy and profane, are overcome and transcended. By contrast, in the classic Jewish understanding, ultimate reality has indelible quality; God is holy—and that means, most closely, that God is good. There is nothing more ultimate. And because God is holy/good,[3] Jews are to be holy/good, which means to do holy/good deeds and create a holy/good human order, which ultimately embraces nature in its fulfillment, with God's help.

Because the holy/good deed has such ultimacy, Jews have made it their primary concern and have now enhanced this traditional activism with the dynamism of modern self-assertion. This existential commitment has provided the motive power for the extraordinary Jewish contribution to modern civilization. Even Jews estranged from their religious tradition tend to measure their worth by what they do for humankind. As a consequence, the almost unanimous response of Jewish thinkers and lay people to the Holocaust has been to try to act to frustrate its goals and prevent its replication. Negatively, that means opposing evil wherever one sees it; positively, it means fostering goodness to the extent that one can. And this form of *Tikkun* has been the most important Jewish response to the Holocaust.

Leo Baeck, the one Jewish theologian (liberal, to be sure) to have been in a concentration camp during the Holocaust and to have survived, wrote these lines as part of the conclusion to his post-Holocaust book of theology:

The great task of dark days, and the greater one of bright hours, was to keep faith with the expectation. Man waits for God, and God waits for man. The promise and the demand speak here, both in one: the grace of the commandment and the commandment of grace. Both are one in the One God. Around the One God there is concealment. He does not reveal Himself, but He reveals the commandment and the grace . . . Every people can be chosen for a history, for a share in the history of humanity. Each is a question which God has asked, and each people must answer. But more history has been assigned to this people than to any other people. God's question speaks stronger here . . . It is so easy to remain a slave, and it is so difficult to become a free man. But this people can only exist in the full seriousness of its task. It can only exist in this freedom which reaches beyond all other freedoms.[4]

With this worldview, the caring Jewish community will overwhelmingly reject the suggestion that, for all the trauma connected with the Holocaust, we ought to understand that it *ultimately* has no significance; or, to put it more directly, that *ultimately* there is no utterly fundamental distinction between the Nazi death camp operators and their victims. For most Jews, a response to the encompassing evils of our day—world hunger, political tyranny, religious intolerance and warfare, the threat of nuclear destruction—cannot properly be made with a consciousness that they are truly second-level concerns, that bringing people to a higher level of understanding is the most significant way to face them. And I cannot imagine them agreeing that the ultimate response to the Nazis would have been for Jews to raise their consciousness from a radically moral to a higher, postmoral level.

Does this then mean, as Masao Abe inquires in his first question, that the Holocaust is an isolated event entirely unrelated to other events in the world and history and thereby has a fixed, enduring absolute evil nature? And if the latter is true, how can the Jewish people come to terms with the Holocaust and with God, who ultimately allowed the Holocaust to occur? In some sense the answer seems reasonably unequivocal. Even Fackenheim, the thinker who has made the strongest case for the qualitative uniqueness of the Holocaust, does not suggest that it was "an isolated event entirely unrelated to other events in the world and history." He and the rest of the Jewish community would not be so sensitive to the Christian background of Nazi anti-Semitism if they thought the Holocaust so unhistorical, nor would they be so concerned that it retain a place in human consciousness to spur people to do the good. Does it, then, have a fixed, enduring, absolute evil nature? Yes and no. It is, as far as we can tell, uniquely significant in telling us about human evil. Until some other, more horrific event occurs—Heaven forfend —and as long as memory recalls it, no small matter to Jews, it seems "fixed [and] enduring." But is it "absolute"? If Abe means, Does it carry the same ultimacy that, for him, Sunyata does and Jewish holiness does not? then I must say, No. In my understanding of Judaism, only God is "absolute," though I would assert that only in a metaphorical, weak sense. (Were God a strong absolute, as Bradley indicated, there could be no creation and no independent human will.[5]) And insofar as the "absolute" God is holy/good, the Holocaust is enduringly evil.

In that event, to continue with the question, "how can [the] Jewish people come to terms with God, who ultimately allowed the Holocaust to occur?" Here, I think, the phrase "come to terms" requires a more intellectual response than the one I gave in my previous discussion of how we "coped." I believe a brief discussion of Holocaust theology and the Jewish community's response to it will be most instructive for clarifying Judaism's distinctive affirmations as I understand them.

To the best of my knowledge only one Jew who has written extensively on the Holocaust, Richard L. Rubenstein, has followed the logic of the problem of evil to the conclusion that God cannot be good. He suggests that, after the Holocaust, God ought better to be understood as

> the Holy Nothingness, known to mystics of all ages, out of which we have come and to which we shall ultimately return . . . The limitations of finitude can be overcome only when we return to the Nothingness out of which we have been thrust. In the final analysis, omnipotent Nothingness is Lord of all creation.[6]

While Rubenstein has not developed this notion fully, there is much in what he did write concerning it that might lead Masao Abe to fruitful dialogue with him.

The Jewish community agreed with Rubenstein that the Holocaust posed a radical challenge to its inherited or reappropriated tradition. But his conception of God found few echoes in what then developed into Holocaust theology. I think it is clear why: it did not provide a ground for qualitatively distinguishing between Nazis and Jews. It had explained logically why "God" could "ultimately allow the holocaust to occur" but had done so only by denying that there was any ultimate reason for being morally outraged to begin with; if ultimate reality is morally neutral—and perhaps negative since Rubenstein calls death the only Messiah[7]—one has as much right to be a Nazi as a Jew. That way of "coming to terms" with the Holocaust was, for all its logical rigor and grim courage, antithetical to the fundamental religious intuition of the Jewish community.

I cannot recall a Jewish thinker who has dealt with Holocaust theodicy who has not begun with a vigorous reassertion of the so-called "free-will defense." Consistent with what has been said above, most Jews see the

Holocaust as an indictment of humankind, specifically of the Nazis for their demonic use of their freedom. For the Jews I know, theological speculation must not be allowed to shift the primary responsibility for the evil from the Nazis to God. Some human beings, often after considerable deliberation, decided to carry out the Holocaust — and many renewed that decision day after day for years. They were the worst. But in a similar but qualitatively different human failure, the Western democracies and even Jewish community leadership did not do what they could to stop or protest the Holocaust; the human guilt is proportional to the human power. While Jews may have been aghast that God would have allowed human freedom to proceed to such evil lengths, no one seriously suggested that a good God should have deprived people of their freedom or, almost the same thing, severely limited its effective scope. The holy/good deed can only come from a free person. That notion is so central to the Jewish intuition of ultimate reality that humankind's action and nature, not God's, must be the primary level of the discussion.

Those Jews who sought a rational understanding of how God could allow the Holocaust found their solution by denying God has encompassing power. They had no difficulty producing numerous citations from rabbinic literature in which God is depicted as limited. Moreover, the notion of a finite, perhaps growing God, had considerable appeal because it heightened the moral responsibility of humankind. One could not now sink into passivity, throwing oneself utterly into God's saving hands and abandoning what one might have done to save oneself and the world. It is a concept that has brought much solace to Jews in a troubled time and, universalized and popularized in Harold Kushner's *When Bad Things Happen to Good People* (New York: Schocken), it has been a healing balm to many troubled Americans.

Surprisingly, considering the alleged rationality of the contemporary Jewish community, the idea of a limited God has not become dominant. For all its helpfulness and logical clarity, it seems to many people to create as many new problems as it resolves old ones. On the human level, it leaves people with no cosmic recourse when they are sorely stricken and have exhausted their human power struggling against their ills. God may then be a co-sufferer but God is also as helpless as we are and thus cannot offer much solace. And it is not clear in a post-Holocaust age that we can count on humankind to perfect God's limitations, since we have so many of our own. How, then, will the Messiah come and history be redeemed from mere neutrality or worse? Moreover, on the ontological level, troublesome questions are raised by the power that is not in God's hands. Is there a force or being over against what we had understood to be the one God? And how shall we now transcend our rationality and have faith that despite God's limited power, God's goodness will ultimately prevail in our universe?

Such questions or their human equivalents have, paradoxically enough, engendered a significant return to the God of the Covenant who, we were told two decades ago, was dead, at least in our time. A minority among us, but an unabating one, is in the midst of a probing spiritual quest. As I have analyzed this movement over the years,[8] it has seemed to me to have been generated by a search for a more adequate ground of value. Once, the high human quality that modern Jews have so prized seemed common to all rational, educated, cultured people; thus humanism could be a substitute for religious faith. In recent years, human frailty and perversity, institutional failure, cultural vacuity, and philosophy's inability to mandate substantive ethics, have increasingly threatened to make our civilization amoral or worse. To be more in touch with what one ultimately believes, to find greater power to resist as one knows one must these corrosive social forces—perhaps even to harness them for human betterment—people have turned to traditional religious belief. Sophisticates who once would have found that unthinkable, given the attractions of radically autonomous human reason and Nietzschean self-assertion, now find those alternatives largely discredited. They have few moral credentials to present to a generation concerned with value. If anything, they are more the problem to be overcome than a proper standard for its solution.

How do these almost-traditional Jewish believers "come to terms" with the Holocaust? Unable to sacrifice God's goodness, or power, or deny the reality of evil, they reluctantly sacrifice the certainty of logic in the face of what they know to be the ultimate commanding power of living in holy goodness. They believe, in their fashion, even though they do not understand in any ultimate way. Like classic Jewish pietists, they hope the goodness of God day by day will set the context for their confrontation with evil. Creating that day-to-day appreciation of God's continual giving goodness is more important to them than understanding the theological ground of the limit case of gross suffering.

Perhaps such a piety, even in its modern guises, sounds strange for a people so proud of its intellectuality. But there is a certain classic Jewish reticence to probe too deeply into God. Christian theologians like Jürgen Moltmann find it congruent with their trinitarian faith to speak of what transpires in God's interior. Masao Abe suggests that from his Buddhist perspective they ought to move on to "the still greater interior of the interior." On this score, the central tradition of the Jewish people has been resolutely agnostic. It does not know much about God's essence because, as a religion of revelation, God did not say much about it. In recent generations, as thinkers have reinterpreted revelation in terms of human religious experience, this aspect of Jewish awe has, if anything, been strengthened. Almost all Jewish thinkers readily acknowledge that they have little knowledge of Godself though they claim empowering understanding of how God wants us to live. The power of the holy/good deed remains that strong among us.

There is an important exception to this characterization of Judaism— namely, Jewish mysticism—and a brief consideration of its career is in order. Our earliest records of the Jewish mystical tradition — from the time of early rabbinic literature — and its first books, focus on how God created the universe and exercises power through it, quite roughly, the classic concerns called *maaseh vereshit* and *maaseh umerkavah*, "the work of creation" and "the work of [God's] chariot" (as per Ezekiel 1). We hear of heavenly palaces and angelic beings, even of the dimensions of God's "body," but not about God's inner life.

About a millennium later, theosophy had emerged as a major Jewish mystical concern with the appearance of the Zohar, the classic work of the Jewish mystical tradition, at the end of the thirteenth century C.E. Strongly influenced by medieval Jewish rationalism's emphasis on unity, the author of the Zohar knows God to be, in utter identity and unbroken unity, both *En Sof* and *Sefirot*. The former term translates easily as "without end" — but thus, if the meaning is taken rigorously, God is the one about whom nothing at all can be said, not even, in a way, this, since saying inevitably suggests limits. Some mystics have even gone on to call God, in this understanding, "Nothing." But they and other Jewish theosophists also radically affirmed that the *Sof* is also the *Sefirot*, the ten "spheres" of interactive divine energy whose configurations and interplay may be described by a range of metaphors so daring and so grossly material they sometimes leave moderns aghast.

In the sixteenth century, Isaac Luria extended the notion of God's pervasive unity to the extent that creation could only by accomplished by God's "contraction" (a sort of "emptying"?) to make "room" for the universe. Two centuries later, the Maggid of Mezeritch, the second-generation leader of the new Hasidic movement, mystically knew that God alone was truly real, and thus in his teaching a clear distinction between a "relative" human level of affairs and an "absolute" divine one holds sway. Much Hasidic doctrine still features this understanding, though the extent to which it remains part of esoteric as against the folksy, exoteric instruction given by Hasidism is unclear. And, it should be noted, for all this doctrine of two levels of reality, Hasidim have been most faithful in their observance of even the minutiae of Jewish law and custom. Masao Abe should find much in this development in Jewish mysticism that is congenial to him though its sense of ultimate reality is that of pervasive fullness rather than that of dialectical emptying.

The bulk of the Jewish community, however, continues to reject such mysticism. Most Orthodox Jews find its teachings about God suspiciously unlike those of the Bible and the Talmud. These Jewish classics accept the reality of creation and the ultimate significance of the holy act. They find this inherited tradition not only self-commending but fully coherent with their experience. Jewish liberals generally find the enveloping mystical sense of God at variance with their own sporadic, tentative religious experience. More critically, knowing God so intimately, Jewish mysticism tends to bend human freedom utterly to God's will. But what if, as in the case of women's rights, people find they must trust their own sense of the holy/ good more than the regulations and customs, indeed more than the "revelation," they have inherited? Again, the primacy of the sense of proper human value reasserts itself and insists upon its central place in any affirmations that are to be made about God. I believe that religious sensitivity is at the root of the general community rejection of asserting God is All-in-All, thereby entailing, ultimately, that there is no real evil—not even the Holocaust. Modernized Jews may wish to make increasing room for God in their lives but, as I understand them, they do not propose thereby to wipe out but to empower what they know to be demanded of humankind: "Seek good and not evil, that ye may live; and so *Adonai*, the God of hosts, will be with you, as you say. Hate evil, love good, and establish justice in the gate" (Amos 5:14-15).

II

I reproduce here the letter I wrote Masao Abe upon reading his paper:

Dear Professor Abe,

Ever since I first read a paper of yours many years ago in *Religious Studies* I have followed your writings with great interest (most recently in vol. 14, no. 3 of *Japanese Religions*). It was therefore with great pleasure that I accepted John Cobb's gracious invitation to be a Jewish respondent to your paper "Kenotic God and Dynamic Sunyata."

Beginning my study of it, I was drawn up short by the places where you cite Nietzsche from *Beyond Good and Evil* dividing history into pre-moral, moral and postmoral periods. You then indicate that he "identifies the first stage of history" with "primitive religions." The following breath-taking statement then appears: "It may be said that this first stage corresponds to the time of the Old Testament which relates stories of this kind of sacrifice in such cases, as Abraham and Isaac. The second state of human history indicates the time of the New Testament and the Christian era following it. . ."

In this context, "the time of the Old Testament," and thus the "Old Testament" itself, and thus the Judaism derived from it are identified with pre-moral religion. Only "the time of the New Testament," and thus the New Testament itself, and thus the Christianity derived from it, are identified with moral religion. The sentence thus perpetuates one of the worst religious canards of Western civilization, one which is a major root of the anti-Semitism that has finally come to be seen as an ugly, discrediting blotch on Christian religious claims.

You specify, "it may be said. . ." By whom? You do not ascribe this to Nietzsche and no note number concludes the paragraph. My cursory survey of the context of *Beyond Good and Evil* did not reveal Nietzsche as its author. In fact, in section 52, some paragraphs before section 55 which you cite, he is relatively positive about the "Old Testament," calling it the great book of justice.

Of course, such statements "may be said"—but they should not be said. If they are said, they should not be repeated. And if they are repeated, they should be clearly repudiated by those doing so.

I can imagine that even if I spent many years seeking to understand Buddhism and the Asian culture in which it arose and now flourishes, I might well blunder in speaking of them despite my best efforts to be faithful to their finest representation. What astonishes me is that the four academics to whom you express gratitude for their suggestions did not call the offensiveness of this material to your attention.

I look forward to hearing from you about this matter.

Due to travel and relocation, Professor Abe was unable to respond to my letter until shortly before this book was to be edited and put into production. While he was then willing to rewrite the portion of the paper in question based on my criticism, it seemed wiser, at this late date, not to prepare a revision of the manuscript already seen by seven other respondents. At Professor Cobb's suggestion, he proposed that the original text be left standing, that I make my criticism of his presentation of Nietzsche's view of the three stages of human history and he would make his response to it in his rejoinder to all the respondents. I agreed to this arrangement.

I wish only to append three brief comments. First, in a discussion of this matter, Milton Himmelfarb was kind enough to point out a historical inaccuracy. The charge that Judaism is "premoral" is not part of classic Christian theological anti-Semitism but is a creation of post-Enlightenment anti-Semitism—and a typical example of secularization, I might add. Second, while it is only one sentence in a demanding, lengthy paper, it will be of some interest to me to see whether any of the Christian theologians responding in this volume noted and reacted to the statement I found so offensive. Finally, in my reading about Buddhism I have occasionally wondered whether Buddhists writing in English mean by such terms as "right conduct" and "right speech" (two major aspects of *sila*, the moral component of the Noble Eightfold Path) or even the more general "compassion" what Jews generally mean by these terms. I shall be less uncertain reading Professor Abe's response.

NOTES

1. Leo Baeck, in *The Essence of Judaism* (New York: Schoeken, 1961), describes the Buddhism of apparently "static" Sunyata as the typological opposite of Judaism; Buber compares and contrasts Zen Buddhism and Hasidic Judaism in his essay, "The Place of Hasidism in the History of Religion," *The Origin and Meaning of Hasidism* (New York: Horizon, 1972).

2. See my *Choices in Modern Jewish Thought* (West Orange, N.J.: Behrman, 1983),

chapter 9, "Confronting the Holocaust," particularly pp. 187-90.

3. I am not satisfied with either the term "holy" or "good" by itself to convey the quality of the mandated, desired Jewish act. "Holy" alone often carries the connotations of "churchy," or of a segregated spirituality. "Good" is too easily secularized into humanistic ethics. The fulfilled Jewish act is more life-involved than the one, more God-oriented than the other. This dilemma surfaces in another way in trying to translate the term *tzedakah*. We variously render it as "righteousness" or "justice," but it is as likely to mean "faithfulness, reliability" and it comes to mean what English calls "charity" (*caritas*).

4. Baeck, *This People Israel* (Holt, Rinehart, Winston), pp. 397 and 402.

5. I discuss the equivocal applicability of the term "absolute" to the God of Judaism in my paper "Liberal Judaism's Effort to Invalidate Relativism Without Mandating Orthodoxy," in *Go and Study, Essays in Honor of Alfred Jospe* (B'nai B'rith Hillel).

6. Richard L. Rubenstein, *After Auschwitz* (Indianapolis, Ind.: Bobbs Merrill), p. 154.

7. Ibid, pp. 184, 198.

8. While this topic is found in many of my articles over the past two decades it was the fundamental theme of my analysis of the situation of American Jewry in *The Mask Jews Wear* (New York: Simon and Schuster, 1973) when Jewish discussions of the death of God were at their height. See particularly the afterword and compare the chapter on the 1980s in the second edition published by Sh'ma, Inc. See the later statements at the end of chapters 2 and 3 in part two of my *Liberal Judaism* (New York: Union of American Hebrew Congregations, 1984).

3

On the Deepening of Buddhism

JOHN B. COBB, JR.

Buddhist-Christian dialogue has been fruitful. This paper of Masao Abe is part of the fruit. It advances the discussion in two major directions.

First, as a Buddhist he has thought and lived deeply into the world of Christian imagery and thought. What he has seen there has been shaped by his Buddhist perspective, but that does not mean that it is invalid. Quite the contrary. We have long known that all of us see what our experience allows and enables us to see. Abe's Buddhist experience allows and enables him to see in Christian tradition what few Christians have seen. That will not replace what most Christians have seen, but unless Christians in the future pay attention to what Abe has seen, their vision will be truncated.

In the past we have recognized that we have something to gain from attending closely to external criticisms. Hostile Marxists have taught us much about ourselves that we have worked to internalize into self-criticism. We expect Buddhists to critique us from without in a similar way and then to internalize this criticism where it rings true to us.

But Abe's work with Christian theology goes beyond that. It is not external in any ordinary sense. It stems from wrestling with our texts as one who seeks their meaning and truth. Nor is this simply a provisional empathetic game. It is fully genuine. As a Buddhist who shares with us the crisis of religion in the modern world, he wants to work with us in the interpretation of our sources to enable them to share their message authentically. He wants to create a context in which we Buddhists and Christians work together in a common task. And he wants to do this, not by finding some superficial commonalities between the two traditions, but by deepening both. Therefore, without ceasing to be a Buddhist, Abe joins us in the work of Christian theology.

Abe's theological proposals are based on very selective use of elements of the Christian tradition, but what he selects are major themes and doctrines. Indeed, he calls Christians back to a wrestling with the central mysteries of the faith. It is in trinitarian and christological thought that he finds the loci where deepening will lead us into insights capable of uniting us with Buddhists and enabling us jointly to reassert religion in the face of scientism and nihilism.

The second direction in which Abe advances the discussion is the interpretation of Buddhism in light of Christian criticisms. He understands these criticisms clearly and he takes them with full seriousness. They are criticisms I have myself directed against Buddhism, and it is with real gratitude that I see so full and open a response.

The response is not defensive in spirit. Abe acknowledges that the criticisms have not expressed mere misunderstanding. He does not belittle them as showing that the critics are dealing only with secondary matters. He acknowledges their force and proposes ways in which Buddhism can and should deal with them.

Such an essay invites Christian engagement at many points. One could, for example, confront Abe's account of Christian theology with another one. But I find most interesting Abe's proposals for developing Buddhism so as to take account of Western and Christian criticism; and I am emboldened by Abe's entry into Christian theology to reply by entering into the Buddhist discussion. My general position is that Abe's adjustments of Buddhism do not go far enough to meet the Christian criticism but that Buddhism is quite capable of taking further steps that would meet these criticisms. As Abe asks Christians to go deeper into our own faith, freeing ourselves from unnecessary commitments and prejudices, so I am asking him to go deeper into his own vision, ceasing to cling to those beliefs and doctrines that block a full appropriation of the truth in Christian criticism.

Abe identifies three criticisms directed to Buddhism by Christians (pp. 32–33). The first is that Buddhism discourages critical rationality. The second is that its transcendence of good and evil blocks development of an ethics. And the third is that its view of past and future as reversible undercuts the concern for history.

The concerns for ethics and for history are so closely connected in Christian thought that I will treat them together. Following Abe, in section I, I will take the Holocaust as a test case of the effectiveness of a response. In section II, I will respond to Abe's comments about the freedom of the will. In section III, I will comment on the potentiality of Buddhism for encouraging and sustaining critical thinking.

I

Let me begin with the most concrete and historically specific feature of Abe's paper, his Buddhist response to the Holocaust. Much that he says seems right to me. We are all bound together in ways that make the Holocaust a matter of our corporate human responsibility, not simply that of the Nazis. Also, the Holocaust does arise out of a level of our human condition, in which we all share, what Christians call original sin. Nothing is more important than that we recognize our interconnectedness with one another and with all things. Abe's Buddhist comments are rich and important for all of us.

But another level of analysis is at least equally important. Original sin and *avidya* have always been with us, but events like the Holocaust are fortunately not everyday occurrences. A specific event requires specific explanation. Awareness of interconnectedness aids in this explanation, but it does not take its place. In the process of that explanation, I find that my own government's policies contributed to the Holocaust by refusing to open our doors to Jewish refugees. I find that anti-Jewish feelings in this country contributed to those policies. Far more important, since my identity as a Christian is deeper than my identity as a citizen, I find that Christian teaching, including the teaching of the New Testament itself, contributed to the Nazi program and its success, that indeed, this contribution was a *major* factor.

I single our these specific causes of the Holocaust because through my identities as a citizen of the United States and as a Christian, I share in responsibility for the Holocaust in special ways. Responsibility means guilt. I do share in guilt. But more important in responsibility than guilt is response. Abe's response is to renew his effort to bring enlightenment to all. It is hard for a Christian not to read this as similar to the pietistic view that by saving each one's soul social problems will be solved. Against this program most thoughtful Christians believe that we need specifically to work to change Christian teaching so that Christian practice will not continue to generate anti-Judaism. Americans need to change the climate of feeling in this country so that we will in the future be ready to receive refugees from terror.

One might argue that the lack of any specific historical project in Abe's response to the Holocaust reflects the fact that Japan and Buddhism were much less directly involved. Yet from a Christian point of view more should be said even there. Japan was an ally of Nazi Germany. So far as I know, it did not protest the Nazi policies or use its influence to change them. Buddhists in Japan in general did not separate themselves from the policies of their government, which directly and indirectly supported the Nazis in their program. And although Buddhism contains no direct anti-Jewish teaching, like that of Christianity, it does seem to contain teaching that leads its followers to be detached from concrete historical involvement in responding to such events as the Holocaust.

I do not by any means wish to suggest that the responsibility of Japanese Buddhists is of the same order of magnitude as that of North American Christians. I am simply trying to contrast the historical response that I favor with the suprahistorical one recommended by Abe. If that really is the Buddhist position, I can only regard Buddhism as inadequate.

Abe also acknowledges a level at which ethical and historical considerations are relevant. He may consider that all that I have proposed belongs there. I do not object. What I do object to is the speed with which that level is passed over in the quest for the ultimate one. For me as a Christian, also, it is important to relativize the ethical, as Abe knows. But the movement to the Christian level from the ethical one deepens the sense of concrete particularity and historical responsibility. The movement to the Buddhist level in Abe seems to leave all this behind.

The most important question is whether the limitations of Abe's response to the Holocaust are necessitated by the Buddhist vision. I do not think so, but I do think that some changes in Abe's formulation would be needed before he or his followers would in fact engage in the discriminating inquiry into particular causes and the particular changes that would reduce the likelihood of a repetition.

The problem would be eased considerably if Abe would draw different conclusions from compassion. These other conclusions have often been drawn in Buddhist writings. Abe writes that "the task for an awakened one is to help these [that is, nonawakened] persons as well 'awaken' to their suchness and interpenetration with all other things" (p. 60). I assume this is part of all Buddhist teaching just as all Christians are called to invite others to faith in Christ. But Buddhists like Christians have spoken of the relief of suffering in other ways as well. Most Christians would regard it as blasphemous to preach Christ to a starving person if one had the power to feed that person and refrained. I think many Buddhists would expect the enlightened one to show compassion in this way as well. Probably Abe's failure to mention this is a mere oversight.

Nevertheless, from a Christian point of view, another step is needed. Alongside spontaneous acts of charity, we need to understand what leads to the suffering we encounter and what contribution we might make to its reduction. In the case of hunger this would draw us into analysis of the production and distribution of food as well as the general question of human sinfulness. It seems that the Buddhist emphasis on nondiscrimination and pure spontaneity discourages this inquiry and this focused action. Abe's paper does not reassure me on this point.

In typical Buddhist fashion Abe concentrates attention on what characterizes every situation whatsoever. This is the place where Buddhism has made its greatest and most profound contribution. I hope I am not understood as belittling this. But when we have recognized how everything is bound up with everything else, so that nothing exists by itself or has any existence in itself, this need not lead us to suppose that everything plays an equal role in the constitution of everything else or that the discrimination of just what role is played by what and when is unimportant. If Buddhism can allow for this mode of inquiry and for shaping compassionate action by its results, then it can provide the sort of guidance we need. I see no reason in principle for Buddhism to refuse this step, but its absence even in a paper such as this concerns me. Is Buddhism so committed to encouraging the realization of the universal condition of all things that it cannot give equal weight to what is particular to each thing? Much of what it teaches suggests quite the opposite—namely, that enlightenment opens one up precisely to the utterly particular. Then why resist the particular analysis and the ordering of compassionate action to its results?

Abe raises the question, "How can Sunyata, as agentless spontaneity, incorporate a personal diety as the ultimate criterion of value judgment in its boundless openness?" That has been a question for me. I have thought that it could do so by recognizing that among the vast number of things that jointly originate the moment of experience, one is the Sambhogakaya or the primal vow. This would then provide the needed ultimate criterion.

Abe does relate the vow to the ultimate criterion, but not in the way I have suggested. We are told that Sunyata in emptying itself turns itself into vow and act. The vow in question is the vow to save one's self and all others, and so to act as to actually pursue the vow. This means that the realization of emptiness cannot be separated from aiming at such realization in all.

Abe does not explain why this occurs, although his account is suggestive. The realization of everything as interdependent and interpenetrating does seem to lead to a preference that all those with whom one is interdependent and interpenetrating would join in realizing that relationship. The vow expressive of this preference leads to judgment "in terms of whether or not a thing or action in question does accord with the vow and act to make one's self and all others awakened" (p. 58).

I would argue that Buddhist judgment is broader and richer than this. It judges positively the relief of suffering in some independence of its connection with awakening. Abe's presentation does not do justice to this characteristic of Buddhist compassion. It therefore does not connect Buddhist compassion successfully to ethics and history. Once again the failure seems to result from unwillingness to consider what particular things and events are of primary importance in the dependent arising of a particular moment.

It is again this refusal to deal with the particularities in dependent arising that blocks the way to a historical consciousness. The realization of the beginninglessness and the endlessness of the temporal process does not have to result in this view. If the inheritance in each moment is different, and this is fully compatible with the interdependence and interpenetration of all things, then the recognition of this difference promotes historical thinking.

Abe acknowledges that "Buddhism is relatively weak in its view of history," and states that this is because "time is understood to be entirely beginningless and endless and thus reversible" (p. 59). This prevents Buddhism from expressing clearly "the unidirectionality of time and the uniqueness of each moment essential to the notion of history" (p. 60). Abe's solution is to distinguish wisdom and compassion. "In the light of wisdom realized in Sunyata, past and future are interpenetrating and reciprocal" (p. 60). This, Abe notes, works against a historical point of view. But compassion is oriented toward the awakening of the unawakened, and this leads to a differentiation of the future as the sphere in which this compassionate work is to be done and thus to history.

This is a fascinating and helpful move, but it does not go far toward a historical consciousness, for two reasons. First, we have already been told that the differentiation of the future from the remainder of the matrix is not ultimately correct. Second, compassion is presented as having only one work, the enlightening of others; and this work is the same at all times and places. Unawakened "persons are innumerable at present and will appear endlessly in the future" (p. 60). Historically diverse circumstances will have no effect on this.

Again, I see no reason why the Buddhist view of history should remain so weak. We are familiar with views of the reversibility of past and future in the West, but I have not found them persuasive. I believe that Buddhists like Westerners can go either way on this doctrine, and I see no advantage in the choice Abe has made. It certainly does not follow from the beginningless and endless character of time. It follows instead from attachment to a metaphysical doctrine, one that seems quite unnecessary.

Second, compassion need not limit itself to concern for what is the universal and unchanging feature of the world—namely, that there are always hosts of unawakened people. It could focus instead on the particular plight of the Jewish people or on the threat of repeated famines in Africa. Indeed, even the presence of unawakened people is not an unchanging condition to be taken for granted. Unless we attend more concretely to the world situation in its uniqueness today, there may not be any people tomorrow awakened or unawakened. This possibility seems not to enter Abe's vision, but there is nothing in Buddhist teaching to counter the apparent fact that the means of self-destruction are now in the hands of unawakened people. Once again, Buddhism need not limit its attention to the general fact of interdependence and interpenetration. It is free to attend to the specificity of what is most important in these interdependent and interpenetrating entities.

Closely related to questions of ethics is that of the freedom of the will. I am particularly grateful that Abe has dealt with this thematically. This is a characteristically Jewish-Christian-Muslim way of framing the anthropological question, and those who frame it this way have had difficulty understanding what Buddhism has to say on this question. Abe's answer is clear and convincing. However, Abe's discussion of the problem depends in part on a formulation of the Christian view that is not quite satisfactory.

First, Abe is certainly correct that the issue has often been couched in terms of "free will." Today, however, this suggests a faculty psychology that is not part of current anthropology, Christian or secular. The question is not whether there is a separate faculty that is free but whether human beings really make decisions—that is, select among real options. The alternative view is that what we experience as decisions are really always the outcome of antecedent conditions and motives. If we select among real options, then we are free in a truly significant sense. If our supposed decisions are predetermined, then we are not. Dominant philosophical traditions in the English-language world hold to the latter position. Many stress that important among the determinants of a decision are antecedent experiences, hopes, fears, and purposes of the person who makes it. Hence they hold that this is not a "hard determinism." But however "soft" the determinism, it remains a determinism, and real freedom cannot be asserted of the human person. The decision cannot constitute an act of self-determination; hence the human person is not truly free.

At this level of the question, the great body of Christian thought seeks to assert human freedom. The conceptuality is often confused and confusing. But there is a strong sense that human beings make decisions for which they are genuinely responsible. The decision is not simply the inevitable result of what has gone before. Human beings are not automatons. And this feature of the human condition, freedom in this sense, is appraised positively.

But much of the discussion among theologians presupposes this ontological freedom and moves on to another level. Granted that we really make decisions and that we are really responsible for the decisions we make, are we able to make the right decisions? Are we able to decide to be what God calls us to be? Here the most powerful traditions in the church answer in the negative. The most sensitive Christians have found themselves unable to choose to love their neighbors as themselves. We are not able not to sin! In this context Christians can speak of the bondage of the will.

This emphasis in Christianity is always conjoined with the emphasis on divine grace. Grace means both that God accepts us despite our sin and that God enables us to some degree to decide as we are called to decide. This latter working of grace in us can be described in such a way that it seems to set our freedom aside, but few Christians intend this. They assume ontological freedom and see grace as freeing us within that context to, in some measure, constitute ourselves as God would have us.

Some Buddhist writings so stress that the present situation is the result of the karmic influence of the past that they seem to deny that there is real freedom in the present. Abe's paper makes it clear that this is a misrepresentation of the true Buddhist position. Karma is bound up with volition, what I am calling deciding. Past decisions play a large role in determining the present, but there is decision now also. This is quite similar to what I regard to be the best account of the situation as experienced by Christians as well.

Abe seems to say that this ontological freedom is appraised negatively by both Christians and Buddhists. I have indicated that I do not agree. *This* level of freedom is positively appraised by Christians. The difference between Christians and Buddhists stems from opposite appraisals of the blind will to live. For Christians life is inherently a good gift of God and the blind will to live is good. What is evil is its distortion into destructive forms. This pervasive distortion is what we call original sin. Grace is required to redirect the will to live toward that which is truly life-fulfilling.

According to Abe the situation is viewed differently by Buddhism. For Buddhists the distinction between good and bad decisions is finally unimportant. As long as there is deciding at all, the blind will to live is gaining expression and this is evil. The goal must be a volitionless state in which the will to live and its expression in deciding are silenced or extinguished. Within this state, Sunyata, there is no deciding at all. This is why there is a discontinuity between the ultimate religious interest and the relative ethical one in Buddhism that is lacking in mainstream Christianity. For Christians the goal is to decide in accordance with the promptings of the Spirit. In this way the blind will to live finds its true fulfillment in real life. But conformation to the Spirit is not cessation of deciding. It is only the cessation of rebellious deciding. The "will" is healed, not eliminated.

I am not persuaded that Buddhism must interpret Sunyata as the elimination of all deciding. It must certainly be the elimination of all self-assertion, of all deciding for me against others, of all struggling to decide rightly. But I believe it can be interpreted as the ideal, spontaneous form of decision in which the decision conforms effortlessly to the primal vow in its concrete meaning for the present situation. If Sunyata can be understood in that way, then it can be highly relevant and valuable to all of us as we try to respond to the concrete reality of our world.

Abe rightly points out that in Christianity there has been a problem about human reason, because it can come into conflict with divine revelation. He notes that Buddhism is free of this problem. Indeed, one of the attractions of Buddhism to Christians and to Westerners generally is that Buddhists seem quite free from the need to defend doubtful doctrines, because of their divinely grounded authority. One of the things Christians have most to gain through dialogue with Buddhists is a similar freedom.

For Christians this is a matter of urgency. Much Christian theology is still tainted with defensiveness in relation to nihilism and scientism. Many Christians seem to fear that the reasons for rejecting these points of view are questionable, so that one must work hard to keep finding rationales. Theology often has the air of making reluctant concessions or describing what we can still believe after all these concessions are made. Buddhism does not appear to be equally vulnerable. It seems to be able to enter deeply into nihilism and come through with its spiritual affirmations strengthened. Through dialogue with Buddhists Christians hope to find ways to affirm their faith that are as pure and convincing as those of Buddhism.

Nevertheless, as Abe recognizes, all is not well with Buddhism with regard to critical reason. It has little to fear from its negative and destructive work, since Buddhism long ago rid itself of all that critical reason might undercut. In this respect it appropriated critical reason from the beginning and has little to learn from the West. But if critical reason also has a constructive role to play, then Buddhism must acknowledge a limitation. It has focused primarily on the unreliability of rational construction, seeking to detach people from clinging to their concepts. Hence, although it has nothing to fear from the advance of science, it has not supported that advance. Nor has it encouraged the construction of relatively adequate worldviews to replace the dualistic and substantialist ones that it so effectively erodes. Having shown that everything interpenetrates everything else, it has not encouraged the development of a cosmology that shows the importance of that insight for the natural and social sciences.

The question is why? The answer is similar to that with regard to the failure to develop concrete analysis of the causes of the Holocaust or any other historical event. The focus is on what is always and everywhere the same. Even though it is emphasized that one of the things that is always and everywhere the same is particularity and uniqueness, this does not lead to a critical account of what is particular in the unique situation. There is a call for openness to that particularity whatever form it takes, but nothing more.

The reason, I think, is that spontaneity and sheer immediacy are so prized that there is no place for critical discrimination. If so, that seems a real weakness. Spontaneity has an important place in the life of the spirit. But we cannot rate spontaneity as the one adequate and satisfactory feature of experience. To do so is to become anti-intellectual. Instead of using enlightened perception to guide the intellect more adequately, it becomes a substitute for careful thought. Religious teaching should do better than that, and Abe offers clues as to how this can happen.

Abe calls for nonthinking, which is beyond the distinction of thinking and not thinking. The point, I understand, is that what we know as thinking is committed to objectifying, separating, substantializing concepts that necessarily and universally distort. Not thinking is avoiding this distortion by not reflecting at all. On the other hand, nonthinking is "primordial thinking prior to the bifurcation between the thinking subject and object of thinking" (p. 35).

Abe sees that some forms of thought developed in the West could be useful for the development of this type of thinking, which has remained mainly a theoretical possibility for Buddhists. A Christian should reply that the West will have much to learn as Buddhists, with their superior realization of the overcoming of the subject-object split and the interconnectedness of all things, bring forth the treasure of thought already implicit in their traditions.

Much as I appreciate Abe's account, I am not entirely reassured. He indicates that a major weakness of Buddhism has been its failure to encourage scientific inquiry. But when he speaks of the forms of reason that

Buddhism might appropriate from the West, he refers only to the transcendental pure reason of Kant and the dialectical self-negating reason of Hegel.

Why this preference for the German idealist tradition so far as reflection on thinking is concerned? Is it because here the object is absorbed into the subject? But Buddhism intends to hold the balance in a quite different way. Is it because here thinking is understood in separation from the particulars that are thought? This is what I fear.

If Buddhism wants to make contact with the kind of thinking that is generative of science at its best, a quite different strategy is needed. Kant's *Critique of Pure Reason* marks the beginning of a split between philosophy and the natural sciences from which both have suffered immeasurably. Buddhism should protest this dualism and the resulting fragmentation of thought as vigorously as it protests other dualisms. It should encourage discriminating analysis of concrete and particular experiences to identify recurrent but not universal patterns or forms. It should encourage reflection about how these forms interrelate with one another. It should also repeatedly remind us that these forms are empty—that is, nonsubstantial and relational.

Buddhism should also warn us against the anthropocentrism of the German idealist tradition. It is ironic that at a time when the West turns to the East to escape this anthropocentrism and to find a worldview that is more appropriate to our scientific and practical needs, Buddhists seem to be succumbing to just that anthropocentrism. Of course, Abe explicitly rejects it in this paper, but it creeps back in not only in his preference for German idealism but also in his account of nature. Here he distinguishes a nonhuman, natural dimension from a transnatural human dimension. According to his account, values apply only to the human dimension. Nature seems to be valueless in itself. Only the human point of view introduces values.

This is standard Western dualism and anthropocentrism. The West has exported them all too successfully to the East. But I would hope for more resistance from Buddhism. Indeed, I would hope for a strong counterargument. Surely from the snake's point of view the swallowing of the mouse is not only "natural" but also good. And surely from the mouse's point of view it is a disaster, however "natural" it is. Why should we assume that human sentimentality provides the only valuation in this situation?

My appeal here, as elsewhere throughout this paper, is that Buddhism go deeper into its own fundamental sense of reality. The Buddhist knows that what I am in any moment, and what everything is, is interconnected with everything else. I do not exist and then act or enter into relations. I am only in my relations and in my act, and in this I do not differ from anything else. The implications of this vision are vast. If thought through, they will transform Western ethics and the natural and social sciences. But they must be thought through. This is unlikely to happen adequately until

Buddhist thinkers are willing to examine what differentiates one entity from another, and the differentiated patterns of relations among them.

Perhaps the deepest problem is the attachment of Buddhists to nondiscrimination. Nondiscrimination is affirmed as a way of breaking attachments, but it seems to become in its turn a new attachment. Perhaps nondiscrimination can be understood after the pattern of nonthinking as primordial discrimination prior to the opposition between subject and object. Perhaps this discrimination can then be encouraged and developed in such a way as to free Buddhism to make the enormous contribution of which it is capable.

4

Scoop up the Water and the Moon Is in Your Hands: On Feminist Theology and Dynamic Self-Emptying

CATHERINE KELLER

Only with a sense of irony—perhaps not unrelated to the Zen smirk—does a feminist add her voice to the Christian-Buddhist dialogue. When this interchange attempts to position itself on a common ground of shared conceptualization (for instance, of Sunyata and kenosis) it neglects the most obvious common denominator of these two world religions: their patriarchalism! The booming chorus of masculine teaching, preaching, leading, and embodying, supporting the time-honored and near universal justification by doctrine of the subordination of women, shapes a common ground so common that it continues to be missed. Therefore, it simply *continues.* Yet might it not present a splendid opportunity for mutual metanoia, for a shared project of post-patriarchal enlightenment?

Happily, though he has not even the faintest feminist concern, Masao Abe takes his stand with that group who call Christianity and Buddhism beyond the mere search for shared givens to a project of "mutual transformation." So perhaps we need not surrender either Buddhism, Christianity, or their emerging dialogue to the androcentric a priori! I am therefore pleased to have the chance to address, in the light of Abe's translation of Christian kenosis by Buddhist Sunyata, some of the snags, snares, and saving graces of the Buddhist-Christian dialogue for women—though of course I can speak only from the perspective of a white middle-class North American feminist, working within the context of a self-critical Christianity. (Perhaps this new habit of locating our perspectives socially, learned especially

102

from liberation theology, is itself a kenotic practice, emptying one's discourse of the false substance of inflated universals.)

Feminism increasingly understands itself as a multidisciplinary, multidimensional, secular and religious movement to subvert—not men—but masculine socio-cultural dominance. Feminist theology takes special responsibility for unmasking the religious justifications of dominance. We recognize in the absence of women among the spiritual leadership of both Christianity and Buddhism a cause of shameful waste and suffering, attributable not to lack of talent but to deprivation of opportunity. And we have come also to realize that the specific oppression of women, as the most universal form of social subjugation, cannot be understood in isolation from the intertwined sufferings imposed by injustice toward all who live in situations of social vulnerability—including not only the poor and those of color, but the earth and all its creatures. Patriarchy, as the original and most pervasive model of systematic exploitation, names the superstructure depending upon all of these sufferings. So any feminist spirituality unfolds in and through an enlarged, politicized, and yet intricately particularized web-consciousness.[1]

How can a feminist position herself in relation to this particular Christian-Buddhist exchange? What gravitational pulls, what attractions, in the kenosis-Sunyata focus, awaken hope for a common cause? The kenotic Christ appeals to the Hebrew tradition of the suffering servant, aligned with the prophetic emphasis upon social justice. Certainly feminist thought evinces a deep kinship to the heritage of the Hebrew protest against injustice, including its recrudescence in Jesus.[2] This despite the fact that the exodus of women from the fleshpots of patriarchy has only just begun, and that the pharaoh has been infinitely instantiated in the teachers of church and synagogue. But we will need to ask whether the kenosis doctrine as Abe interprets it helps or hinders the prophetic purposes of women.

As to Buddhist Sunyata, feminism must acknowledge exciting and irreducible affinities. If "the freedom of the Buddhist is found in the awakening to the nonsubstantiality and the interdependence of everything in the universe,"[3] the freedom of women lies in our awakening to the powers of our interconnection—to self, body, sisterhood, society, and cosmos. Thus the metaphor of the web has become central to feminist sensibility, pervasive to its discourse, and expressive of the political and cosmic extensions of personal and interpersonal liberation.[4] We may welcome Abe's dynamic interrelatedness as stemming from a tradition with real resemblances to the emerging feminist ontology, in which selfhood cannot be construed in isolation from its network of relationships. Over a millennium ago, the Chinese Hua-yen Buddhists drew inspiration from the image of Indra's net to express the "intercausation and interpenetration" of all beings.[5] The realization of such causal interrelatedness, as Abe explains, results in the realization that all things are empty, *sunya*. For there is no-thing and no-self—if to be a thing or a self means to have a substantial, separate, and self-identically enduring existence.

Yet if feminist theory cannot easily make the move to Sunyata—as I believe it cannot—it is not just for lack of enlightenment. I shall argue that if Sunyata must be understood as a state of absolute selflessness, Abe's move will tend to reinforce the more patriarchal implications of the kenotic Christ idea. But inasmuch as his strategy serves to underscore the panrelational interdependence in the universe, then the implicit iconoclasm of dynamic Sunyata can support a feminist revision of kenosis.

In proposing this sort of argument, with its inherently politicized criterion of truth as that which furthers individual and social liberation, I am proceeding from a starting point necessarily different from Abe's. He finds the major obstacle to his agenda, that of interreligious dialogue, in irreligion. His essay pursues a subtle dialectical confrontation with the problems of nihilism and scientism. His absorption of the scientific and atheist critiques of religion into the radical *Aufhebung* of emptiness, characteristic of Kyoto School Buddhism, presents a useful ploy for twentieth-century religious intellectuals, in an age in which interreligious exchange is both possible and crucial.

But I find this way of posing the project slightly anachronistic for the present historical circumstance. At the moment the great obstacles to interreligious exchange lie not so much in sophisticated irreligion as in a barbaric rereligion. That is, we face a massed force of religious reaction in occidental culture, most dangerously in U.S. Christian fundamentalism. This sort of reaction can be happening, Abe might contend, only because Christianity has so far failed to present a compelling alternative to scientism and nihilism. Abe's proposal would also appear to the normal Christian to be nothing but a thinly disguised atheism. The attraction of so many needy persons to fundamentalism has altered the religious landscape, and the academy cannot escape—especially inasmuch as academic theology depends to some extent on church-related seminaries and schools of theology, which cannot survive the indefinite continuation of the present trend. This religious reaction opposes "secular humanism," but thrives in an ominous symbiosis with high technology—and so paradoxically with that nihilist scientism that Abe addresses. The new apocalypticism supports the terminal exploitation and maldistribution of the planet's resources and the risk of nuclear exchange as God's will for "these last and evil days."[6] Of course accompanying Christian, Muslim, and Jewish fundamentalism is a virulent antifeminist agenda. And the same exclusivist biblical literalism that abuses the rights and spirits of women also must shun any interreligious dialogue that does not aim at conversion. The politics of interreligious exchange is not to be underestimated.

Though I would evaluate the context of the exchange differently, it can, if pursued in a shared commitment to all levels of liberation, help to articulate authentic and novel forms of spirituality grounded in global responsibility. The commitment of mainline Christianity at its higher levels to social justice has, to the detriment of its own agenda, so far failed to nurture a spiritual base for its prophetic ideology. In both the Christian and Buddhist situations, the interchange can lead to a crucial enrichment of the religious project: "a global practical theology is telling Christian social prophets that they must be more contemplative, and Eastern mystics that they must be more prophetic."[7] "Praxis" must then refer not only to political activism but at the same time to some sort of nondualistic spiritual discipline that heightens our awareness of ourselves as inseparably linked to body, other culture, world, earth. Meditation leads the Buddhist to the experience of Sunyata, the emptiness of the illusion of separateness, of own-being (*svabhāva*). Abe himself shows little interest in praxis of either sort, being primarily concerned with the possibility of a creative conceptual convergence. His strictly theoretical focus supports his diagnosis of the relevant crisis as one of meaningful religion versus an intellectual irreligion. But apart from the difference of approach, does his choice of convergent ideas further the full scale of liberation required by a viable feminist theology?

Abe's interpretation of the kenosis passage in Philippians brings us (inadvertently) to the very heart of women's disenchantment with traditional religious categories, but also of our hope for certain radical revisions. I will first analyze the problem, and then conclude by suggesting the promise. His reading of kenosis in terms of agape certainly remains faithful to the Pauline text. And when he highlights the self-sacrificial, self-humbling, and obedient aspects of agape, he continues a strong heritage of Christian hermeneutics. The text itself unfolds the meaning of Christ's incarnational self-emptying in terms of the motifs of servanthood, self-humbling, and obedience unto death. We are told to "have this mind in you" — that is, to instantiate this Christic obedience.

But unfortunately it is with just this aspect of the tradition that feminist theologians have had their longest-running quarrel. Elizabeth Cady Stanton already in the mid-nineteenth century faced head-on the oppressive use of the Christian rhetoric of self-sacrifice and humble service to keep women in their place. She told a reporter to "put it down in capital letters: SELF-DEVELOPMENT IS A HIGHER DUTY THAN SELF-SACRIFICE."[8] In 1960 Valerie Saiving inaugurated a new wave of feminist theology by challenging the applicability to women (within patriarchy) of the traditional emphasis upon sin as prideful self-assertion.[9] The call to agapic self-sacrifice may indeed provide the proper corrective to the hypertrophic masculine ego, which patriarchal society eggs on to inflated forms of ego development. But women sin in the opposite and complementary direction: that of the underdevelopment of the self.

In a social situation of women's subordination, when the male preachers and teachers exhort the predominantly female flock to deny themselves and practice obedience, they reinforce woman's already unhealthy dependency upon men for spiritual, cultural, and economic identity. The politics of kenotic humility incarnates itself all too clearly in the willingness of most male ministers, especially but not exclusively within theologically conservative churches, to deal with situations of physical, often life-endangering, abuse by counseling the woman to remain and submit. Christianity has been perennially tempted to glorify victimization in its glorification of its central victim. The cross, when rendered normative rather than descriptive, can indeed work to create submissive martyrs rather than revolutionary risk-takers. The root of compulsive self-victimization lies in the underdevelopment of the self.

Often one hears "women need to have a self before they can sacrifice it." Yet this sentiment falls short of what I take the more radical feminist project to be: the reconstruction of the very notion of self.[10] For despite the pressures of professionalism, women have little desire to develop a masculine ego. The masculine ego-ideal is precisely of that substantial, skin-encapsulated and self-identically enduring subjectivity that Buddhism decries as ignorance and Christianity as sin. For women the route to maturity hardly lies in first developing this mode of sinful ignorance and then overcoming it! Nor does it lie in acquiescence in the passivity, diffusion, and eager-to-please dependency of traditional femininity. Increasingly women are realizing that we have a unique opportunity to transform our profound relational sensitivity and affective vitality from a weakness into a strength, and thus to offer both women and men a new norm of selfhood. So it is perhaps evident why we will not be able to return now or—I hope—in the foreseeable future, to embrace any ideals of self-sacrifice, self-denial, and selflessness that have not first thoroughly struggled with the concrete contexts in which selfhood is *engendered.*

In this way I fear that Masao Abe's coupling of Christian self-sacrifice with Buddhist *anatta* attenuates the problem. Will the Christian-Buddhist dialogue offer the worst of both worlds to women? How can the two patriarchies, with their common problem of the inflationary male ego and their common solution of selflessness, fail to redouble the oppressive irrelevance of the "world religions" for the liberation of women? Or indeed of any persons already suffering from their internalization of the role of the victim?

Because the Buddhist analyzes selfhood in terms of the *dharmas* that produce and reproduce delusion from moment to moment, can one imagine adding to the list a few *skandhas* of sexist complementarity? Could Buddhism address specifically the karmic bondage of men in their illusion of independence who are dependent upon submissive women to sustain that illusion for them, while those women, often embodying the survival power of the family, needing to cultivate a sense of their own weak dependency? Certainly the Buddhist metaphysic elucidates the relational interdependency and causal network in which the sense of self—and its neurotic clinging to its own illusions—comes to be. At this level the feminine self in its solubility and the masculine self in its separativeness may be equally and jointly implicated in the delusions that heap up suffering. But before Western women can hear the liberating words of Buddha to the situation of false dependency and false independence, the deep disjunction of feminist and Buddhist projects must be faced, as it must also be faced in relation to Christian teachings.

If one were to list the marks of feminist selfhood (for both men and woman) it would consist of a series of retrievals. And note that it would need to reclaim almost equally from traditional Buddhism as from traditional Christianity. These feminist desiderata seem to mark the "wrong" way for both. Feminism reclaims the body, its wisdom, desires, and pleasures, knowing its obsessions to represent imposed distortion. It emphasizes the particularity of social location, of difference, of otherness. It blesses emotion — anger and tenderness are "angels, not polarities."[11] Unlike most traditional forms of prayer or meditation, it celebrates imagination. It cultivates a spiritual and practical connection to the natural environment. It decries the futility of all thought or spirituality that sinks into quietism. Action seeks to transform the structures, psychological or social, that create unjust suffering. And above all it strengthens both the sense of attachment and the sense of self, seeking not to overcome self but to experience and to articulate an extensively relational self. Its selfhood is a dynamic becoming, not a static ego. Precisely in its impermanence, the moment of self is to be affirmed. Classic Christianity, in its burdensome dependence upon an Aristotelian substance metaphysic and in its failure to reform its own image of the warrior Lord, has only inconsistently affirmed the fluidity, communality, and bodiliness of selfhood. This in spite of the obvious biblical impetus to bodiliness and community as instrinsic, not merely instrumental, values. The incarnation and the passion of the deity are often isolated — though precisely not in the kenosis teaching — from their anthropological implications.

And I also am aware that while Buddhism acknowledges passion, embodiment, sociality, as ontological facts it seems to disdain them as delusions of the still-attached ego, miserable distractions from the attainment of nirvana. Though Abe rightly stresses that Sunyata can be experienced only in conjunction with *tathata* — the vivid particularity of finite existence here and now — one nonetheless cannot evade the severe implications of nonattachment. Even Buddha identifies the transient with the miserable: "whosoever of the monks or the priests regards the delightful and pleasurable things in the world as impermanent, miserable, and without an ego, as a disease and sorrow, it is he who overcomes the craving."[12] I may be taking the text out of context, and realize that the point of overcoming craving is to move in the world with an ecstatic and compassionate wisdom, not with a sour otherworldliness. But nonetheless there are tensions between the feminist pursuit of a relational self and the Buddhist pursuit of a nonself whose relationality discloses its emptiness of any own-being. At least for women and others who have developed the habit of self-denigration, to *own* one's life, one's experience, is to creatively overcome dispossession. It will be for Buddhist women to address these issues on their own terms, not on the terms of Christian feminists.[13]

The underlying metaphysical tension can be stated in this way: feminism can find more in Buddhist ontology than in any classic Christian metaphysic as to the radical and fluid interconnectivity in the universe. But whereas for Buddhism this interdependency (*pratitya samutpada*) functions as a radically deconstructive analysis, for feminism it functions as our most radically constructive vision.

In some respects such tensions merely echo the tension between East and West, and will appear in the interchange with other forms of Western thought, even of the antisubstantialist variety. For instance, Whiteheadian and Buddhist thought share strikingly an ontology of cosmic interdependency and dynamic becoming. Feminist cosmology, as it emerges, will deeply resemble both: the idea of interconnectedness requires that of process. But whereas Western process thought, like much feminist thought, fundamentally embraces the creativity inherent in the universe as an ultimate truth, deeper than illusion, Buddhism seeks to liberate us from the cycle of perpetual becoming. And where process thought, like recent feminism, greets the momentary individuals issuing from the process of interconnectedness as what is real, Buddhism uses the analysis of interpenetration to stress the unreality of any kind of individual existent. To affirm the self, precisely as awakened to its "suchness and interpenetration," is impossible. For Buddhism this is just where we must extinguish the rhetoric of self. Is this just a semantic difference? Or is there not rather a fundamental move in Buddhism, including Abe's variety, toward the obliteration of all differentiation from the perspective of the absolute—that is, the realization of Sunyata?[14]

Theologically related tensions come into play when Abe interprets God's radical self-emptying as an absolute identification with the world. Such a move parallels the fundamental understanding of selfhood as emptied into a decentered selflessness. Abe contends that his kenotic God is fully personal, because so fully loving as to be "identical with everything."[15] But what does "love" mean when it dissolves into sheer identification? How can we not diagnose this deity, even in its "boundless openness," as a projection of narcissistic merger? Certainly such a vision offers a useful corrective to the dualistic separations of a transcendent deity from "his" creation, reflective of the masculine ego structure. But has psychoanalytic theory, especially in its object relations and feminist revisions, not taught us to beware any "oceanic feeling," which violates the otherness of the other? Without the love of the other as other, made possible only when self is distinct from other, "love" turns out upon closer inspection to be a case of egoistic self-love, which attempts to encase the other within the self. In Abe's paradigm, neither divine nor human individuals can love each other in each other's *difference* from each other.

Difference requires no dualism, but neither does it brook absolute non-dualism. To apply Abe's method, in three propositions:

> The self is not the self unless the other is other. But difference is not the same as separation; and nonseparation is not the same as non-differentiation.
>
> God is not God unless God is other. But God is not separate from the world.
>
> Because God is in everything, God is fully immanent. Because God is *in* everything, God is not identical with anything. Because God is in *everything,* God transcends anything. God is fully transcendent because fully immanent.

Feminist theology, with its strong immanentism emanating from its discovery of the sacredness of all connection and its repudiation of androcentric dualism, is often accused of pantheism. Some feminist spiritualists would gladly accept this "charge."[16] But if a feminist theologian, or if Abe, really wants (as he asserts he does) to avoid pantheism, then such a one must find a way to evoke a genuine dialectic between world and deity, based on a relationship rather than an act of mere identification. This implies attributing personality to the sacred. Should we — as feminists or as Buddhists — want to implicate ourselves in Hebrew-Christian faith patterns so far as to affirm a personal deity, it seems crucial then to take the metaphors and the analysis of the personal, with its interpersonal dynamic, with utmost seriousness. Here the meaning of Abe's "interpenetration and reciprocity" reverberates with yet unfulfilled promise.

Whether divine or human "persons" are at stake, one wonders whether genuine reciprocity is possible when no individual (person or group) has any distinct contribution to make, as even a momentary "ownbeing" is ruled out, or temporality is understood as concentrated in a present moment in which past and future are reversible.

Reciprocity seems to me to imply a causal flow from present to future, in which that present is becoming irreversibly the past, and so giving way through the reciprocity of influences with others, to a new present. Abe wants to strengthen the sense of history in Buddhism, as he also wishes to create a common ground with theism in the struggle against irreligion. These are related, as the biblical God is deeply involved in historical time. Feminism has a hard time affirming, as would Abe, "the God who acts in history," if that means the all-powerful agent of miraculous intervention, or of unremitting control. But time is the dimension of relatedness, if relatedness is the stuff of the creative process. Time becomes irreversible only when the particular, unique *difference* of this momentary event — my self here and now—transmits its sense of irreducible value. Theism grounds that value in an ultimate relationship.

But even without an explicit theism, an outspoken cosmic Thou (which many feminists can certainly do without), that difference which I make in the future of my world, my relationships, cannot be reversed. Our causal—ethical—responsibility is in this sense nonnegotiable. My effects on the world can be altered, negotiated, diminished or augmented, but what I become and do here and now cannot be retroactively annihilated. The intuition into the irreversible spiral of time may be essential not only to a feminist sensibility, which concerns itself with relational responsibility intimately and collectively, but also to any liberationist commitment to justice in history. Abe's Buddhist case study of the Holocaust takes up this matter of historical responsibility with sensitivity and boldness, addressing the purported underdevelopment of Buddhist social ethics. He builds his case upon the distinction between the relative perspective, in which good and evil are distinguishable, from the absolute perspective in which all distinction—even, I presume, that between relative and absolute, samsara and nirvana—is emptied out. And it is of course to the level of the relative that he would relegate "women's concerns"—if indeed he could even recognize an evil in sexism at all. Feminism is also committed to overcoming the sort of ethical dualism in which I call the other "evil," create of the other a scapegoat to bear my shadows, and therefore eliminate my own responsibility. We do not wish to continue the pattern, even in the tempting reversal of identifying patriarchy with evil. So feminist ethics may best define "evil" as that which projects its evil onto another; therefore evil is the effect upon the network of relationships of an individual or systemic denial of interrelatedness itself. In Ruether's words, "sin exists precisely in the distortion of relationality, including relation to oneself."[17] But this does not represent the two-tiered system that Abe seems to be suggesting, between a level in which distinctions of better and worse matter and another, even construed as pure "interpenetration," in which they do not. Is it not precisely because of our interpermeation that ethical considerations matter? Though from the vantage point of the whole web, the distinctions are of course relative, they remain also relational, and therefore *real.* Whereas the logic of Sunyata seems to move in the opposite direction: relative, relational, therefore empty—where in its negative sense Sunyata carries the taint of unreality.

In general, I must continue to ask whether Abe's revision of Buddhism can finally valorize—as it does indeed wish and claim to—the particularity of individuals, groups, and historical moments. Particularity is affirmed as "suchness"—but is such suchness too undifferentiated (even in its capacity for vivid presence)? How can it be interpreted to support historical projects of transformation? Is there not a danger that the dualism of "relative" and "absolute" will function as just that—a dualism? The absolute is within the relative, and Sunyata only realized in and through samsara (as the realm of God is among us, now and coming). Sunyata itself is emptied into samsara. But does it not dissolve the web of karmic-causal relationships as it flows back into them? Does not the enlightened one work *outside* the causal net of influences? "Vow and act" notwithstanding, or rather in the light of them, how can the one who is "enlightened" (and should we wait to attain this state before attempting "right action"? How Long?) find the motivation to work in and through history, institutions, ongoing relationships? Though Abe has not ignored or devalued such questions, I suspect that the reversibility of time and the supremacy of an undifferentiating absolute can work as a kind of solvent on the historical sensibility, even as it is trying to emerge.

But let me empty this response of any futile opposition to Sunyata. For as its subtlest apologist, Nagarjuna, responds to the (then Indian) opponents of emptiness: Time and again you have made a condemnation of emptiness, but that refutation does not apply to our emptiness. Therefore I hope that the foregoing remarks will be read not as judgments but questions, not polarizations but creative tensions.

In conclusion let me celebrate more specifically ways in which I think the Buddhist-Christian dialogue, and Abe's brilliant contribution to it, enhance the feminist project.

1. The hermeneutic of Sunyata can refresh and radicalize the metaphor of the kenotic Christ. If freed of the emphasis upon self-sacrifice, the notion of divine self-emptying can subject traditional christology to a gentle and needed iconoclasm. To empty the christological kenosis into the essential function of the deity shores up a high christology, but leaves the figure of Jesus its full, finite, and particular humanness. While Christian feminists can enjoy the distinctive maleness of Jesus himself, the deification of Jesus, which yields the divinization of masculinity, has a most unsaving and unsavory effect upon the gender balance. Abe's version of the incarnation and kenosis of the second Person of the Trinity can at least have the effect of emptying deity of its anthropormorphic (andromorphic) projections. More existentially, it helps to free us from the deifying and subsequent reifying of the male ego structure as something substantial, independent, and dominant.

To claim that God is always and everywhere self-emptying, in essence and not only in one saving event, relieves christology at once of its exclusivism and of its triumphalism. Non-Christians and Christian feminists alike can benefit from this move, for it points to a cosmic generosity rather than a divine stinginess in matters of revelation and salvation. Yet if "God" is to remain a metaphor for something personal in the universe, then perhaps God should be conceived as *truly* "dynamically self-emptying" — that is, symbolizing a movement into the world of becoming, by which the deity becomes part of all that is, but also by which all that has become becomes a part of the deity. Such a theology makes way ontologically for an endless and needed pluralism of metaphors for deity — arising from inorganic nature, biological life, and both genders of person.

2. Buddhism shares with feminism an unconditional no to all suffering. Christianity, by contrast, has been tempted to glorify suffering as redemptive in order to recycle the suffering and death of the redeemer. Feminist theology has contributed to the strong case against scriptural validation of such sadomasochistic theology.[18] Rather than shoring up the self-sacrificial motif of agape (which contributes also to its opposition, to eros), the discourse of self-emptying can help to undo all commitment to suffering. Suffering may be redeemable, but is not intrinsically redemptive. Buddhism teaches a way that leads beyond needless suffering, and so can counteract the neurotic clinging to guilt, masochism, and self-deprecation that traditional Christianity so readily breeds.

Moreover, as Buddhism continues to become a force for social transformation in the world (as for example in the Third World liberation Buddhisms of Sri Lanka and Thailand[19]) its commitment to end suffering, combined with its profound grasp of interdependence, is moving to undo the institutional causes of suffering as well. In this it does and can ever more join forces with the prophetic biblical denunciation of all unjust suffering. As this happens, women become forces for transformation rather than scapegoats for the intolerable.

3. Feminist theology, psychology, and philosophy are groping toward an ontology of relationship. Yet we remain anxious that our emphasis upon interconnectedness may be a function of our role within the Western patriarchal tradition, which denied relatedness and left it to women. There is thus a certain epistemological advantage in finding an ontology of relationship already long at hand, arisen out of separate circumstances, and indeed in many ways moderating and correcting the prevenient patriarchalism of Hinduism. The differences between the feminist affirmation of interrelatedness, as a normative vision, and the deconstructive, Buddhist use of *pratitya-samutpada* — the chain of dependent co-origination that demonstrates the bondage of all creatures as their interdependence — remain. They may, however, reflect the patriarchal context that Buddhism no more overthrew than did Christianity in its analogous situation. But such a possibility should motivate rather than discourage further dialogue.

4. The feminist affirmation of eros, body, emotion, relationship, self, and the like, does as noted earlier present a prima facie contradiction to traditional Buddhist (and to some extent Christian) value and practice. However, feminists need not simply celebrate all manner of affect or connection, like cheerleaders, for every intense and undervalued experience. At this point we can afford to be — indeed cannot afford not to be — discerning, careful, and conscious in the pursuit of all such neglected aspects of culture and personality. To put it more directly: we need to be (and I think are) increasingly discriminating in the affirmation of emotion and relation. We learn, usually the hard way, that even as high-consciousness feminists passionate emotion can sell us short and even sell us out. And so we begin to

distinguish between healthy uses of anger, for instance, and the sort of anger that merely consumes our energies or our relationships. In Buddhist parlance, we learn to take note of our anger, not to repress it, but neither to magnify it. We find that surrendering to depression is a way of clinging to pain. We learn that some kinds of intimacy leave us drained, anxious, and obsessed, and others free us, glowing, to pursue our work in the world. We learn that "falling in love" is likely to trap us, radical feminist or not, lesbian or heterosexual, in modes of dependency and desperation to which the Buddhist diagnosis of *avidya* well applies. We learn that real loving (unlike the "falling" kind) has emptied itself of dependent attachment, neurotic projection, and the frustrating cycle of greedy and needy desire. Feminist praxis can learn from Buddhist ontology and spirituality as we move toward a more refined vocabulary of emotion and relation. This is essential not just for personal well-being (itself certainly essential!) but for the revolutionary work of undoing the internalized patterns of self-denigration and self-destruction that keep the systems of suffering intact.

5. Some version of Buddhist meditative praxis, or some Western variation that perhaps works especially for our peculiar dilemmas and dualisms, is essential to enlightenment. We may affirm a dynamic process of enlightening rather than a final, qualitatively removed product. Would not an evolving process of coming to wisdom and compassion, always exercising the "vow and act," best coordinate with Abe's dynamic Sunyata? The Buddha's ancient lesson on "right attention"—noting moment by moment your breath, your perceptions, sensations, emotions and thoughts, not struggling against them but staying aware of them and always returning to breathe— is a perfectly good starting place. Without such spiritual practice, political praxis is prone to become an ineffectual, polarizing rhetoric, and simply to burn out. Moreover, such practice allows us to process the pain involved in global awareness (for instance, reading the newspaper!) much more effectively, without being consumed and depressed by it. So we are more likely to stay informed and active.

6. Abe's thoroughgoing insistence on the dynamism of dynamic Sunyata is to be applauded. Moreover, he suggests that we translate it with the verb form of "self-emptying," rather than the noun form "emptiness." This is salutary at many levels. First, if we are committed to the wider spread of Buddhist concepts in the West (beyond the academy), we must cultivate a sensitivity to metaphor. "Emptiness" does not and cannot *work*—in English it conjures stagnation, boredom, dispersion (quite the opposite of Sunyata, but just exactly what most nonmeditators first experience when trying to meditate!). "Self-emptying" is free of these linguistic associations. It evokes a perpetual call to "boundless openness"—to let go of all that binds or abuses us, to let the past enter into the future and the future turn into the past, to step free of the inner effects of oppression in order to undo the outer causes. Could Abe allow for such historicizing of dynamic Sunyata as to let it apply to the institutional structures of religion as well? Can it empty

out the idolatrous fixities of the Christian faith—by which, for example, finite masculine images (father, son, lord, pope, or the baritone voice of the preacher) become the *pars pro toto* of spiritual authority? Can it empty out the patriarchy of the Buddhist tradition as well? For as long as world religions transmit the karma of masculine acquisitive greed for power over women, how are they liberating? As long as they leave unrecognized and unextinguished the dependent co-origination of sex role stereotypes, of gender complementarity and hierarchy, what ego have they overcome?

7. Can we hear in this dynamic self-emptying, both in self and in deity, a rhythm of emptying and filling, which only extinguishes the self as it realizes it, which empties the moment's self-actualization not into nothing but into the future shared by the community of all becoming? If times are relational rather than reversible, the self becomes before it perishes. It is no-self if "self" means a self-encapsulated and enduring ego; but that is just the meaning that must be emptied. Though it will immediately drain through our cupped fingers, we scoop up the water and the moon is in our hands.[20]

NOTES

1. See Rosemary Ruether, *New Woman New Earth* (New York: Seabury, 1975) for a classic statement of the originality of sexism; and see Charlene Spretnak, ed., *The Politics of Women's Spirituality* (Garden City, N.Y.: Anchor, 1982), and Robin Morgan, *The Anatomy of Freedom: Feminism, Physics, and Global Politics* (Garden City, N.Y.: Anchor, 1982) for key discussions of the political-personal-spiritual holiness of feminist consciousness.

2. See especially Rosemary Ruether, *Sexism and God-Talk* (Boston: Beacon, 1983) for a feminist exposition of the prophetic principle.

3. Abe, see above p. 31.

4. My *From a Broken Web: Separation, Sexism, and Self* (Boston: Beacon, 1986) cites numerous feminist evocations of the web—notably in the poetry of Adrienne Rich and the thought of Mary Daly.

5. See Steve Odin, *Process Metaphysics and Hua-Yen Buddhism* (Albany: SUNY Press, 1982), pp. 16f.

6. Grace Halsell, *Prophecy and Politics: Militant Evangelists on the Road to Nuclear War* (Westport, Conn.: Lawrence Hill, 1986).

7. Paul Knitter, *No Other Name? A Critical Survey of Christian Attitudes toward the World Religions* (Maryknoll, N.Y.: Orbis, 1985), p. 229.

8. Quoted in Carol Gilligan, *In a Different Voice* (Cambridge: Harvard University Press, 1982), p. 129.

9. Valerie Saiving, "The Human Situation: A Feminist View," in *Womanspirit Rising: A Feminist Reader in Religion*, C. Christ and J. Plaskow, ed. (San Francisco: Harper & Row, 1979). Judith Plaskow extends and systematizes Saiving's insight, working out a debate with Reinhold Niebuhr and Paul Tillich on the basis of criteria derived from women's experience of self and of transcendence. See Plaskow, *Sex, Sin, and Grace: Women's Experience and the Theologies of Reinhold Niebuhr and Paul Tillich* (Washington, D.C.: University Press of America, 1980).

10. Such reconstruction is the project of my book, mentioned above.

11. Adrienne Rich, *"Integrity,"* *A Wild Patience Has Taken Me This Far* (New York: Norton, 1981), p. 8.

12. Dwight Goddard, ed., *A Buddhist Bible* (Boston: Beacon, 1938), p. 31.

13. See, for instance, the work of Rita Gross. Feminist issues for Buddhist women seem to surface most concretely around matters of community—patterns of monastic authority, Theravada refusal to ordain nuns, and the role of interpersonal friendship.

14. Steve Odin has lucidly demonstrated in the case of Hua-Yen Buddhism that the difference between Whitehead and Buddhism lies in the Whiteheadian affirmation of a form of momentary creative *svabhava,* which in Buddhism is exhaustively factored into nothingness *(Process Metaphysics and Hua-Yen Buddhism).*

15. Abe, see above p. 18.

16. Such as Starhawk or Naomi Goldenberg. Ruether, by contrast, could be accused of pantheism for her strong ecocentric immanentism in *Sexism and God-Talk,* but would rightly deny the applicability of the category.

17. *Sexism and God-Talk,* p. 181.

18. See Elizabeth Schüssler-Fiorenza's *In Memory of Her: A Feminist Reconstruction of Christian Origins;* Rita Brock, *Journeys by Heart: A Christology of Erotic Power;* Mary Daly, *Beyond God the Father.*

19. See Joanna Macy, *Dharma and Development: Religion as Resource in the Sarvodaya Self-help Movement* (W. Hartford: Kumarian Press, 1983).

20. From the *Zenrinkushū,* a collection of Zen sayings.

5

God Is Unselfish Love

JÜRGEN MOLTMANN*

It is unusual, nevertheless I want to begin with a personal comment: one can only congratulate Masao Abe for this Buddhist-Christian study. There are few Christian theological studies about the kenosis of Christ and the kenosis of God according to Philippians 2 that are so profound and precise as this work of a Buddhist scholar concerning the central topic of Christian faith. His presentation of the dynamic Sunyata is so lucid that every Christian theologian can understand it. Here reciprocal understanding is not only furthered, but Christianity and Buddhism in their immiscible difference are led into a common reality. In light of this common reality, perhaps a mutual transformation does not yet begin, but certainly a reciprocal liking and opening for each other.

This has always been the tendency of the dialogue between Christians and Buddhists. Masao Abe has been one of the first to complete this step. It is an intellectual pleasure to discuss with him on this level and to think further, stimulated by him. In this response I want to most of all focus on his understanding of "kenotic God," but I also want to say something about his presuppositions and his consequences.

THE SITUATION OF RELIGIONS IN TODAY'S WORLD

Masao Abe has defined the common situation of religions, especially of Christianity and of Buddhism, in contemporary civilization through the modern critique of religion: (1) through *scientism* and its interpretation of religion as "unscientific" and in a scientific civilization, therefore, irrelevant; (2) through modern *nihilism* in the sense of Nietzsche and its destruction of religion as an "enemy of life" because it is an "enemy of power."

---

*English translation by Marianne M. Martin.

In his presentation of the problems of Buddhism in modern civilization he is then more concrete: Buddhism has indeed taught a deep religious wisdom, but it has not produced the modern notion of autonomous human reason as in the sense of Kant. Buddhism has indeed taught the cosmic community of all living things, but it has not created the modern notion of the responsible person. Buddhism has indeed cosmically interpreted the problem of evil with the help of the term karma, but with that, it has too quickly disregarded the moral and political dimension of evil.

From the perspective of Christianity, the situation of the modern world looks somewhat different. Because it has arisen at least to a large extent from the Christian world of the West, Christians today see the contradictions of this modern world more than its advances. Not science itself is a problem of the world, but rather science in its "scientific-technological civilization." Not reason itself is a problem of religion, but rather reason in its function in the world which is dominated by it. The metaphysical nihilism of the thinking of a Nietzsche is not the problem of humanity today but rather the political and economical *exterminism* which is practiced. The modern world which is characterized by reason, science, and metaphysical nihilism, has (1) produced the misery of the "Third World" and increases it from year to year, has (2) produced the nuclear terror system and threatens the world from year to year with stronger weapons of annihilation, has (3) brought about the ecological crisis through which from year to year more types of plants and animals are exterminated and the atmosphere is fatally poisoned. What one hundred years ago was the hopeful "modern times," has today become the "end time" of humanity. That means, the era in which the end of humanity is nuclearly always possible and in one hundred years is ecologically almost inevitable, if it does not come to a global change in the thinking, intentions, and being of humans. To initiate such a change is the task of religion in the present-day world.

There are religions and cultures which enter into the age of this modern "scientific-technological civilization" only today. But there are also religions and cultures that were involved in the birth of this civilization and which therefore see its victims especially clearly and search for a new civilization of common survival for humanity and nature. For Western religions and cultures, the new interest in the religions and wisdoms of the East arises out of the critique of the contradictions of "modern" civilization and the quest for a "postmodern" world of peace and reconciliation of contradictions. The true interest in the wisdoms of Buddhism and of Taoism in the West is not to be found with the "drop-outs" who are tired of civilization, but rather with the worried and knowing who search for a new civilization that serves life and no longer death.

THE DIVINE KENOSIS

For the modern Western religion of scientific-technological civilization, *God* is *the Lord,* the *omnipotent* one. The transcendent God stands over against the world. It is God's property. This monotheism of modern Western religion has disenchanted the world (Max Weber), deprived it of all divine attributes and secularized it. Through this monotheism, the modern mechanical worldview is made possible. This worldview, in turn, became the basis of the modern world conquest by Western people. If humans are "God's likeness," then they must strive to conform to their God and to be like their God. If God is the Lord of the world, then the human must become the lord of the earth. If God is owner of heaven and earth, then the human must become the owner of the nature of the earth. Just as God rules the world as absolute subject of the world, so humans as subjects of knowing and wanting must learn to rule themselves.

Apart from the devastating ecological consequences of this modern conquest-religion of the West, the division of person and nature was sealed through it. The human person is understood as natureless and nature as personless.

Masao Abe has, with a secure sense, taken up and interpreted the very different fundamental idea of Christianity: the kenosis of Christ in which the kenosis of God is revealed. The Christ hymn of Philippians 2 is also the most impressive and touching passage in the Bible for me. First, I confirm and deepen its meaning:

1. Christ's emptying himself is not a partial or an ostensible self-emptying, but a whole and genuine emptying of his divine form and his divinity as well as his divine power, as it says in a Christian Christmas song. He becomes a servant without power or rulership, the powerless crucified one:

> He empties himself of all his power,
> becomes humble and low,
> and takes upon himself the form of a servant:
> the creator of all things.
> N. Herman

Or, as it says in the modern Anglican "Hymne to the Creator" by W.H. Valstone:

> Thou art God, no monarch Thou,
> Throu'd in easy estate to reign;
> Thou art God, whose arms of Love
> aching, spent, the world enstain.

2. But because this *emptying of himself* to the point of death on the cross happens in obedience to God, one must say at the same time that the *self-realization* of the Son of God is also accomplished in it. It is an active kenosis of the divine which only the Son of God himself can accomplish.

3. But if his emptying of himself is at the same time his self-realization, then it is based not in his arbitrary action, but rather in the spontaneity of

his eternal being. As Professor Abe says, "the Son of God becomes flesh simply because the Son of God is originally self-emptying." There is no imaginable condition of the Son of God in which he would not exist in this self-emptying surrendering.

4. If this is right, then divinity itself is from eternity nothing other than self-emptying and, in that, unselfish love. A glance at the Gospel of John confirms this: "For God so loved the world that he gave his only Son . . ." (John 3:16), and "God is love" (1 John 4:16). God's love subsequently consists in surrendering. God does not love arbitrarily, but God's whole being "is" love, and that means surrendering. God's freedom is God's love and God's love is God's freedom.

5. If loving surrendering, that is kenosis, is not only an act but the being and existence of God, then this must also be the fundamental idea of the Christian doctrine of the Trinity. In fact, in the Western doctrine of the Trinity since Augustine, the doctrine of the Trinity has always been developed in terms evoking an image of the intrinsic love of God:

> You see the Trinity,
> when you see the love;
> Because three are the loving one,
> the loved one and the love.
> Augustine

6. Masao Abe is correct when he says: "Kenosis . . . is . . . the fundamental nature of God." But then in his friendly critique of my theology of the cross,[1] he has taken up the Christian doctrine of the Trinity only in the rudimentary form of the well-known statement from Tertullian: *Tres personae - una substantia*. This is insufficient. Christian theology has gone far beyond this early statement. Taking up the ideas of the Middle Ages and modern times, I developed a *social doctrine of Trinity* in 1980, for which the *perichoretical community* of the three persons stands in the center, not the divine substance as with Tertullian.[2] The beginning point is again the Gospel of John: "Father, thou art in me, and I in thee . . . we are one," says the Son of God according to the Gospel of John (17:20ff). I understand this as follows: The Son does not exist in himself, but by virtue of his unselfish love entirely in the Father. The Father does not exist in himself, but by virtue of his unselfish love entirely in the Son. The Holy Spirit does not exist in itself, but entirely in the Father and the Son. So the three persons are by virtue of the essential surrendering different and yet entirely one.

The surrendering of the Son to death on the cross is included from eternity in the exchange of the eternal love that constitutes the divine life of the Trinity. It is the divine being of the Father, the Son, and the Holy Spirit to surrender entirely to the other person and in this way to achieve self-realization only in the other persons.[3] The unselfishness in the eternal love and unity of the trinitarian God is *perichoresis*: community in mutual interdependence and interpenetration.

7. Masao Abe has called the substantial unity of the trinitarian God the "great zero," and drawing upon Meister Eckhart and Jakob Böhme he has interpreted it as the *nothingness* or the *groundlessness* of the divinity. In place of the interpersonal categories of the social doctrine of the Trinity, he has used the natural categories of substance metaphysics because they come closer to the Buddhist understanding of ultimate reality. I do not agree with this because with it one loses the possibility of balancing person and nature. According to the Christian doctrine of the Trinity, "person" is a *hypostatic nature* or, said differently, "nature is captured in person." In this way, a necessary split between person and nature or making person and nature antithetical is rendered impossible. In person, nature comes to itself. In nature, person realizes him/herself. One can not reduce a hypostatic nature to a non-hypostatic form of nature. Therefore, the trinitarian formula of Tertullian (*tres personae - una substantia*) is insufficient. If one takes away the divine persons, then no divine substance remains. The divine "substance" can only be searched for in the community of the three divine persons and this is unselfish, surrendering love.

Meister Eckhart's explanations of the "abyss" of the divinity behind the three divine persons are just as insufficient. When one recognizes the common divinity of the three divine persons *in* their hypostatic community, then this divinity certainly displays those characteristics that Meister Eckhart and Jakob Böhme attempted to describe: unselfish love and surrender to the other as the highest form of *negation*, while self-denial is at the same time the highest form of affirmation, the affirmation of others in their otherness.

In this respect, the divinity of the trinitarian God is kenosis. This divine kenosis is being as well as non-being. It is neither being nor non-being. It is the unfathomable secret of love, which one cannot comprehend, but rather only worship in amazement. Because all our notions create idols, only amazement understands the secret of reality.

8. God is not subject, *God is community*. Therefore the divine persons are not only the reference point for the prayer of people, but their community is also the presence, the space, and the environment in which people can pray. Christian prayer, like the Christian knowledge of God, has a trinitarian structure: in the power of the Spirit people pray through the Son to the Father. People pray not only *to God*, but also *through God* and *in God*. In no other way could they pray to God. Christian meditation makes those who pray conscious that they pray *in God* to God.

9. Christian existence is *existence in God*: "who abides in love abides in God" (1 John 4:16). Here God is neither "subject," as Hans Kung assumes, nor "predicate," as Masao Abe suggests. The reciprocal inhabitation of humans in God and of God in humans, as it is effected in the "community of the Holy Spirit," happens here. The mutual *perichoresis* of the Father

and the Son is so deep that it is wide open for the entire creation: "Even as thou, Father, art in me and I in thee, that they also may be in us" (John 17:21).

In summary: God is unselfish love. Kenosis is the mystery of the trinitarian God. By virtue of God's unselfish love, God permeates all creatures and makes them alive. In this way God lives in the creation community and allows the community of all God's creatures to live in God. In reciprocal permeation everything that is exists and lives. The unselfish empathy of God awakens the sympathy of all creatures for each other. Perichoresis is also the mystery of the creation.

10. If one starts with this, then one arrives at a new understanding of the *world as God's creation in God*.[4] Buddhist and Jewish-Christian thought can mutually deepen each other here. (a) Creation means: everything that exists is contingent. (b) Nothing that exists has its cause in itself; rather, the cause is in something else and nothing is *causa sui*. (c) Whatever is contingent and cannot exist out of itself has its existential basis in something else. All creatures exist in mutual dependence. Everything that exists is reciprocal. Life means to exist with the other, for the other, and in the other. Creation is a single creation community. It is a perichoretical network of reciprocal sympathy.

In addition (d), the sum of all relationships and all things that we call "the creation" cannot have its existence in itself and from itself, but rather is indebted to the kenosis of the God who is love. "Creation" denotes not only a "work" of God, but also the community of God with the world. Of this divine creation community it is said: "In him we live and move and have our being" (Acts 17:28). (e) With this creation mystery—and this mystery of God—Sunyata appears to come so close to creation that Christians can learn from Buddhists how to handle and how to live in this creation community. If all existing things exist reciprocally in each other and in God, then this world has no center in itself. It is "excentric." In Sunyata the perichoretical structure of all things is realized.

All egocentrism (f) of human persons and all anthropocentrism of humankind subverts the creation community of the kenotic God. Any being that leaves the creation community and makes itself dependent on itself or self-centeredly appropriates something else to itself falls into decay. Self-adulation is the death of every creature. And if by "greed" the idolization of an object or a self-adulation is meant, then greed is the beginning of suffering and of decay. Opposed to this, true love is the unselfish surrender to another person or other beings for their own sake. Reciprocal kenotic love sustains the world. It depletes the world "in reference to inherent existence" while it enlivens the world through the realization of perichoristic community.

THE GRACE OF SPONTANEITY

In his presentation of "dynamic Sunyata," Masao Abe compares Buddhist and Christian conceptions of salvation and finds in Christianity a personalistic divine-human relationship (I-Thou-relationship). He says that Christianity has a theistic view of the "one personal God as the ultimate reality" and he speaks of "God as creator and ruler of the universe," which Buddhism does not know. These statements about Christianity are inconsistent with those statements about the "kenotic God" that Masao Abe himself has developed from the New Testament.

In order to correct him, I wish to raise briefly the following points:

1. The Christian notion of redemption includes person and nature, soul and body, humanity and cosmos. Already for Paul (Romans 8:19ff.), there was a deep solidarity between the humans and all other creatures in suffering from the annihilation as well as in the hope of redemption in the glory of God. The ancient Church developed the so-called doctrine of "physical redemption," teaching that humans were not only redeemed personally from their sins, but also naturally from transitoriness and mortality. The redemption of humans is only the personal side of the redemption of the whole cosmos. But Christian theology does not reduce the personal dimension to the transpersonal cosmic side of redemption, but retains an understanding of a differentiated unity of person and nature.

2. The theism of the "one personal God as the ultimate reality" is propagated through Islam. Christianity is trinitarian because it must see God in Jesus and Jesus in God. The doctrine of the Trinity connects organically the transcendence and the immanence of God in the world. I have written about the consequences above. The image Masao Abe uses is of the Christian God as transcendent "Creator" and "ruler" outside of the world is incorrect and provides no basis for a productive dialogue.

Masao Abe's critical comments about the weaknesses of Buddhism with regard to the formation of modern rationality, human personality, and the problem of evil are helpful because they are not meant apologetically but invitingly. I find that the interests of Christians and Buddhists intersect here. Christians are fascinated with the Buddhist idea of the cosmic community of all creatures—that is, with the Buddhist understanding of nature. But Buddhists ask obviously in view of civilization about the Christian understanding of person, because in the Christian understanding of person the development of modern subjectivity and rationality is based. In view of the ecological crisis of modern civilization, we need a new understanding of nature. But because there is no alternative to modern civilization we need a new integration of person and nature, of humanity and earth. I want to discuss this in regard to two concrete issues.

1. *Auschwitz:* Masao Abe is Japanese, I am German. He is Buddhist, I am Christian. I indeed understand his interpretation of Auschwitz as a problem of karma. Because everything that happens stands in reciprocal relationship with everything else, he identifies himself with what happened there in that he feels the blame of the Holocaust and feels responsibility for it. But according to this karma interpretation, Auschwitz loses its horrible uniqueness and becomes relative, because in the endless process of

karma everything is relative. What is said in this manner about the Holocaust can also be said about every other occurrence.

As a German and as a Christian I can not speak about Auschwitz in this way. I belong to the people who committed these crimes; I belong to the generation from which the murderers came even if I personally had nothing to do with them. I therefore live in the shadow of Auschwitz and exist in the presence of those who were gassed and murdered.

Before I can accept Masao Abe's karma interpretation of what happened there, I must see it from the point of view of God's justice. Then, on the one hand, I see a burden of guilt which can not be carried; and, on the other hand, I see the God who will not allow the murderers to triumph over their victims. The question of God becomes for me then the question of my right to live in the light of Auschwitz and the question of justice for the dead. Accordingly, the Protestant Church in Germany published a *Confession of Guilt* in 1945.

The Protestant Churches in Japan (Kyodan) published a confession of guilt concerning Japanese imperialism and the massacre in China twenty years after the end of World War II. I see no other possibility than such confessions if one is to come to terms with this past. Masao Abe has indeed taken up Jewish thinking on the Holocaust from my friend Emil Fackenheim, but has not considered another side — German and Christian thinking on Auschwitz.[5]

2. *The Grace of Spontaneity:* The explanations of *jinen* in the realization of Sunyata appealed to me very much because they come very close to the Christian understanding of living by the grace of God. I was also reminded of Kierkegaard's three stages. (1) There is the childlike stage of natural spontaneity, the "dreaming innocence," as Tillich has called it. (2) There is the adult stage of reflection and of morality. Here childlike spontaneity is broken by self-consciousness. Conscious and intended action takes the place of childlike spontaneity. (3) Finally, there is the stage of grace. In faith a new, transmoral, divine spontaneity comes forth. Therefore the images for the faith take up the stages of childhood: "Unless you turn and become like children. . ." in faith. What happens there? "Suddenly," that is, unintentionally and without forcing it, humans experience the grace of God. They can "let go" in this experience. They become unselfish and free from fear for themselves. They open themselves to love for all God's creatures. They no longer abuse creatures for their own selfish purposes, but allow them to be God's creatures. *Sua sponte* ("on its own"), says Luther, it happens. It is the new spontaneity in the Spirit of God which allows humans to live no longer in themselves but in God. The law of morality is then overcome because the blessed do justice and the good "automatically." *Ama et fac quod vis* ("Love and do what you will"), said Augustine, because in this love your will is not your will but God's will.

Such living by the grace of God is not the return to childlike naturalness. Instead, it presupposes reflection and morality. This new spontaneity is not animal-like instinctive spontaneity, nor "spontaneity based on primordial naturalness," as Masao Abe says of *jinen*. As spontaneity of grace, it is the beginning of redemption. Only in the glory of the new creation will everything live in this spontaneity.

In closing, I want to thank Masao Abe once again for his new interpretation of dynamic Sunyata. The best thanks is the question which arises from thinking with him. I therefore close with two questions: (1) Can Sunyata be interpreted "dynamically" without paying heed to the uniqueness of each occurrence and the finality of the redeeming future? (2) Can Sunyata be understood "dynamically" without expanding the naturalist categories through personalist categories?

NOTES

1. Jürgen Moltmann, *The Crucified God: The Cross of Christ as Foundation and Criticism of Christian Theology* (New York, 1972).

2. Jürgen Moltmann, *The Trinity and the Kingdom* (San Francisco: Harper and Row, 1981). See also my "The Unity of the Triune God" and the responses of John B. Cobb, Jr., Susan Thistlethwaite, and John Meyendorff, in *St. Vladimir's Theological Quarterly* 28 (No. 3, 1984).

3. *The Trinity and the Kingdom*, pp. 174ff.

4. Jürgen Moltmann, *God in Creation: A New Theology of Creation and the Spirit of God* (San Francisco: Harper & Row, 1985).

5. See E. Kogon and J. B. Metz, *Gott nach Auschwitz: Dimensionen des Massenmords am jüdischen Volk* (Freiburg, 1979). See also R. Rendtorff and E. Stegemann, *Auschwitz - Krise der christlichen Theologie* (Munich, 1980).

6

Faith in God and Realization of Emptiness

SCHUBERT M. OGDEN

I welcome the opportunity to respond to my friend Masao Abe's "Kenotic God and Dynamic Sunyata." Having engaged with him for some years in various forms of critical discussion, I have never failed to learn from him, whether in person or through his writings, and I have nothing but admiration both for his integrity as a thinker and for the seriousness of his commitment to broadening and deepening interreligious and intercultural understanding. More than that, I entirely share his belief—so prominent in his essay—that Buddhists and Christians alike must take responsibility for validating their claims to truth, and that they cannot possibly acquit themselves of this responsibility unless they situate their dialogue with one another in the larger context of critical discussion with all other persons of good will, religious and antireligious, who make or imply the same kinds of claims.

But these are not the only reasons I welcome this opportunity to continue my discussion with Masao Abe. Through him, above all, I have become increasingly convinced that, for all the obvious differences between their respective formulations, there are striking similarities between the understanding of human existence for which he and other members of the Kyoto School typically argue and what I as a Christian theologian take to be our authentic self-understanding as human beings. Applying, as I do, then, my existentialist equivalent of a pragmatist criterion of meaning—according to which different formulations that make no difference in how one must understand oneself to appropriate them only verbally different—I conclude that such real differences as there are may be between the two self-understandings can only be rather subtle and, therefore, all the more worthy of continuing discussion. Of course, my understanding of authentic existence is not the only Christian understanding of faith in God, any more than Abe's understanding of authenticity is the only Buddhist understanding of realization of emptiness. But fully recognizing that our discussion is only part of the larger Buddhist-Christian dialogue, I nonetheless regard it as of the utmost significance for my own continuing attempt to understand the differences as well as the similarities between Christian and Buddhist understandings of authentic existence.

As it happens, however, Abe's focus in this particular essay is not so much existential or religious as metaphysical. There are good reasons for this, for any self-understanding purporting to be authentic necessarily has metaphysical implications; and just as Christian talk of faith as authentic necessarily implies certain claims about self, world, and God, so Buddhist talk of realization as authentic necessarily implies certain claims about self, world, and emptiness. But it is fair to say, I think, that the immediate reason for Abe's focus on God and Sunyata rather than on faith and realization is the larger context of discussion with the antireligious ideologies of scientism and nihilism in which he feels obliged to develop his argument. From the standpoint of these ideologies, what is most problematic about both Buddhism and Christianity are their strictly metaphysical claims about the ground of ultimate reality, whether emptiness or God. Because Abe is concerned not only with the mutual transformation of Buddhism and Christianity, but also about validating his claims in face of the counterclaims of such religion-negating ideologies, he understandably takes up the task of developing a "revolutionary reinterpretation of the concept of God in Christianity and the concept of emptiness in Buddhism" (p. 4).

The gist of his reinterpretation is well expressed by the title of his essay. From his own standpoint as a Buddhist as well as from the standpoint of modern scientism and nihilism, the big problem with Christianity is its claim that the ground of ultimate reality is God as the sole primal source and the sole final end of self and the world:

> Buddhism is *fundamentally* not theistic and does not accept one personal God as the ultimate reality . . . One God as absolute good cannot be accepted in Buddhism because, speaking from the perspective of dependent co-origination, a notion such as the one God as the absolute good who must be independent is nothing but a reification and substantialization of something ultimate as the only entity that has its own being . . . One God as the absolute good appears as a special form of attachment in the religious and transcendent dimension"(pp. 48-49).

In Abe's view, in other words, faith in God as Christianity has traditionally conceived God attaches the self to yet another thing delusively supposed to be independent and self-existing, and thus cannot overcome but only intensify the self's profound estrangement from itself and the world.

The fact remains, however, that this traditional concept of God is not the only or the most adequate way of conceiving the God necessarily implied by Christian faith. On the contrary, Abe argues, the New Testament, and specifically the Pauline, teaching of the kenosis, or self-emptying, of Christ clearly indicates another and more adequate concept insofar as it logically requires that "the kenotic God" as the ground or the "root source of the kenotic Christ."

So far from being the one God who as absolute good must be independent of everything, the God necessarily presupposed by the self-emptying of Christ is the self-emptying God, the God of "unconditional love" who "through complete self-abnegation . . . is totally identical with everything, including sinful humans." By "kenotic God," then, Abe means this alternative concept of God that he takes to be more deeply and truly Christian than the traditional theistic concept. At the same time, he holds that it

> opens up for Christianity a common ground with Buddhism by overcoming Christianity's monotheistic character, the absolute oneness of God, and by sharing with Buddhism the realization of absolute nothingness as the essential basis for the ultimate (p. 17).

By dynamic Sunyata, on the other hand, Abe means a concept of emptiness that, in his view, is more deeply and truly Buddhist than any other traditional concept, even while it also opens up for Buddhism some common ground with Christianity as well as with all that is positive in modern scientism and nihilism. This it does by overcoming the negative aspect of the Buddhist notion of Sunyata, the failing to grasp the positive significance of reason, free will, and history, and by allowing for any suggestions Christianity may have to offer about properly providing "a ground for human ethics and modern rationality" (pp. 37f.).

Although Abe is emphatic that the Mahayana tradition has always held that "true Sunyata is not a static state of emptiness but a dynamic movement of emptying everything, including itself," he is nevertheless frank to admit that "the dynamic character of the Buddhist notion of Sunyata" has also been overlooked (pp. 42, 36).

Thus Sunyata has been understood simply or undialectically as the negation of self and the world, instead of being conceived dialectically as the negation of their negation, and hence as also their affirmation. The result is that realization of emptiness has in its own way failed to overcome the self's estrangement from itself and others and, by falsely attaching the self to a static emptiness, has only exacerbated its estrangement. The proof of this is that throughout its long history Buddhism has not positively grasped either human reason or human will and has been "relatively weak in its view of history" (p. 59–60).

To this extent, Abe concedes the validity of Western and Christian criticisms of much traditional Buddhism. But the purpose of his argument is to show that, when emptiness is conceived dynamically and not statically, as it can and should be conceived, all such criticisms can be answered. Realization of emptiness is then seen to involve compassion as well as wisdom, a turning toward self and the world as well as a turning away from them, and on this basis Buddhism can properly affirm both reason and will and develop its own view of history, and so provide the ground for responsible thought and action in the world.

Such, as I understand it, is the burden of Abe's argument—although I am painfully aware that so summary an interpretation cannot begin to do justice to the nuances of his own statement. Before I now try to express my main difficulties with it, I want to make two somewhat briefer comments, also by way of criticism.

First of all, as much as I applaud Abe's concern to confront the objections raised by antireligious ideologies, I do not see that anything he has to say is very effective in meeting them. Although he asserts that his reinterpretation of God and emptiness can overcome scientism and nihilism, he does not seem to me to provide adequate evidence or argument to support his assertion. In fact, when he argues at one point that "the notion of the kenotic God can overcome Nietzsche's nihilism" because "the kenotic God sacrifices Godself . . . for *absolute* nothingness, which is at one and the same time absolute Being," it is hard to take him seriously (p. 16). This is particularly so if one considers that the whole point of Nietzsche's nihilism is to deny the positive soteriological meanings that Abe insists derive from absolute nothingness when it is properly conceived as dynamic Sunyata.

Secondly, and more positively, my difficulties with his argument do not keep me from feeling very close to what I take to be his basic intentions. I, too, would want to argue that the ground of ultimate reality, however conceived, cannot be conceived rightly as long as the self can be really related to it only by being the more completely estranged from itself and the world. And I would want to argue further that an essential test of whether any self-understanding, Buddhist or Christian, involves such self-estrangement is whether it so allows for the affirmation of human reason and will, and of the reality and significance of history, as to ground the responsible thought and action apart from which we human beings can neither live nor live well nor live better in this world. My question, however, is whether Abe's argument and the conclusions he draws from it are the only or the most adequate way of realizing these intentions, or whether, on the contrary, they can be adequately realized only by way of a rather different argument and conclusions.

I press this question, for one reason, because of the difficulties I have with his argument for "kenotic God." Despite the fact that he appeals to Philippians 2:5-11 as the ostensible basis for his argument, it is obvious that the conclusion he draws is controlled less by a historical-critical exegesis of this passage than by his own Buddhist beliefs concerning the nature of ultimate reality. Integral to these beliefs is the assumption that anything divine, just like anything natural or human, neither is nor can be independent and self-existing, but has to be interdependent with literally everything else and, therefore, empty in itself. Thus Abe can say that what "the religious dimension" signifies for him as a Buddhist is not "a God who is loving and just," but "the boundless openness or emptiness that is neither God, human, or nature, and in which all things, including the divine, the human, and the natural, are all interrelated with and interpenetrated by each other" (p. 51). Given this assumption, it clearly could make sense to talk about a self-emptying God; for then even God would be simply one individual among others faced with the same fundamental option between inauthentic self-affirmation and ignorance of emptiness, on the one hand, and authentic realization of emptiness and self-denial, on the other. But what reason does Abe give either for thinking that such talk could make sense on any other assumption or for supposing that this same assumption is somehow integral, if not to the beliefs expressed by Philippians 2:5-11, then to the necessary implications of Christian faith in God?

In my judgment, anything like his notion of a self-emptying God, implying as it does that God is at best a particular individual who at least could be self-assertive instead, is not only not necessarily implied by Christian faith but also necessarily precluded by it. Because such faith is the unreserved trust and loyalty for which the ground of ultimate reality is the boundless love decisively represented through Jesus Christ, the God whom faith necessarily implies cannot be conceived as merely one particular individual among others but only as the universal individual in whom both self and the world and anything else that is so much as possible have their sole primal source and their sole final end. But one of the defining characteristics of God so conceived is that God can no more be estranged from others than from Godself and, therefore, not only does not need to be self-abnegating but also does not have the possibility of being so. Thus from the standpoint of Christian faith any individual who could conceivably be the kenotic God could not really be God at all but only an idol in whom faith could believe only by ceasing to be itself.

But what about Abe's claim, made especially in his criticism of Karl Rahner, that if God is really unconditional love, the self-emptying must be total, not partial? Even assuming that I am right, that the God in whom Christian faith believes could not be coherently conceived as self-emptying, I nonetheless see a valid point in this claim. If God is really unconditional love of others, then God must be really, internally related to others and insofar as God is dependent on them, God is not independent of them. Moreover, if unconditional love of others as well as of self is not merely an accident in God but, as Christian faith seems to me to imply, the very essence of God, then God's real, internal relatedness to others and dependence on them is itself essential to God and not merely accidental (see my

"The Metaphysics of Faith and Justice," *Process Studies*, 1985, 14, 2:87–101). But if this means, as Abe validly urges against Rahner, that God's "infinite unrelatedness" cannot have priority over God's "relatedness with the other," it does not mean, as Abe seems to suppose, either that there can be no such thing as God's "infinite unrelatedness" or that God's essential "relatedness with the other" is one and the same with God's being completely interdependent with others and so "totally identical" with them. On the contrary, because God's love of others is indeed "unconditional" and hence real no matter what else is or can be real, it has to have an aspect in which it is independent of everything, actual or possible, and, therefore, precisely, "infinitely unrelated." Likewise, real, internal relation to others of the sort that God's unconditional love indeed involves necessarily implies God's difference from others, not God's identity with them. As between the extreme contraries of "infinite unrelatedness" and "total identity," God's unconditional love — in its concrete aspect, as distinct from the infinite unrelatedness of its abstract aspect — is more appropriately described as God's "infinite relatedness."

Abe would no doubt object to this that, despite my insistence that God really is unconditional love, mine is a view for which God's love "is still somewhat conceptualized or objectified," and thus leaves behind "traces of dualism, a dualism of God and the other, the infinite and the finite, immutability and change, within and without, and so forth" (pp. 15f.). But whatever force this objection may have against other Christian concepts of God (including, I do not question, even Rahner's kind of revisionary theism), I find it lacking in force against the concept for which I am concerned to argue. Of course, if anything other than "total identity" could only be "dualism," then, since I deny that God is simply identical with self and the world, mine could only be a dualistic view. But not to be simply identical is not necessarily to be totally separated; we should recognize the important conceptual difference in God's being neither identical with self and the world nor separated from them, but related to them and, therefore, also distinct from them.

In short, duality is not dualism (see C. Hartshorne, "Duality versus Dualism and Monism," *Japanese Religions*, 1969, 5, 1:51–63); and what is necessarily implied by Christian faith in God as unconditional love is precisely duality. God is indeed distinct from self and the world, but only because God is really, internally related to them and therefore inclusive of them. To be sure, as the strictly universal individual, God could and would be thus related to anything that is so much as possible. And this means, as I pointed out before, that there must indeed be an abstract aspect in which God is not really, internally related to anything and therefore is exclusive of everything. But because this aspect of God is precisely abstract, here, too, there is not dualism but only duality; for, like everything else, God's "infinite unrelatedness" is included in the "infinite relatedness" of God's concrete aspect, and so is distinct without being separate. On the other hand, because God's love of self and the world is not identical with them but distinct from them, and because anything even conceivable could not fail to be included in this love, there is an intelligible ground for the kind of unreserved trust and loyalty that are distinctive of Christian faith. Its radical freedom from self and the world and its equally radical freedom for them are both grounded in God's boundless and all-inclusive love.

This brings me to the other reason for pressing my question about the adequacy of Abe's argument and conclusions—namely, my difficulties with his claim that "dynamic Sunyata" provides an adequate ground for responsible thought and action in history. Here, certainly, I want to emphasize that the difficulties I have are mine and that they may not be much more than that simply because I have failed to understand Abe's meaning. In general, I find the Buddhist concept of "emptiness" extremely hard to understand because it appears to involve the same kind of paradoxes or self-contradictions that are familiar in the metaphysics of Advaita Vedanta—with the notable difference that, although both kinds of thinking tacitly presuppose the same distinction between parts and the whole, Vedantism takes the parts to be "appearance," while Buddhism insists that the whole is "absolute nothingness." In either case, one is met with a distinction that is not really a distinction after all, and therefore with a relation, or an apparent relation, that is wholly unintelligible. All in all, I confess that I have the same difficulties with Abe's talk of "dynamic Sunyata," at least insofar as I take it to be properly metaphysical talk. But whether the reasons for my difficulties are due to his inconsistency or lack of clarity or simply to my own failure to understand is not easy to decide. Consequently, all I can do is to explain why I am not convinced by his claim and then leave it to our continuing discussion to shed further light on the reasons for this.

The nub of my difficulties is easily identified. As I understand it, the concept of the "emptiness" of all things is of a piece with the doctrine that nothing whatever is or can be independent and self-existing, because everything is interdependent with and interpenetrated by everything else. This doctrine, in turn, is necessarily implied by, if indeed, it is not simply another way of formulating, the fundamental Buddhist doctrine of "dependent co-origination." According to Abe, this most basic doctrine not only holds that "everything without exception is co-arising and co-ceasing, impermanent, without 'own being,' empty," but also clearly emphasizes that "everything without exception is interdependent with every other thing; nothing whatsoever is independent and self-existing" (pp. 48–49). But, as Abe himself recognizes, thus to affirm the interdependence and interpenetration of everything is also to affirm "the mutual reversibility of things. . . . Accordingly, time and history are not simply understood to be linear and unidirectionally moving toward a particular end, but are understood to be reciprocal and even reversible" (p. 31). It is more than mildly surprising, then, that Abe should subsequently conclude that, inasmuch as Buddhism affirms time to be thus reversible, "the unidirectionality of time and the uniqueness of each moment essential to the notion of history are not clearly expressed in Buddhism" (p. 60). Surely, the conclusion indicated by his argument is that in his Buddhism, even as, presumably, in Buddhism generally, these essential conditions of the notion of history are all too clearly denied.

Such a denial seems to be necessarily implied, at any rate, by his metaphysics of universal interdependence and interpenetration. If the ultimate metaphysical truth is that everything without exception is interdependent with and interpenetrated by everything else, then each thing simply *is* every other thing, and any real differences between parts themselves, as well as between parts and the whole, disappear. But this means, then, that any differences between things sufficient to ground responsible and, therefore, differential thought and action with respect to them can only be delusive. Indeed, from the standpoint of Abe's metaphysics and unqualified interdependence, even the absolutely fundamental difference between enlightenment and ignorance must be empty, and any concern or action for the first rather than the second either in one's own case or in anyone else's is ultimately groundless and arbitrary.

If I understand him correctly, Abe's way of seeking to meet this objection even while, in effect, conceding it is to distinguish between different "dimensions," specifically, between "a more fundamental religious dimension" that is "ultimate" and "absolute" and a "moral" or "ethical dimension" that is "historical" and "relative." Thus he seeks to make clear that, although in the ethical dimension one can and should distinguish between good and evil, "ultimately," in the religious dimension, "the distinction between good and evil in the ethical dimension is relative, not absolute." Specifically, he argues, "while in a human moral dimension the Holocaust should be condemned as an unpardonable, absolute evil, from the ultimate religious point of view even it should not be taken as an absolute but a relative evil" (p. 53).

But what could Abe mean by this if not that from the ultimate religious point of view, authorized by the emptiness and interdependence of all things, even "absolute" moral differences cease to make any difference? After all, any "relative" difference they could make would have to be a difference within the ethical dimension, not the religious one. Abe does say at one point that the affirmation of all things in "their suchness and *jinen*" is "not an uncritical affirmation of the given situation," but "on the contrary ... is a great and absolute affirmation beyond—and thus not excluding—any critical, objective, and analytical distinction" (p. 32). But not to exclude something is one thing, to include it, something else; and Abe's way of expressing himself seems entirely fitting, for it is hard to see how the great and absolute affirmation of all things in their complete emptiness and interdependence either does or could include any critical and analytical distinction between them that is also properly objective. (I should add, perhaps, that I do not consider the little I have said to be an adequate discussion of Abe's view of the Holocaust, which depends on his under-standing of "the universal or collective karma innate in human existence" as well as on his metaphysics of thoroughgoing interdependence (p. 52).

Of course, Abe's whole point is that a concept of Sunyata as "dynamic" removes any reason for objecting that it is merely negative in its implications for thought and action. But suppose we grant this and allow for the sake of argument that his metaphysics indeed need not imply that we are to be concerned for nothing at all. The question remains, I submit, whether it could logically imply anything more than that we are to be equally con-cerned for everything—an implication that, in my opinion, is hardly less stultifying of responsible thought and action. To think and to act, even as simply to live, is inevitably to do so differentially, to be concerned for some things more, other things less. Nor can it be otherwise even for someone who has been liberated from bondage to self and the world so as to be able to think and to act responsibly for them. For even for such a person—in fact, especially for such a person—the many differences between things and persons are real and significant, and if one's thought and action are to be at all relevant or to have any point, everything turns on one's being able to effect what Reinhold Niebuhr used to speak of as "the nicely calculated difference between less and more." Yet all that Abe's metaphysics allows for, if it allows even for that, is the "transmoral" compassion that is based on "the great affirmation of all things realized through wisdom" (p. 32). Just as "by virtue of wisdom, all things including the natural, the human, and the divine, regardless of their differences, are each equally affirmed in their suchness and *jinen*," so in the light of the compassion with which wisdom is "inseparably and dynamically connected, . . . the dominant-sub-ordinate relationship among things in the ordinary and relative sense is freely turned over, and moral and ethical judgments in terms of good and evil, right and wrong on the human, historical dimension, are transcended in the ultimate dimension" (p. 32). Abe claims, reasonably enough, that "one can work toward bettering both humans and nature most effectively and appropriately when unattached to human self-interest." But what he never makes clear, at least to me, is how the "universal compassion" that may indeed overcome attachment to self-interest can possibly provide the ground for the differential thought and action apart from which all our meliorative efforts are quite impossible.

So far as I can see, then, even "dynamic Sunyata" is no more adequate than "kenotic God" as a concept of the ground of ultimate reality as Abe and I both intend to think and speak about it. Because the metaphysics of which it is a piece implies that any thought and action for which there are real differences between things and persons can only be delusive, it is so far from providing a ground for responsible thought and action as to under-cut them. To say this, however, is in no way to question that Abe is as sincerely committed as I am to an understanding of human existence for which efforts to better humans and nature are of the essence of authenticity. On the contrary, to read what he has to say about Sunyata having to empty itself into "the vow and act to make oneself and all others awakened," and about how actually doing this involves "both promoting 'valuable' things and transforming 'antivaluable' things," is to have all the evidence one needs that his understanding of authentic existence intends to be, in its way, "formative," and even "world-formative," not merely "avertive" (pp. 57f.; see N. Westerstorff, *Until Justice and Peace Embrace* [Grand Rapids: Eerdmans, 1983], pp. 5, 10). But the question persists whether the metaphysics necessarily implied by just this understanding must not be rather different from the explicit metaphysics which Abe argues. If my answer to this question should prove to be correct, it certainly would not be the only case in which an inherited metaphysics finally proved to be inadequate to the self-understanding whose implication it was supposed to make explicit.

7

Kenosis, Sunyata, and Trinity: A Dialogue with Masao Abe

DAVID TRACY

It is an honor to provide some reflections on the important essay "Kenotic God and Dynamic Sunyata" of my friend and colleague, Masao Abe. Abe has been a model of the kind of serious interreligious dialogue necessary to our present moment. Both his courage and his serenity are altogether rare virtues—and rarer still in combination. Indeed to read his present essay, as well as his other work, is, from a Christian perspective, rather like reading a patristic text. For Abe's text, like Origen's, is so unforced in its spiritual sense, so clear in its outline and correctly obscure in its substance, so assured in its willingness to employ and, when necessary, to invent concepts that fit the firm intellectual-spiritual awareness that pervades the whole text.

This is not to suggest, however, that Abe's work is not a thoroughly modern one. His insistence on a dialogical moment with the other ways is quintessentially modern. So is his concern with the "antireligious" movements of contemporary secularism as determining much of the horizon today for any serious religious thinker in any tradition. So, too, is Abe's ready use of both classical and modern Buddhist categories as well as, as always with the entire Kyoto School, the categories and concerns of modern Western thought. The "mixed discourse" of Abe's text—that same combination of speculative serenity and modern concern—is a deeply enriching one. Indeed, that same unlikely combination provides no little of the persuasive power of his essay. It leads to awareness.

And yet, I am not persuaded. More exactly, I am not persuaded that Abe's interpretation of the Christian belief in God is the way for Christians—even modern, dialogical ones—to think about God. Impressed and thankful one cannot but be for Abe's work and person. Indeed, as I shall clarify below, Abe has helped me to change my former Christian theological understanding of God in ways that needed changing. But I do not believe that Abe's formulation of the kenotic God and the kenotic Christ is the route for Christians to take.

I am, however, somewhat hesitant here. For anyone aware of the historicity of all thought cannot but wonder: if Christian speculative thought had emerged in East Asia rather than West Asia, might it not have taken a course very like the one which Abe suggests in our late-twentieth-century dialogical world? It might have. But it did not. And however honestly and gropingly we now strive to understand the remarkable range and speculative power of Indian, Chinese, Thai, Tibetan, and Japanese religious thought, we Christian thinkers (even Asian ones) know that we are forever religiously grounded in the world of Israel and we have been formed by the intellectual world of the Hellenistic West. We must be open to the possibility that we should abandon that Greco-Roman intellectual world for a more adequate speculative alternative. We must even be open to any Buddhist critique of our Jewish religious roots—but the latter option, unlike the former, would mean the end not only of classical theism but of any theism worthy of the word "ultimate."

And so part of our contemporary Christian theological journey may be to strive to rethink the fullness of our tradition even while we try to honor and understand the otherness of the other great ways. A large part of that contemporary retrieval and inevitable self-critique for Christians is likely to be as a result of challenges like Abe's. At the heart of that attempt is dialogue. We are in the midst of dialogical understanding of all our own pluralistic and ambiguous histories occasioned by a dialogue with the other whose own history—in all its plurality and ambiguity—we finally begin to sense. My response to Abe's paper, therefore, must take a rather circuitous route.

More summarily, my response has three parts: first, a necessarily somewhat autobiographical account of my own journey to understand God theologically—a journey significantly challenged, even transformed, by the work of Abe and his Kyoto colleagues; second, an interpretation of the significant differences and similarities between Meister Eckhart and Jan Ruuysbroec as the clearest analogue in Christian thought to the challenge Abe presents to my own way of thinking; third, a more direct response to Abe's paper on the kenotic God and dynamic Sunyata in which, following his example, I shall presume to return his gracious compliment to Christians and to give a Christian reading of his Buddhist position on dynamic Sunyata.

After several drafts of trying to write the present third section as the whole essay (as I originally preferred), I regretfully discovered that the very power of Abe's thought and the seductiveness (for me) of its reading of the kenotic God forced me to be more reflective of my own theological journey than I would ordinarily wish to be. I found myself trying to understand our late-twentieth-century dialogue by returning to a dispute between Eckhart and Ruuysbroec in that other *fascinans et tremendum* century, the fourteenth century—our "distant mirror" as Barbara Tuchman correctly named it. Part of the reason for that change, I now know, is the result of the Buddhist-Christian dialogue upon my Christian theological understanding of God. How that happened and with what results, I shall now attempt to explain.

A CHRISTIAN UNDERSTANDING OF GOD:
ONE THEOLOGIAN'S JOURNEY

As a Roman Catholic theologian, I studied philosophy for two years before studying theology proper. In those years (the late 1950s) that meant a study of neo-Thomism. Fortunately, for myself, this did not mean a study of the decadent neo-Scholasticism of the then prevailing "manuals." Rather, it meant a study of the kind of neo-Thomism represented best at that time by Jacques Maritain (in political theory, aesthetics, and metaphysics) and Etienne Gilson and Frederick Copleston (in the history of Thomism within the Thomistically-construed context of Western philosophy). The understanding of God I there received was one now known as "classical theism." In my present judgment, there are good reasons (*pace* Hartshorne, Tillich, and even Gilson!) to doubt whether Thomas Aquinas himself was a neo-Thomist classical theist (see Preller for an extreme reading and Burrell and Rahner for more persuasive ones). Thomas was more neo-Platonic (Fabro and Geiger) than the empirico-Aristotelian neo-Thomist version suggests. Thomas was also more apophatic than most neo-Thomists and anti-Thomists are yet willing to concede (Preller, Burrell, Rahner).

But for the neo-Thomists of my youth, Thomas was a—indeed, *the*—classic classical theist: God's transcendence was secure (*Ipsum Esse Subsistens*)—the one being whose very essence is to be. God's immanence was also affirmed, though in muted tones. God's relations to the world were conceptually external if religiously (for the Thomists, "metaphorically") internal. The journey into the self of Augustine, like the "turn to the subject" of modernity, was judged a seductive but eminently resistible temptation. God affected all reality but was not affected by it. The list could go on but the point is clear, as Thomists and anti-Thomists admitted, Thomas Aquinas was *the* classical theist. My own resistance to neo-Thomism in those years was real but unfocused: more exactly, I did my "thesis" on Kierkegaard to distance myself from the neo-Thomist philosophical position that I could neither accept nor refute.

The four years of theological study at the Gregorian University in Rome changed all that. First of all, the years I studied there (1960-64 and 1965-67) largely coincided with the years of the Second Vatican Council. It was odd and, I confess, exhilarating to see all change so suddenly. Indeed those years taught me the truth of Wordsworth's famous refrain on his own youth during the French Revolution: "Bliss was it in that dawn to be alive—but to be young was very Heaven."

Part of what changed through that remarkable Council was the hegemony of neo-Scholasticism in general and neo-Thomism in particular in Catholic philosophy and theology. At the time, few took any notice of the difference that meant for the understanding of God. Classical theism, however, at least in its neo-Thomist version, is now in widespread disarray in Catholic theology. A new form of Thomism—the transcendental Thomism of Rahner and Lonergan—became the dominant (but not sole) way of thinking about God among Catholic theologians. This is not the place to rehearse the complex developments of Rahner and Lonergan in the understanding of God. But this much needs saying: the transcendental turn to the subject of Rahner and Lonergan dealt a death-blow to the empirico-Aristotelian reading of Thomas Aquinas. With the modern turn to the subject, Augustinian interiority returned into Catholic theology. I believe one can read Lonergan's developing thought as an increasing turn to interiority until, at the end, love had prevailed over knowledge for understanding God, feeling had a prominence it once totally lacked, and a mystical theology of God was beginning to emerge.

In Rahner—whose thought was always more directly theological than methodological, more speculative than historical (the exact reverse of Lonergan)—the matter is even more clear. However much Rahner attempted to hold on to the classical theism of the scholastic tradition (as he did), his theology, at its deepest and most original, resisted that same classical theism. In his last several years, Rahner shifted mightily in his understanding of God: all theological thought became a "reduction to Mystery," which was clearly not identical to the intellectual "mysteries" of the neo-Scholastics. The more comprehensible God was, the more incomprehensible God became; indeed, even in the Beatific Vision, Rahner surmised, God would be more incomprehensible still—not Cartesianly clear as the neo-Scholastics hoped. This "mystagogical" turn in both Rahner and Lonergan (and Maréchal before them), like the "mystico-prophetic" turn of their Catholic successors (Metz, Schillebeeckx, Dupré, Gutiérrez, and many others—including myself) made "classical theism" either explicitly or more usually implicitly suspect as *the* Catholic understanding of God.

By the time of his summary volume (*Foundations of Christian Faith: An Introduction*, German edition, 1976; English translation, 1978), Rahner had become something like an anonymous process theologian. At the same time, and thanks to my new setting of the University of Chicago, I (and other Catholic theologians) became and, to a certain extent, remain an explicitly process theologian. At least, I remain a process theologian in the following senses: First, I accept the now familiar criticisms of neo-Thomist "classic theism" by process thinkers. (I still wonder about Thomas Aquinas himself for the reasons cited above.) Second, insofar as classic theism is largely

determined by categories of "substance" rather than "event" and "relationality" (as it was and is), I believe that there is no good philosophical
defense of its position. Third, to render coherent the central Christian
metaphor, "God is love," demands relational, dynamic, process categories.
For only then can one show how God both affects all and is affected by all
(as love logically must be). Fourth, process thought defends the major
insight of classical theism—that "perfection-language" is necessary for the
Christian understanding of God as transcendent. The choice of "creative
synthesis" (Hartshorne), for example, as a central process category allows
for the insistence that God is perfect in being unsurpassable by all others
but surpassable by Godself. Fifth, the divine transcendence is thereby
affirmed without the loss (or, at the least, the muting as in classical theism)
of the divine relational immanence in all reality. Sixth, the dipolar character
of God's reality can assure the reality of God's love (and its attendant
attributes such as internal relations with the world—the consequent pole)
without the loss, but with the reinterpretation, of the classical attributes of
eternity, omniscience, omnipotence, and the like (the primordial pole).

In sum, the process theology I discovered at Chicago represented a
decided improvement on most classical Christian theological understanding
of God, especially that now correctly called classical theism. And yet I am
unsatisfied with the process position as a fully adequate understanding of
the Christian God. Part of my dissatisfaction is that I do not understand
how Whitehead's "creativity" and Whitehead's "God" relate. John Cobb's
distinction, in his important dialogues with Buddhists, between "Ultimate
Reality" (Sunyata) and "Ultimate Actuality" (God) seems to me, now in
more recognizably Christian theological terms, to disclose the same kind of
ambiguity. It may be, as Cobb argues, that I, like most Western thinkers
since Aristotle but before the discovery of matter as energy in relativity
theory and quantum mechanics, am unable to conceive of Ultimate Reality,
"Emptiness," in terms of "material causes" (energy-matter) and thereby
am unable to conceive of God as that aspect of reality (Ultimate Actuality)
best conceived in terms of formal, final, and efficient causation.

One can only agree with Cobb that God, as understood by Christians,
must be ultimate as the one to be trusted and worshiped, as the trustworthy
source, ground, and end of all reality. But I fail to see how to make coherent
sense of that kind of ultimacy (as "Ultimate Actuality") in relationship to
the "material" Ultimate Reality. The latter is *esse* for Aquinas, Creativity
for Whitehead, and dynamic Sunyata for Abe (and perhaps Cobb). But if
ultimate reality is to be trusted and worshipped, it (he/she) must also be
God. That Aquinas and, I suspect, Abe affirm. That both Whitehead (with
his distinction between creativity and God) and Cobb (with his distinction
between Ultimate Reality and Ultimate Actuality) deny. The exact relationship of the metaphysical distinctions proposed by Whitehead and Cobb
remain unclear to me. Moreover, the Christian theological implications of
the distinction are troubling. It is the latter I now wish to address in order

to show why my response to Abe can learn from, but finally not take the same form as Cobb's — or any other process thinker. Here, I fear, I must describe myself — to change respectfully a famous process phrase — not as a process theologian, but perhaps as a "fellow-traveler who sometimes understands."

In this curious theological journey toward an understanding of God, I now find myself — in part, as I shall try to show below, thanks to Buddhist thought — rediscovering the oft-forgotten if not repressed neo-Platonic spiritual-theological tradition of Christian thought. In one sense, as John Macquarrie argues in his elegant defense of this tradition under the rubric of "dialectical theism," process theology is a part of this neo-Platonic heritage. Given Whitehead's love of Plato, this should cause little surprise. But my hesitancy fully to affirm process theology is not dependent only on my failure to accept the metaphysical distinction between creativity and God or ultimate reality and ultimate actuality. It is dependent on the failure of process theology, as Christian theology, to develop, with the rest of the neo-Platonic tradition, a fully Trinitarian understanding of God.

In one sense, of course, process theology, as Macquarrie justly observes, is, at the very least, "binatarian." At least, the dipolarity of the process God bears striking affinities to the classical neo-Platonic understandings of "Logos" and "Spirit." But the affirmation of "creativity" or "ultimate reality" in distinction from the same dipolar God (as ultimate actuality) suggests that the Father (or Mother) is not merely distinguished from Logos and Spirit within God but distinguished as another (I do not say separate) ultimacy from Logos and Spirit. This, I suggest, should be troubling to any fully Christian understanding of God. It is also vulnerable not merely to the criticism of classical Trinitarian theologians but also to Buddhist thinkers. The latter can ask as well as a Christian theologian (witness Abe on Moltmann) whether the Christian understanding of God must be Trinitarian (this Abe seems to affirm about Moltmann despite his critique on the "fourth"). One may ask whether process theology, without rethinking its distinction between "creativity" and God or "Ultimate Reality" and "Ultimate Actuality" can become properly Trinitarian.

I realize that this critique can sound like a rather extrinsic one to many process theologians — indeed one which Catholic theologians with their presumed desire to affirm the classical doctrines may be expected to introduce. But the facts are not as simple as that. Indeed, I cannot but agree with Moltmann (and indeed with that other "dialectical theist," Hegel) that the Christian understanding of God *is* intrinsically Trinitarian precisely as dynamic and/or dialectical. Neither the process understanding of God nor the classical neo-Platonic dialectical understanding of God is classical theism. Neither, despite the criticisms of classical theists, is pantheistic either: the first is panentheistic; the second is dialectically Trinitarian theism. But why should we choose the second option rather than the first?

Insofar as Christians accept the reality of God's self-manifestation in

Jesus Christ, they accept a Trinitarian (and not merely monotheistic) understanding of God. Insofar as metaphysicians accept a dynamic and anti-substantialist understanding of all reality, they are well suited to understand God in dialectically Trinitarian terms—*unless* they distinguish "creativity" and "God." Or unless, as Eckhart sometimes does, they distinguish the "Godhead" of "God" by relating *esse* to the "Godhead" rather than to the Father as creative, self-manifesting source of the Trinity. Insofar as Christian theologians attempt to develop conceptualities appropriate to the self-disclosure of God in Jesus Christ, they are prepared to accept an "economic" understanding of God as Trinitarian. Insofar as the same theologians, informed philosophically by a dynamic understanding of God as necessarily manifesting Godself in Source, Logos and Spirit, they may also come to believe that the "economic" Trinity is also our central clue to God's own reality: the divine reality in itself and not merely as manifested to us in creation and redemption.

Such "insofars" are the basic (and, to be sure, debatable on inner-Christian grounds) reasons for my proposal to Abe on how to interpret the Christian understanding of God *as Christian* (which he clearly wishes to do in his section on the kenotic God and the kenotic Christ). Such, in fact, is also why I propose, in the next section, to try to clarify that dynamic and/or dialectical understanding of God as necessarily both trinity and unity by reflecting on the differences between Eckhart and Ruuysbroec.

But first this description—at once too brief and too long—of my own Christian theological journey to understand God must end. I have described one theologian's journey and some of the principal influences on it—from neo-Thomist classical theism through "transcendental Thomism" become mystagogical to process theology to an attempted recovery of the neo-Platonic Trinitarian dynamic and dialectical theism. I have not yet, I realize, stated how Buddhist thought has complicated this journey. For the moment, perhaps the following comments will suffice. In my present attempts to retrieve and critically rethink the neo-Platonic tradition, I have found myself, with relative ease, able to understand and, in my own way, to appropriate the contributions of the "image" and the "Trinitarian" and the "love" speculative neo-Platonic mystical theologians. In the obvious sense that all Christian theologians acknowledge the reality of God as ultimately a mystery (more exactly *the* Ultimate Mystery) for all our understanding of God, I have also always understood and partly appropriated the "apophatic" moments in the whole theological tradition, especially the neo-Platonic.

But not until two further and more recent challenges did I begin to wonder about the radicality of the apophatic neo-Platonic traditions' understanding of God in Pseudo-Dionysius, John Scotus Eriugena, Ruuysbroec, Cusanus, and especially, Eckhart. Those two challenges, although markedly different in both conceptuality and spirituality, nevertheless bear remarkable affinities: first radical postmodern thought on difference and negativity

(Derrida and Deleuze); second, Buddhist—more exactly, Kyoto Mayahana Buddhist—thought. The radical negativity in Deleuze's notion of "difference" and Derrida's non-category of *différence* challenges, after all, not only all "substantialist" thought but also relational thought, both process and dialectical. The Buddhist insistence—in Abe on Pseudo-Dionysius, in Nishitani on Nietzsche—is that Western thought tends to end in an impasse of "nihility" but not "true nothingness." This is genuinely analogous to, but admittedly more radical than, the insistence of the "new Nietzscheans" that the "old" existentialist and nihilistic Nietzschean position is as dead as the God it buried. Rather we must learn with the "new Nietzsche" to laugh and dance over the abyss. Indeed, we must learn to cease to cling to our Western logocentrism.

Derrida's refusal to be interpreted in terms of "negative theology," like Abe's refusal to accord the "nothingness" of Pseudo-Dionysius and other apophatic neo-Platonic theologians the status of true nothingness as dynamic Sunyata, are distinct but parallel refusals.

Derrida's refusal emerges from a radically secular form of postmodern thought, Abe's emerges from a deeply religious form of thought. Both, however, challenge both substantist and relational-dialectical thought, although Abe, rather like Nagarjuna, does so (ironically?) through the instruments of dialectical thought itself.

I do not hesitate to state that it is Buddhists who helped me reread and begin to understand the most radical apophatic Christian theologian of all, Meister Eckhart with his initially very strange talk of the "Godhead beyond God" and his even stranger prayer "I pray to God to free me from God." It is Abe's present essay on the kenotic God and dynamic Sunyata that helped me understand why, finally, I am with Ruuysbroec and not with either Eckhart or Abe—although, as in Ruuysbroec himself, I have come to believe that such a position is possible, if at all, only for one who has tried to think with Eckhart and, today, with Abe. This is the uncanny dilemma in which I find myself in relationship to Abe's paper. I must now try to explain my response to the dilemma by first interpreting the Eckhart-Ruuysbroec dispute in Christian theology and then reflecting on Abe's own position from my own Christian theological perspective.

THE CHRISTIAN-BUDDHIST DIALOGUE RECONSIDERED

The Buddhist-Christian Dialogue and Modernity

The Buddhist-Christian dialogue, as conducted by Abe Masao, helps to clarify certain principles which may also be restated in Christian theological terms.

1. The historical division between spiritual practice and theory needs reconsideration in Christian theology. As the Kyoto thinkers, including Abe, amply demonstrate, religious thinking should bring together religious

practice and critical reflection if the thinker is to render properly one's buddhological or theological position. I agree with Abe in his consistent insistence on this central methodological point. Indeed, only by rethinking our own heritage in analogous terms can Christian theologians hope to enter fully into the demands and the promise of Buddhist-Christian dialogue. This entire subject demands new attention in both Protestant and Catholic theology (less so in Orthodox theology)—for Protestants under the rubrics of "piety" (Schleiermacher) and theology, for Catholics under the rubric of spirituality" and theology. Alternatively, if these terms do not suffice, the recent recovery of the role of "praxis" for theology is a helpful entry into the kind of dialogue needed. As a single instance of this rethinking, I have chosen to concentrate, in my own theological contributions, on two theologians, Eckhart and Ruuysbroec, who share Abe's dual insistence on practice and the search for fitting conceptualities.

2. The insistence on existential practice as driving the theological task, as Abe insists, frees theology from the linked temptations of either divorcing spiritual practice and thought or reifying the conceptualities employed. Whatever their other difficulties, the neo-Platonic tradition of Christian theology never made that fatal error—which shows, once again, its promise for the Buddhist-Christian dialogue.

3. One can maintain both former points and still insist, as both Abe and most modern Catholic and Protestant theologians do, that modernity has made several crucial differences for all religious thought. As Abe insists, several "antireligious" ideologies of modernity demand that religious thinkers, in intellectual honesty, defend the religious dimension of existence in terms which are acceptable, in principle, to all reflective persons.

The basic claim of all modern Western Christian thinkers has been the claim of Kierkegaard: that a loss of religion is also a loss of our humanity. That claim has been defended in myriad ways by all forms of modern Christian theology: through a defense of the "limit-questions" and "limit-experiences," or the depth-experiences or questions of ultimacy disclosive of a religious dimension to our existence through more immediately praxis-oriented existential displays of the religious dimension of all human existence (Dostoevsky or Merton). The failure to realize this challenge of modernity means the ultimate failure of traditional religion for modern persons, whether Buddhist or Christian, or in any other great way. The attraction of Eastern Orthodox theology or, in Catholic theology, the unrevised neo-Platonic position of Hans Urs Van Balthasar or, in Protestant theology, the neo-Reformed theology of Karl Barth, is clear. These theological traditions do keep together the spirituality (Orthodoxy and von Balthasar) or the piety (Barth) or the community's narrative (Frei, Lindbeck, and Hauerwas) and the attendant theological conceptualities. The loss in these theologies is just as clear: by refusing an "apologetic" task on other than an ad hoc basis, these theologies, however great their attractiveness, are insufficient on their own for modern Christians. Abe's comments on the Buddhist need to show the appropriate range and limits of "discursive" reason (both transcendental and speculative) in relationship to the Buddhist vision suggests (as does his comment on the necessity of taking seriously the antireligious ideologies) that he, too, demands something like a revised correlational model for religious thought.

More exactly, insofar as religious thinkers take reason and modernity seriously and insofar as religious thinkers feel responsible to respond to the antireligious ideologies of modernity, they perforce demand an "apologetic" aspect to the theological task. They demand, in sum, a theology that attempts to establish mutually critical correlations between an interpretation of the heart of the tradition (for example, dynamic Sunyata) and the rational and responsible search of modernity (for example, on values, on science, on reason—as in Abe's final thoughts on the need for revision in traditional Buddhist thought).

A fair generalization is the following: modern Christian liberal theologies have been strong on the apologetic task and hermeneutically and historically conscious on the modern complexities in the interpretation of the heart of the tradition. But, as the recent explosion of interest in the role of praxis for all theory and the role of piety, spirituality, or existential religious awareness make clear, Christian liberal theology has become relatively under-developed in its attempted critical retrievals of Christian spirituality.

Here the Buddhists (especially revisionary ones like the Kyoto School) have much to teach us—how to unite those two so long kept asunder, reason and passion (Wesley). Abe, with his implicitly correlational and explicitly revisionary stand, does not hesitate. Neither should revisionary Christian theologians—as Karl Rahner shows far more than Hans Urs von Balthasar, as Paul Tillich shows far more than Karl Barth. Correlational Christian and Buddhist thinkers are more likely to be open to serious interreligious dialogue than traditional religious thinkers are. But if that dialogue is not to evaporate into mere good intentions and fine feelings, all partners to the dialogue must be willing, as Abe and his Kyoto colleagues clearly are, to speak explicitly of the relationships of spiritual praxis and all conceptualities and the relationship of both to modern critical reason. This is surely no easy task. But, as Abe shows, it is the only way for serious interreligious dialogue in our uncanny situation.

Can Mystics Read Prophetic Texts? The Christian Neo-Platonists and the Buddhists

The prior and more methodological observations may suggest one way to retrieve one neglected strand of the Christian theological tradition: the Christian neo-Platonic tradition from Pseudo-Dionysius through John Scotus Eriugena, Eckhart, Ruuysbroec, Cusanus, to important aspects of Hegel, Whitehead, Heidegger, Rahner, and Tillich. For whatever else the

Christian theological tradition is, as Christian, it is also an interpretation of the Christian scriptures. Unlike Zen Buddhism and more like such forms of Buddhism as Tibetan, Theravadan, or even Pure Land in relationship to debates on the sutras, Christians as Christians find themselves responsible to showing how their interpretations of all reality cohere with the Scriptures. Clearly this need not lead to either a fundamentalism nor even to a purely "narrativist" biblical theology. This is the case, in scriptural terms alone, insofar as the scriptures, however prophetic and narrative they are in their core readings of God's self-manifestation in the history of Israel and the life, message, ministry, death, and resurrection of Jesus Christ, are also texts that lend themselves readily to meditative or even speculative readings.

Nor need the defense of Christian neo-Platonic readings of the scriptures be so general and indirect. For both Testaments also contain writings that can only be named meditative, often speculative. and sometimes even mystical: the Wisdom tradition of the Hebrew Scriptures, the meditative theology of manifestation of John, and the dialectical thought of Paul and the Pauline tradition. Even in terms of the gospel, there is not one narrative, but four: the apocalyptic, interruptive, non-closure text of Mark; the salvation-history, identity-formation text of Luke-Acts; the community-formation, new Torah text of Matthew; and the meditative narrative of John. It is little wonder that the early patristic writers turned most frequently to John and parts of "Paul" (especially Colossians and Ephesians) to inaugurate their neo-Platonic mystical and speculative readings of Christian existence. For however strained Gregory of Nyssa's reading of Moses in the apophatic dark cloud of unknowing in the Book of Exodus may be, in modern critical hermeneutical terms, he was surely correct to find his "image" theology, his love, and his Trinitarian reflections and even his apophatic insistence in the great "mystical" readings of the common gospel narrative by John and "Paul." For the neo-Platonists, Christ as Logos is the very self-expression, the identical image of God. Human being, in Christ, is, in its essence, an *imago Dei* and Christian life is a life *ad imaginem Dei*. For the love uniting the Father (Source) and Logos, manifests Godself in the very love that, as both *agape* (pure gift) and *eros*, should define the heart of the Christian spiritual life, both personal and communal.

The core of the neo-Platonist reading of the Scriptures is not a mere imposition of Hellenistic Platonism upon Jewish-Christian prophetic texts. Rather as both the Wisdom tradition and the Johannine and Pauline traditions testify, a mystical reading of the Scriptures, if faithful to the heart of the matter, is fully appropriate. All the great strands of Christian mysticism, I believe, are grounded in legitimate readings of John and Paul and the Wisdom literature: the image mysticism of Gregory and Origen and Irenaeus; the Trinitarian theology of Orthodoxy and the Western tradition of the Victorines and Ruuysbroec; the love-mysticism of Bernard of Clairvaux and the later Carmelites, John of the Cross and Teresa of Avila; the apophatic theologies of Pseudo-Dionysius, John Scotus Eriugena, and Meister Eckhart. Modernized remnants of these same traditions can be found in the Trinitarian dialectics of Hegel, the dipolar God of Whitehead, and the apophatic meditations of Heidegger and Wittgenstein as well as the theologies of Rahner and Tillich.

The intellectual situation of the patristic and medieval neo-Platonists encouraged Platonic readings of the Christian scriptures. The Scriptures allow for those readings: hence the neo-Platonic appeal to the Logos of John, the "image" of Colossians and Ephesians. Hence their insistence on the Trinitarian reality of God as Source, Logos and Spirit and their ability (through the many medieval debates on the relative priority of "love" and "knowledge") to develop both love-mysticism (Bernard) and apophatic intellectualist mysticism (Eckhart). The neo-Platonic mystical theologians, more than more traditional theologians, have always realized how inadequate all our "names" for God are. They have not resisted, therefore, apophatic demands as long as those demands are grounded in the Christian communal spiritual experience of (1) Christ as Logos, as the Image of God, the Second "Person" of the Trinity, and (2) the Christian spiritual experience of love in the Christ as an experience of God's own self as Spirit— the Spirit who, as God, lovingly unites us to Father and Son even as the Spirit unites Father and Son to one another in God.

However theologically defensible the neo-Platonic Christian tradition is (even on emanation as *one* way to interpret creation) on inner-Christian, indeed scriptural terms, it is also, of course, true that it is just as dependent on the Greco-Roman culture within which such Christian speculative thought emerged. In that intellectual context, it is hardly surprising that the Logos and the *imago dei* should prove so central to the tradition—even if the extraordinary developments of the Trinitarian, love, and apophatic strands of the diverse Christian neo-Platonists are genuinely distinct and sometimes conflicting developments beyond the original Logos tradition.

This Greco-Roman cultural and intellectual background makes all the more intriguing the thought that if Christian theological speculation occurred in an East Asian cultural and intellectual context, a radically kenotic theology like that developed by Abe rather than an image-theology may well have developed.

In the meantime, the clearest analogue in the Christian tradition to Abe's position may be found not in the image, Trinitarian, and love strands of the Christian neo-Platonists but in the radically apophatic strands culminating in the intellectualist and spiritual journey of Meister Eckhart. As several Buddhist and Christian thinkers, including Abe, have acknowledged, Eckhart remains the clearest Christian *analogue* to the kind of radically kenotic interpretation of the Christian understanding of God that Abe articulates. Hence a brief recall of the terms of the debate between Eckhart and Ruuysbroec may help to illuminate my own Christian theological differences from Abe's daring dialectical speculations on the kenotic God.

THE ECKHART-RUUYSBROEC DEBATE AND DYNAMIC SUNYATA

The complexities of Eckhart's position continue to puzzle interpreters. Indeed, the complexities are such that Rudolph Otto could compare Eckhart to Shankara while D.T. Suzuki found the more apt comparison to be Nagarjuna. There remain, as well, continuing debates over the accuracy of the posthumous papal condemnation of some propositions of Eckhart in the bull *In Agro Dominico*. Moreover, in philosophy and in Christian theology, the more radical recent readings of Eckhart tend to compare his position to the more radical—that is, apophatic—side of Heidegger (Caputo and Schurmann) while other interpreters (McGinn and Colledge) argue for the importance not only of the more apophatic of the vernacular sermons but also of the scholastic categories of the more systematic Latin works.

I cannot presume to resolve the difficulties of the expert interpreters. Fortunately, for the present limited purposes, that is unnecessary. Rather, informed by my own reading of the relevant texts and some principal interpreters, I shall confine my comments on Eckhart to two principal questions relevant for the dialogue with Abe. The first issue may be called one of spirituality. What strikes a reader most about Eckhart's texts (as indeed of Abe's) is a spirituality (or religious awareness) that is marked, above all, by two characteristics: intellectualism and radical detachment. Here a rigorous intellectualism not only is not divorced from the spirituality but is a central element in it. For Eckhart, this shows his fidelity to his Dominican tradition in contrast to the greater love orientation of Bernard of Clairvaux and the Franciscans. For Abe, this shows his fidelity to the disciplined and spiritual intellectualism of the Zen tradition in Buddhism. This intellectualism, in turn, leads to a spirituality, in Eckhart, of radical detachment that bears remarkable resemblances to the non-attachment, non-clinging spirituality of all forms of Buddhism. Like the Buddhists and unlike the love-mystics, Eckhart sometimes seems to accord a "higher" spiritual role to radical detachment than to Christian love. This causes serious consequences in his theology. On the one hand, he is far more apophatic in his language than even such apophatically inclined love-mystics as John of the Cross. On the other hand, unlike some but by no means all Christian mystics, Eckhart is not interested in such intense experiences as rapture or ecstasy but, like Zen Buddhists, far more interested in illuminating our true awareness of the everyday. In the Buddhist case, nirvana and samsara are one. In Eckhart's case, the disclosure of the Godhead beyond God is, at the same time, the disclosure of our release to the everyday life of activity-in-the-world. His remarkable reading of the Martha-Mary story is especially illustrative here for, in his reading, it is the active-contemplative Martha and not (as for many Christian contemplatives) the purely contemplative Mary who is the best illustration of the Christian contemplative's life as a life-in-the-world "without a why."

These affinities (not *identities*) in the kind of spiritual awareness of Eckhart and Zen make plausible the appeal of Eckhart to Buddhist thinkers. This same kind of spirituality of radical detachment and intellectualism leads to some of the more radically apophatic conceptualities of Eckhart, especially his famous insistence on the "Godhead beyond God" wherein even the names Father, Son, and Spirit are deemed inappropriate. Although Eckhart does not make this characteristic move in the kenotic lines favored by Abe, he does make it in such manner that the language of "nothingness" receives an unusual radicality for a Christian thinker. To be sure, as Buddhist thinkers have been quick to note, even Eckhart's "nothingness" is not the "absolute nothingness" of Zen thought.

That this is true can be seen in the fact that, however radically apophatic Eckhart is for a Christian thinker, he remains a God-obsessed thinker who constantly shifts, in different contexts, his language of transcendentals for both God and the Godhead beyond God: not only Nothingness but One, Intelligence, and *Esse* seem to him appropriate if always inadequate language. Whether all Eckhart's language can be rendered coherent without either loss of all *Christian* God-language or without reducing his position to some more familiar Christian understanding of God remains the principal question still under dispute, despite *In Agro Dominico*. What is relatively clear, however, especially but not solely in the Latin texts, as McGinn argues, is Eckhart's unique use of the languages of predication, analogy, and dialectic.

The dialectical language of Eckhart bears some striking resemblances to Abe's own use of dialectic for both the kenotic God and dynamic Sunyata. But, in Eckhart's case, all such dialectical language for the Godhead and God can occur only after the possibilities and limits of predication and analogy have been tried. What is striking, for example, about Eckhart's use of analogy is its difference from his Dominican forebear, Thomas Aquinas. For Eckhart, however faithful to Thomas' language of analogy, exactly reverses its meaning: only God can provide the proper analogy. Indeed, this is true for Eckhart to the point where we are left with "extrinsic" attribution language rather than either Thomist "intrinsic" attribution or "proportionality."

But lest one think that Eckhart is an early proponent of Barth's *analogia fidei* against *analogia entis* one must note that this "failure" of traditional analogical language (and, before it, of traditional predication) becomes, for Eckhart, an occasion to note the need for a radically dialectical language. Here is where he makes his most original moves—for the Godhead as One is indistinct and precisely as such is distinct from all reality (and vice versa). In more familiar dialectical terms, precisely the divine transcendence of all reality renders the divine reality immanent to all reality (and vice versa).

This radically dialectical understanding of indistinction and distinction, of immanence and transcendence, allows Eckhart to interpret both the *bullitio* of the emergence of the divine relations of the Trinity and, in creation, the *ebullitio* of the birth of the Word in the soul. In the return spiritual-intellectual journey, the soul returns to the Trinity and, in a final negation of radical apophatic detachment and radically apophatic dialectical thought, even breaks through to the Godhead beyond God. Thus can Eckhart, in a final paradox, *pray to* God to free him *from* God.

Even in the abbreviated form given above, one cannot but find Eckhart's intellectual-spiritual journey a remarkable one for a Christian. He can even be said to go a long way—although not all the way—with Abe's kenotic God. For Eckhart's dialectic, so similar to Abe's, nonetheless demands a move which Abe's does not: the self-manifestation of the Godhead in the distinct *bullitio* as the Trinity and the *ebullitio* of the creature. To be more exact, Abe's dialectic of dynamic Sunyata may have a similar self-manifestation character insofar as dynamic Sunyata manifests itself *as* wisdom and *as* compassion to the enlightened one. But this is still unlike Eckhart's explicit revision of neo-Platonic "emanation" language into the more radically dialectical language of *bullitio* and *ebullitio* (and, allied to that, on the human side of awareness, the birth of the Word in the soul and the "breakthrough" of the soul to the Godhead).

In Buddhist terms, Eckhart's "Godhead beyond God" is a route to, but is not finally an awareness of, "absolute nothingness." In Eckhartian Christian terms, Abe needs to show how *dialectically* "dynamic Sunyata" is not only immanent in all and thereby transcendent (and vice versa) but how that immanence-transcendence discloses itself as wisdom and as compassion. Here Christian neo-Platonism, especially in its more intellectualist, detached, and apophatic expressions, may have more to suggest to Abe than even his own dialectical reflections in the *"total* kenosis" of Christ and the "total" kenosis of God. For, as far as I can see, Abe can disclose the wisdom and compassion of the kenotic God but, paradoxically, cannot (or, at least does not *dialectically*, as distinct from spiritually) show why dynamic Sunyata is necessarily disclosed *as* wise and *as* compassionate.

But this "Eckhartian" criticism of Abe is not my central point. For, impelled by the Buddhist-Christian dialogue, to rethink Eckhart, I nevertheless remain puzzled whether the Christian understanding of God can receive as radically an apophatic character as Eckhart sometimes insists upon. I say this not to doubt the greater need to recover the apophatic tradition in Christian theology nor to doubt that no-thingness needs to be thought seriously in that tradition in relationship to such traditional (but difficult!) language as One, Intelligence, Being, or Creativity.

It is possible (I suspect, but do not yet know) that Eckhart's "Godhead beyond God" language may be appropriate Christian theological language—not merely in the relatively easy sense of one way to acknowledge the radical inadequacy of all our God-language, but in the more difficult dialectical sense of a more adequate naming of what Christians call God. For that reason, at this time and prior to further reflection impelled by the Buddhist-Christian dialogue and the rethinking of the apophatic tradition, I find myself, in Christian theological terms, more with Jan Ruuysbroec than with Meister Eckhart. To continue the parallel with Eckhart (and with Abe), one may furnish the Christian theological reasons to move in Ruuysbroec's direction for understanding the Christian God in terms of both spirituality and theology. In the Christian spiritual life (here Merton in his famous dialogue with Suzuki clearly agrees with Ruuysbroec), the move to radical negation and nothingness is construed by the Christian as one important moment of awareness in the larger sphere of awareness of the fuller Christian life. Even Eckhart, with his language of *bullitio* and *ebullitio* may agree here.

In the Christian construal, the most radical negations of the cloud of unknowing and the acknowledgment of nothingness must, through its own power of awareness, yield to the self-manifestation (emanation, *bullitio-ebullitio*, revelation) of the Divine Reality (whether named Godhead or God).

Theologically, this means, as Ruuysbroec clearly sees, that the radical indistinction, the no-thingness of Eckhart's Godhead-beyond-God, will necessarily manifest itself in the Christian life as the self-manifesting Father-Son-Spirit. Where Eckhart is unclear in his language about applying his diverse transcendental terms (One, *Esse*, Intelligence), sometimes to the Godhead and sometimes to the Father-Source, Ruuysbroec is clear. In Christian terms, all our language for God is inadequate. The radical negations of the spiritual life demand radical negations of all our names for God. And yet the Christian experience and thereby awareness of God's wisdom in the Logos and God's love in the Spirit remain our central clues to the reality we hesitantly name God. Insofar as Christians experience Godself as Source, Logos, and Spirit they find their central insight into God's own reality as always self-manifesting. That self-manifestation of the Father as Logos-Image is the Son. That relationship of divine self-manifestation is the Spirit. Christians find these conceptualities for understanding the divine reality through their very experiences and awareness of wisdom and love. Those clues to the source, order, and end of all reality allow them to name God as an always self-manifesting God—as Father-Son-Spirit (or Mother-Daughter-Spirit or Source-Logos-Spirit).

In traditional theological terms, the "economic" Trinity is our main clue to the "ontological" Trinity of God's own reality. Nor need one fear (as Abe does) that there will always be a "fourth"—the divine essence in all Christian Trinitarian understanding of God—insofar as one grasps, as Ruuysbroec clearly does, that God's essence *is* dialectically self-manifesting and thereby is necessarily Father-Son-Spirit.

I believe, furthermore, that Macquarrie (and Hegel and the entire neo-Platonic tradition before him!) is correct to state that this Christian insight

implies that "natural theology" should also feel obliged to show the intrin- /
sically incarnational and relational Trinitarian structure of all reality.
Unlike not only the Barthians but also the Thomists (with their distinction
between "natural" mysteries and "supernatural" mysteries), the neo-Platonists (including, here, Hegelians and some Whiteheadians, Rahnerians,
and Tillichians) develop philosophical positions that attempt to show, min-
imally, the reasonableness (and not merely the Thomist non-contradiction)
of an incarnational, relational, and Trinitarian understanding of all reality.
Such an enterprise, to be sure, demands a full incarnational metaphysics
of relationality, which may or may not cohere with Buddhist metaphysics.
That is clearly another discussion for another time and place.

In the meantime, precisely the Christian Trinitarian (self-manifesting,
radically relational) understanding of the Divine Reality so well expressed
by Ruuysbroec may suggest that Buddhists too may find such understanding
suggestive for their very distinct enterprise. For insofar as Abe's Buddhist
thought is dependent on Buddhist practice and spiritual awareness, then
the Buddhist awareness of Sunyata as wise and compassionate may suggest
the need for Abe to develop his transcendent-immanent dialectic further
into a dialectic of Sunyata as ultimate source-wisdom-compassion.

Clearly, even if this suggestion were agreed to, the Buddhist and the
Christian would still not be saying the same thing. But the radically relational and self-manifesting *structure* of Ultimate Reality would be commonly
affirmed. And that would render further conversation on such distinct
issues as the "duality" of God and all creatures (in the Buddhist critique
of Christianity) and the coherence of radical relationality and radically
autonomous "suchness" and its puzzling "freedom" and "nonfreedom" (in
the Christian critique of Buddhism) more intelligible—or at least, more
discussable in mutually intelligible terms. But that hope is dependent on
the fruitfulness (or lack thereof) of my suggestions on dynamic Sunyata as
wisdom-compassion via Ruuysbroec and Eckhart. It is time, however, to
turn to a more direct response to Abe's dialectics of the totally kenotic
God.

THE DIALECTIC OF THE KENOTIC GOD

The differences between Eckhart and Ruuysbroec illuminate two ways
in which Christian theology acknowledges the dialectic of the dynamically
self-manifesting Divine Reality. As noted above, I believe Ruuysbroec's
Trinitarian mysticism is even more appropriate than Eckhart's—but only
as dialectically related to the profound negations of Eckhart's apophatic
way (as Ruuysbroec's, unlike many other Trinitarian positions). Moreover,
both Eckhart and Ruuysbroec develop dialectical positions that show how
wisdom (Logos) and love (Spirit) *must* be characteristic of ultimate reality.
These latter Christian Trinitarian dialectics may prove suggestive for how
Abe might further develop his own Buddhist dialectic to show not only the

total immanence and transcendence of dynamic Sunyata but also its necessary character as wisdom and compassion in inner-Buddhist terms.

At the same time, Abe's original interpretations of the totally kenotic God and the totally kenotic Christ cannot but remind the Christian theologian that even the complex apophatic dialectic of Eckhart and the Trinitarian dialectic of Ruuysbroec do not suffice on inner-Christian grounds. For Abe is correct to cite Rahner and Moltmann on the theological implications for our understanding of God in the face of the cross and death of Jesus Christ. In terms of the Christian symbol system, one cannot understand the incarnation or resurrection without the cross (or vice versa). Here Abe's "high christology," or at least, his "christology from above, not below" strikes me as exactly right. For a christology—even a valuable one "from below"—the message and ministry of Jesus must also be a "christology from above" if it is not finally a mere Jesusology. The "kenotic christology" of Philippians has been and remains one of the most fruitful scriptural texts where Christian theologians may learn to reflect anew on how the "christology from above" and the "christology from below" actually meet—in the central notion of kenosis.

With this particular inner-Christian christological debate (on "from above" and "from below"), Abe, unlike Moltmann or even Rahner, is relatively uninterested. For his interest, as always, is meditative and, in the best sense, speculative on the possible dialectical implications of a kenotic christology for reinterpreting the kenotic God as total kenosis. It is hardly surprising that a great Buddhist thinker would move with natural affinity to this Pauline text and would interpret it as total kenosis of both Christ and God. It is more surprising—but from my Ruuysbroec position—happily surprising, that Abe would basically affirm the importance of Moltmann's insistence on the Trinitarian implications of the cross. But as Abe's curiously underdeveloped criticism of any Trinitarian understanding (and not only Moltmann's) suggests, he has not understood the intrinsically dynamic, self-manifesting, and dialectical character of any good Christian Trinitarian understanding of God: either that of Ruuysbroec or the distinct one of Moltmann. How otherwise can we understand Abe's strangely uncomprehending remarks on the "fourth"—the "essence"? The divine essence *is* intrinsically self-manifesting and thereby dynamic, relational, and dialectical; and necessarily Father, Son, and Spirit. And even if Abe would have us shift from Ruuysbroec's Trinitarian dialectic to the "Godhead-beyond-God" of Eckhart (as he surely would, given his comments on the "deeper interior"), a further question from the Christian theologian—even Eckhart—remains. Here the problem is not Abe's undialectical assumption of the divine essence as a "fourth" but his insistence on the divine reality (the deeper interior, even perhaps, the "Godhead beyond God"?) as Zero. Yet Eckhart, with his dialectical understanding, so similar to Abe's, of distinction-indistinction (or transcendence-immanence), could surely reply that Abe does not understand dialectically at all why One is not a numerical but a transcendental category—indeed, the principal Eckhartian category that allows the Christian to affirm the radical indistinction and distinction of the "Godhead beyond God"—even as *Nichts*, but never as Zero.

The introduction of kenotic categories moreover deepens the mystery of the divine self-manifestation in Jesus Christ but does not radically alter the fundamentally Trinitarian structure of the dialectical character of that self-manifestation. For the cross (which neither Eckhart nor Ruuysbroec emphasized as strongly as Tauler or John of the Cross, much less Luther or Jüngel and Moltmann) does, for the Christian, demand new reflection on the character of the divine self-manifestation in Jesus Christ. That it is proper to speak of God's suffering is a thought that the traditional neo-Platonic thinkers resisted. But as such *modern* neo-Platonists as Hegel and Whitehead correctly insist on modern philosophical (or "natural theological") grounds, there is no intrinsic dialectical reason to reject that conclusion. If God *is* love, it is difficult, indeed impossible, to conceive coherently how God is not affected by all reality.

This crucial move—which, note, can be made on both Hegelian and Whiteheadian modern and revisionary grounds—does challenge the vestigial (and incoherent) character of traditional neo-Platonists. Indeed, that tradition—with its "natural theology" of radical relationality and thereby the Incarnation and Trinity and their "scriptural" grounding in the Logos, Trinitarian, love and apophatic strands of John and Paul—should be revised, for its own coherence, in either a Hegelian or Whiteheadian neo-Platonic direction.

The insistence—with Paul and Luther—on the *cross* of Christ as the central disclosure of God's own reality is, indeed, an insight that the traditional neo-Platonists did not possess. That insight, as Paul in Philippians shows, is one that can lead into a meditation on the meaning of the cross of Christ that throws new light on both "Incarnation" (the "form of a servant"), the ministry and message of Jesus, and the dialectic of cross-resurrection as a dialectic of "humiliation-exaltation." That same mode of reflection can lead a modern theologian—like Rahner or Moltmann in their distinct ways—to reflect on the kenosis of Christ as the kenosis of God. But, in Christian theological terms, this need not lead in Abe's "totality" direction. Rather, a kenotic Christology of the cross can deepen one's understanding of the mysterious character of the divine self-manifestation as self-sacrificing love—affecting all and affected by all. Thus does love become not merely the divine reality of Spirit as the necessary relationship between Source and Logos, nor merely God's purely agapic gift to creatures. Rather, in the cross of Christ, the Christian understands that God's *love* is total. Indeed, God's decisive self-manifestation is in the servanthood, suffering, and death of this Jesus who is no other than the Christ.

This total love as self-manifesting, self-sacrificing love does not radically alter the Trinitarian dialectic but deepens one's partial spiritual and theological understanding of the nature of God as love. There is no "fourth."

There is no Zero. There is, therefore, no *total* kenosis.

The Christian reflects now not only on the earlier clues of the neo-Platonists on Logos, love, Trinity and apophaticism, but the clue of the cross as illuminating the deeper nature of Logos, of love, and of Trinity and demanding further apophatic negations. Only then can one understand love as suffering and thereby develop further metaphysical-theological reflections on love as radical relationality (affecting and affected). All this kind of revisionary thought—as such Trinitarian theologians as Moltmann, Rahner, and Jüngel show—is prompted by deeper reflection on the cross. Here Paul—with his "Christ and Christ crucified" theology—led the way as Luther insisted and as such later apophatic mystics as John of the Cross also sensed. But only if the Trinitarian dialectic of the dynamic self-manifesting God (now reconceived as the totally loving kenotic God) is misconstrued in a direction it *need* not take can either Altizer's "death of God" reading or Abe's Buddhist reading of the "kenotic God" hold.

To be sure, for Abe my reading will inevitably mean that, for the Christian, there is still a "duality" between the loving and beloved God and the beloved and loving creature. And this is true. But duality, as the entire neo-Platonist tradition dialectically shows, need not mean the dualism of classical theism.

The further issue between the Buddhist dialectic of dynamic Sunyata and the Christian Trinitarian dialectic of the totally loving kenotic God, I am persuaded, lies in the direction of a careful comparative analysis of the Buddhist dialectic of non-duality and the distinct Christian dialectic of identity-in-difference. These are clearly not the same dialectics—which is why I cannot accept Abe's reading of the kenotic God. But, as Abe has helped me see by driving me back to Ruuysbroec and Eckhart, these two dialectics are also not simply opposite to one another. Perhaps they are even "not-two"—at least that is the impression I receive from the very different reading of Buddhism given by Tanabe. I suspect that Abe must disagree with Tanabe's reading of our age and our need for "other-power" as much as he consistently disagrees with any duality at all (even identity-in-difference) of Western Christian thinkers. But that comparative dialectical analysis is a further discussion and one that, if fruitful for the Buddhist-Christian dialogue, will need once again the wise and compassionate dialectical spirit of Abe Masao.

PART III

A Rejoinder

A Rejoinder

MASAO ABE

I take great pleasure in writing this rejoinder to responses by eminent theologians with diverse religious backgrounds. I appreciate the acknowledgment by several respondents of my contribution to interfaith dialogue. Jürgen Moltmann writes, "Here reciprocal understanding is not only furthered, but Christianity and Buddhism in their immiscible difference are led into a common reality." Eugene B. Borowitz parallels Moltmann from his Jewish point of view: "Decreasing the linguistic barriers to greater understanding, as Masao Abe has so well done here, seems to me one of the most realistic and important aims of inter-faith dialogue."

What is more important, however, is that I have received responses that are critical, insightful, and provocative. I am pleased that my essay, "Kenotic God and Dynamic Sunyata" not only stimulated penetrating criticisms of my understanding of the Christian view of God and faith but also elicited Jewish and Christian discussion of Buddhism.

This latter facet appears distinctly in John Cobb's response. Referring to my serious acceptance of Christian criticisms of Buddhism, Cobb writes: "Abe acknowledges that the criticisms have not expressed mere misunderstanding. He does not belittle them as showing that the critics are dealing only with secondary matters. He acknowledges their force and proposes ways in which Buddhism can and should deal with them" (p. 92). He then emphatically states:

Such an essay invites Christian engagement at many points. One could, for example, confront Abe's account of Christian theology with another one. But I find most interesting Abe's proposals for developing Buddhism so as to take account of Western and Christian criticism; and I am emboldened by Abe's entry into Christian theology to reply by entering into the Buddhist discussion. My general position is that Abe's adjustments of Buddhism do not go far enough to meet the Christian criticism but that Buddhism is quite capable of taking further steps that would meet these criticisms. As Abe asks Christians to go deeper into our own faith, freeing ourselves from unnecessary commitments and prejudice, so I am asking him to go deeper into his own vision, ceasing to cling to those beliefs and doctrines that block a full appropriation of the truth in Christian criticism [p. 92].

This statement is encouraging as well as challenging. It is my conviction (shared particularly with John Cobb and others) that Buddhist-Christian-Jewish dialogue should go beyond the stage of promoting mutual understanding between the two religions and must aim at mutual transformation. This is especially the case today as we face the challenge of antireligious ideologies. A suggestion of mutual reinterpretation or mutual deepening of these faiths through the exchange of criticism is most welcome.

It is not, however, an easy job for me to present a full rejoinder to all the responses. Presented from various theological standpoints, they are divergent, and yet equally insightful. In what follows I will focus on what I take to be major issues. This rejoinder will consist of eleven sections.

THE CONTEXT FOR BUDDHIST-CHRISTIAN DIALOGUE

Before discussing the kenosis of God and dynamic Sunyata as Christian and Buddhist notions that may provide a profound point of contact between the two religions, I emphasized the necessity of approaching interfaith dialogue in the wider context of contemporary spirituality. This is a socio-historical context in which religion is challenged by a number of irreligious ideologies, such as scientism, Marxism, traditional Freudian psychoanalytic thought, and Nietzschean nihilism. Having a great impact in our present world, these ideologies deny the raison d'etre of religion on theoretical grounds. Accordingly, I insisted that we should engage in Buddhist-Christian dialogue in light of the wider socio-cultural problem of religion versus irreligion.

Reading through the responses to my essay, I received the impression that all the respondents agree with my insistence on this context for our dialogue, although some of them did not explicitly mention this methodological consideration. Three respondents, however, explicitly acknowledged the importance of such a wider context for our interfaith dialogue: Schubert M. Ogden, John Cobb, and Jürgen Moltmann. In the opening paragraph of his response, Schubert Ogden stresses the need for Buddhists and Christians to validate their truth claims and "situate their dialogue with one another in the larger context of critical discussion with all other persons of good will, religious and antireligious, who make or imply the same kinds of claims" (p. 125).

After evaluating my basic approach to Christianity, John Cobb writes: "As a Buddhist who shares with us the crisis of religion in the modern world, he wants to work with us in the interpretation of our sources to enable them to share their message authentically" (p. 91).

Jürgen Moltmann agrees that both Christianity and Buddhism are facing common challenges in the form of modern critiques of religion, notably scientism and nihilism à la Nietzsche. He goes on to point out how the Christian reaction to the contemporary situation differs from the Buddhist reaction:

> For Western religions and cultures, the new interest in the religions and wisdoms of the East arises out of the critique of the contradictions of "modern" civilization and the quest for a "postmodern" world of peace and reconciliation of contradictions. The true interest in the wisdoms of Buddhism and of Taoism in the West is not to be found with the "drop-outs" who are tired of civilization, but rather with the worried and knowing who search for a new civilization that serves life and no longer death (p. 117).

In the remarks of these three theologians I hear the serious voice of the Western conscience, which Buddhism must assimilate into itself.

My emphasis on the wider context for interfaith dialogue is not free from criticism, however. Schubert Ogden makes the following comment:

> As much as I applaud Abe's concern to confront the objections raised by antireligious ideologies, I do not see that anything he has to say is very effective in meeting them. Although he asserts that his reinterpretation of God and emptiness can overcome scientism and nihilism, he does not seem to me to provide adequate evidence or argument to support his assertion. In fact, when he argues at one point that "the notion of the kenotic God can overcome Nietzsche's nihilism," because "the kenotic God sacrifices Godself . . . for *absolute* nothingness, which is at one and the same time absolute Being," it is hard to take him seriously (p. 128)

I admit that although I tried to show how the notion of the kenotic God goes beyond Nietzsche's nihilism and can embrace the autonomous reason of modern science, and how the notion of dynamic Sunyata includes discriminating thinking and can deal with the problem of free will and evil as well as the problem of time and history, my discussion does not sufficiently "provide adequate evidence or argument" to support my assertion. In this rejoinder I will attempt to develop a fuller discussion of how the notions of kenotic God and dynamic Sunyata can effectively meet the challenge of irreligious ideologies, especially scientism and nihilism.

Another criticism of my insistence on Buddhist-Christian dialogue as a part of the wider, socio-cultural problem of religion versus irreligion comes from Catherine Keller, a feminist theologian. In her response, she states that my approach is "slightly anachronistic." With this criticism, Keller argues that religious fundamentalism is a more serious obstacle to interfaith dialogue.

At the moment the great obstacles to interreligious exchange lie not so much in sophisticated irreligion as in a barbaric rereligion. That is, we face a massed force of religious reaction in occidental culture, most dangerously in U.S. Christian fundamentalism. This sort of reaction can be happening, Abe might contend, only because Christianity has so far failed to present a compelling alternative to scientism and nihilism. Abe's proposal would also appear to the normal Christian to be nothing but a thinly disguised atheism. The attraction of so many needy persons to fundamentalism has altered the religious landscape (p. 104).

I agree with Keller—we must take the problem of fundamentalism into account in our interfaith dialogue, for we cannot afford to overlook the politics of interreligious exchange.

KENOTIC CHRIST AND KENOTIC GOD

My treatment of the notions of kenotic Christ and kenotic God was discussed by the respondent theologians more intensively than I expected. Correctly citing the Buddhist disagreement with the notion of a personal God who is self-existing and absolutely good—a disagreement based on the Buddhist principle of dependent co-origination—Schubert Ogden points out that I propose "the kenotic God" as an alternative to the traditional theistic notion of God:

This traditional concept of God is not the only or the most adequate way of conceiving the God necessarily implied by Christian faith. On the contrary. Abe argues, the New Testament, and specifically the Pauline, teaching of the kenosis, or self-emptying, of Christ clearly indicates another and more adequate concept insofar as it logically requires "the kenotic God" as the ground or the "root-source of the kenotic Christ." So far from being the one God who as absolute good must be independent of everything, the God necessarily presupposed by the self-emptying of Christ is the self-emptying God, the God of "unconditional love" who, "through complete self-abnegation ... is totally identical with everything, including sinful humans" (p. 127).

In conjunction with this, I do not accept Jürgen Moltmann's criticism of the inconsistency of my statements concerning the Christian notion of God. Moltmann writes:

He [Abe] says that Christianity has a theistic view of the "one personal God as the ultimate reality" and he speaks of "God as creator and ruler of the universe," which Buddhism does not know. These statements about Christianity are inconsistent with those statements about the 'kenotic God' that Masao Abe himself has developed from the New Testament. (p. 122).

I hope it is now clear that I am proposing the notion of kenotic God as the most adequate interpretation of God in Christianity in place of the traditional theistic view of God, and thereby no inconsistency is involved in my discussion.

In many respects, however, Jürgen Moltmann does understand and sympathize with my notion of kenotic Christ and kenotic God. He makes the following observations to deepen the meaning of the Christic hymn of Philippians 2, observations with which I completely agree: in the kenosis of Christ he empties his whole divinity and becomes the powerless crucified one; in "obedience" to God through emptying himself to the extent of dying on the cross, the "self-realization" of the Son of God is also accomplished; thus kenosis is based in the spontaneity of his eternal being; from eternity the divinity itself is unselfish love. God's whole being "is" love, meaning surrendering. God's freedom is God's love and God's love is God's freedom; loving surrendering—that is, "kenosis"—is not only an act but the being and existence of God, and hence it must also be the fundamental idea of the Christian doctrine of the Trinity. Moltmann then criticizes my understanding of the doctrine of the Trinity as going no further than Tertullian, who wrote, *Tres personae—una substantia.*

David Tracy criticizes my interpretation of the trinitarian doctrine of God, though welcoming my notions of the totally kenotic Christ and the totally kenotic God. In this connection, he introduces the notions of "high christology" or "christology from above" and "christology from below," and emphasizes that in the notion of kenosis these two christologies can meet each other. Then, expressing "happy surprise" at my basic affirmation of the importance of Moltmann's insistence on the trinitarian implications of the cross, Tracy makes the following critical comments on my understanding of the Trinity:

> But as Abe's curiously underdeveloped criticism of any Trinitarian understanding (and not only Moltmann's) suggests, he has not understood the intrinsically dynamic, self-manifesting, and dialectical character of any good Christian Trinitarian understanding of God. ... How otherwise can we understand Abe's strangely uncomprehending remarks on the "fourth"—the "essence"? (p. 152).

Facing these strong criticisms by Moltmann and Tracy concerning my understanding of the Christian doctrine of the Trinity, I heed what they say and will revise and deepen my interpretation. At the same time, I should also like to clarify further the points of my own understanding of the Christian doctrine of the Trinity and my Buddhist criticism of it. Since this issue is one of the highlights of our present dialogue, I will discuss it under the following two sections, "Trinity and Kenosis" and "Trinity and Sunyata."

TRINITY AND KENOSIS

As I stated before, Moltmann argues that my treatment of the Trinity does not go beyond Tertullian's formulation: *Tres personae — una substantia*. Moltmann then presents his own dynamic interpretation of the Trinity and emphasizes perichoresis: "The unselfishness in the eternal love and unity of the trinitarian God is *perichoresis*: community in mutual interdependence and interpenetration" (pp. 119–20). Moltmann also criticizes my construing the one God in the Trinity as the "great zero" and as *Nichts* or *Ungrund* based on Meister Eckhart and Jacob Boehme.

While explicitly emphasizing an attempted recovery of neoplatonic trinitarian, dynamic, and dialectical theism, David Tracy takes a similar stand concerning my understanding of the Christian doctrine of the Trinity:

> The divine essence *is* intrinsically self-manifesting and thereby dynamic, relational, and dialectical; and necessarily Father, Son, and Spirit. And even if Abe would have us shift from Ruuysbroec's Trinitarian dialectic to the "Godhead-beyond-God" of Eckhart (as he surely would, given his comments on the "deeper interior"), a further question from the Christian theologian — even Eckhart — remains. Here the problem is not Abe's undialectical assumption of the divine essence as a "fourth" but his insistence on the divine reality (the deeper interior, even perhaps, the "Godhead beyond God"?) as Zero. Yet Eckhart, with his dialectical understanding, so similar to Abe's, of distinction-indistinction (or transcendence-immanence), could surely reply that Abe does not understand dialectically at all why One is not a numerical but a transcendental category — indeed, the principal Eckhartian category that allows the Christian to affirm the radical indistinction and distinction of the "Godhead beyond God" — even as *Nichts*, but never as Zero (pp. 152–53).

My response to the above criticisms by Moltmann and Tracy can be summarized in the following four points:

1. In my essay I cite the Tertullian formula of the Trinity, "the unity of three persons in the one God or Godhead" as a starting point for my consideration of Moltmann's view of the Trinity, not as my own understanding. It may be my failure not to take Moltmann's own social doctrine of the Trinity as a starting point, but when I raised the issue of "whether the trinitarian interpretation as illustrated by Moltmann is a *real* solution of that paradoxical statement of God" (a statement essential to the traditional doctrine of God's two natures: God is "dead" on the cross and yet is not

dead), I thought it better to start with the traditional trinitarian formula of Tertullian.

2. I now realize that my usage of the terms "fourth" and "zero" is misleading. I was, however, aware that in the trinitarian doctrine "one" and "three" are not numerical but transcendental categories. I articulated the *substantia* by one God and the *hypostatis* by three persons, as can be seen in the following quotation.

> In the doctrine of the trinity it is clear that the one God is not the fourth person or the fourth being. One God is the common *substantia* or *essentia* whereas the three persons are three distinct *hypostatases* (p. 24).

It is this substantialist interpretation of the Trinity that is attacked by both Moltmann and Tracy as inadequate. As I stated a little earlier, this Tertullian understanding of the Trinity is not my own, and thus I made the following criticism that is different from that of Moltmann and Tracy:

> Although there are clear differences and mutual relationships among the three persons, the one God is the undivided essence, indicating the unity of God. The distinction between *essentia* (which is one and unity) and *hypostasis* (which is three and trinity) is indispensable and should not be confused in the doctrine of the Trinity. If this distinction is vital, however, the one God as *essentia*, though clearly not the fourth being, is not completely independent of [devoid of] or free from the character of the fourth being. In my view, in order to overcome the presence of the character of the fourth being, the oneness of this one God must possess the characteristic of zero. The one God in the Trinity must be great zero that is free even from the oneness as distinguished from the threeness.
>
> This means that only when the one God is understood to have the characteristic of zero can the doctrine of Trinity be fully and dynamically realized. This is because three distinctive beings—Father, Son, and Spirit—are then clearly and thoroughly realized in their distinctiveness without any possibility of being reduced to one Godhead, and because at the same time the oneness of the one God is completely preserved from the haunting presence of the fourth being (p. 24).

Careful reading of the above quotation, I hope, will make it clear that with the notion of "Zero" or "great zero" I reject the understanding of the one God as *substantia* or *essentia* as distinguished from the three persons as *hypostases*, and regard the one God as *nonsubstantial* and dialectically identical with three persons: Father, Son, and Spirit. Only through a clear realization of the *nonsubstantiality*—the characteristic of zero—of the one God, I believe, can we say with Tracy, "the divine essence *is* intrinsically self-manifesting and thereby dynamic, relational, and dialectical and necessarily Father, Son, and Spirit" (p. 152). This is why I state:

> In order for the trinitarian structure to be truly possible, that one
> God should not be *essentia* as distinguished from *hypostasis*, much less
> *substantia*, but *Nichts* or *Ungrund*. Only when the doctrine of Trinity
> of God is understood in this way are the unity and the trinity of God
> fully and harmoniously realized without conflict. And only then is the
> event of the cross in God's being, as Moltmann requires, understood
> in *both* trinitarian *and* personal terms, or "simultaneously in both
> christocentric and trinitarian terms" (p. 24).

3. A further point to be clarified in my response to the criticism by
Moltmann and Tracy is that of how clearly the dialectical relationship
between the Godhead (the one God in my discussion) and Father-Son-Spirit is realized in my interpretation of the Trinity. Emphasizing that "he
(Eckhart) can be said to go a long way—although not all the way—with
Abe's kenotic God," Tracy states:

> Eckhart's dialectic, so similar to Abe's, nonetheless demands a move
> which Abe's does not: the self-manifestation of the Godhead in the
> distinct *bullitio* as the Trinity and the *ebullitio* of the creature. To be
> more exact, Abe's dialectic of dynamic Sunyata may have a similar
> self-manifestation character insofar as dynamic Sunyata manifests
> itself *as* wisdom and *as* compassion to the enlightened one. But this
> is still unlike Eckhart's explicit revision of neo-Platonic "emanation"
> language into the more radically dialectical language of *bullitio* and
> *ebullitio* (and, allied to that, on the human side of awareness, the birth
> of the Word in the soul and the "breakthrough" of the soul to the
> Godhead) (p. 149).

Tracy, however, does not stop here but moves from Eckhart to Ruuysbroec, for he finds Ruuysbroec clearer than Eckhart in his language of
Christian awareness. According to Tracy, in Ruuysbroec "God's essence is
dialectically self-manifesting and thereby is necessarily Father, Son, Spirit."
Moreover, "Insofar as Christians experience Godself as Source, Logos, and
Spirit, they find their central insight into God's own reality as always self-manifesting. That self-manifestation of the Father as Logos-Image is the
Son. That relationship of divine self-manifestation is the Spirit" (p. 150).
This is a fascinating and extremely insightful interpretation of the triune
God. Neither my understanding of the Christian doctrine of the Trinity nor
my interpretation of the Buddhist notion of dynamic Sunyata is as clearly
dialectical as Ruuysbroec's standpoint. Buddhists will be able to learn many
things from Tracy's dialectical interpretation of the Christian Trinity.

4. An issue arises concerning Ruuysbroec's and Tracy's interpretation

of the self-manifesting God as Father-Son-Spirit. When Ruuysbroec or Tracy talks about the self-manifesting God as Father-Son-Spirit, where does he find himself? Does he take his stand outside God's self-manifestation or inside? If he takes his stand somewhat *outside* of the self-manifestation of God as Father-Son-Spirit he must be objectifying or conceptualizing God's self-manifestation. This stand is not acceptable, however, for it is devoid of reality. In order to be free from objectification or conceptualization and fully realize the reality of God's self-manifestation as Father-Son-Spirit, one must be existentially *identical* with the self-manifestation of God. Through this existential identity does the person not realize that at the very root of the self-manifestation—that is, prior to the self-manifestation—God is neither Father nor Son nor Spirit? Is it not precisely because God is neither Father nor Son nor Spirit that God manifests Godself as Father-Son-Spirit? The self-manifesting God must be a self-emptying God. A dynamic Trinity must be based on kenosis. Divine self-manifestation without the realization of self-emptying—that is, kenosis—is something substantialized—something objectified or conceptualized. Is not the fact that God is neither Father nor Son nor Spirit and is thus absolute no-thingness the reason why God manifests Godself as Father-Son-Spirit in full reality? This is not merely the "ontological" Trinity of God's own reality but also the "economic" Trinity, for it includes an incarnational, relational, and trinitarian understanding of this reality.

There are two more issues to be discussed under the theme, "Trinity and Kenosis." One is Moltmann's notion of creation and the other is Tracy's reaction to my emphasis on the totality of kenosis.

I find a great affinity with Moltmann when he states:

The divinity of the trinitarian God is kenosis. This divine kenosis is being as well as non-being. It is neither being nor non-being. It is the unfathomable secret of love, which one cannot comprehend, but rather only worship in amazement. Because all our notions create idols, only amazement understands the secret of reality (p. 120).

Moltmann also emphasizes a new understanding of the *world as God's creation in God* and suggests that "Buddhist and Jewish-Christian thoughts can mutually deepen each other here" (p. 121). His idea of "creation" is strikingly similar to the Buddhist notion of *pratitya-samutpada*, dependent co-origination, for he writes that creation means that all existing things are contingent, nothing is *causa sui*, and all creatures exist in mutual reciprocal sympathy. Buddhists can learn from Christians about the notion that "God is community" and the perichoretical structure of the creation community. My only question in this regard is this: when Moltmann states that "everything that exists, exists reciprocally in each other and in God," what is the relationship between each thing and God? Is the relationship between each thing and God reciprocal or not?

My emphasis on the *total* kenosis of Christ and the *total* kenosis of God is accepted and rejected by Tracy. As I stated before, he accepts it by stating:

Abe's original interpretations of the totally kenotic God and the totally kenotic Christ cannot but remind the Christian theologian that even the complex apophatic dialectic of Eckhart and the Trinitarian dialectic of Ruuysbroec do not suffice on inner-Christian grounds. For Abe is correct to cite Rahner and Moltmann on the theological implications for our understanding of God in the face of the cross and death of Jesus Christ. In terms of the Christian symbol system, one cannot understand the incarnation or resurrection without the cross (or vice versa) (p. 152).

In another section of his response, however, while equally emphasizing the crucial importance of the cross of Christ as the central disclosure of God's own reality, Tracy states:

In Christian theological terms, this [meditation on the meaning of the cross of Christ] need not lead in Abe's "totality" direction. Rather a kenotic Christology of the cross can deepen one's understanding of the mysterious character of the divine self-manifestation as self-sacrificing love—affecting all and affected by all. Thus does love become not merely the divine reality of Spirit as the necessary relationship between Source and Logos, nor merely God's purely agapic gift to creatures. Rather, in the cross of Christ, the Christian understands that God's *love* is total. Indeed, God's decisive self-manifestation is in the servanthood, suffering, and death of this Jesus who is no other than the Christ (p. 153).

I am puzzled as to whether these two paragraphs are consistent and whether my emphasis on *total* kenosis is properly understood by Tracy. Insofar as I understand Tracy's point, he apparently wants to insist:

1. The introduction of kenotic categories does not weaken but rather deepens the mystery of the divine self-manifestation in Jesus Christ.

2. It does not radically alter the fundamentally trinitarian structure of the dialectical character of the divine self-manifestation in Jesus Christ, which is God's love.

3. The emphasis on the total kenosis of both Christ and God based on his Buddhist standpoint moves in an unnecessary direction: not to the totally loving, kenotic God but to an intellectual, radically detached notion of the kenotic God that is less dialectical.

If this third point correctly reflects Tracy's criticism then I must say he misunderstands my emphasis on the total kenosis of Christ and God.

In my article, I emphasized the totality of Christ's kenosis for the following three reasons:

1. Christ's kenosis is a transformation not only in appearance but in substance or reality, and it implies a radical and thoroughgoing abnegation of the Son of God.

2. The Son of God is *essentially* and *fundamentally* self-emptying: it is not that the Son of God became a person through kenosis, but that the Son fundamentally *is* a true person and true God at one and the same time in his dynamic work of kenosis.

3. Through *total* kenosis the Son of God negates himself and dialectically affirms himself as the Christ.

Consequently, I formulated the doctrine of Christ's kenosis as follows:

> The Son of God is not the Son of God (for he is essentially and fundamentally self-emptying); precisely because he *is not* the Son of God he *is* truly the Son of God (for he originally and always works as Christ, the messiah, in his salvational function of self-emptying) (p. 12).

Likewise, I emphasized the totality of God's kenosis as follows:

1. The kenosis of Christ was accomplished on the basis of God's *will*, but in the case of God, kenosis is implied in the original *nature* of God that is *love*.

2. God is God, not because God had the Son of God take a human form and be sacrificed while God remained God, but because God is a suffering God, a self-sacrificial God through *total kenosis*.

3. Only through total kenosis and God's self-sacrificial identification with everything in the world is God truly God. Here we fully realize the reality and actuality of God which is entirely beyond conception and objectification.

Accordingly, concerning faith in God I affirm that God is not God (for God is love and completely self-emptying); precisely because God is not a self-affirmative God, God is truly the God of love (for through complete self-abnegation God is totally identical with everything, including sinful humans). In this interpretation, although the trinitarian structure of God's essence is not discussed, God and Christ are understood quite dialectically without neoplatonic intellectualism and detachment, and the cross of Christ is fully realized as God's love. It is through the *total kenosis* that both Christ and God can be understood in radically dialectical language.

TRINITY AND SUNYATA

As I mentioned before, Tracy offers the criticism that my interpretation of dynamic Sunyata is not clear enough in terms of how dynamic Sunyata emerges *as* wisdom and *as* compassion in the enlightened one:

In Buddhist terms, Eckhart's "Godhead beyond God" is a route to, but is not finally an awareness of, "absolute nothingness." In Eckhartian Christian terms, Abe needs to show how *dialectically* "dynamic Sunyata" is not only immanent in all and thereby transcendent (and vice versa) but how that immanence-transcendence discloses itself as wisdom and as compassion (p. 149).

Then Tracy suggests that the Trinitarian understanding of Divine Reality may contribute to a more dialectic understanding of Buddhist Sunyata.

In discussing the soteriological significance of Sunyata, I stated that it signifies the realization of *suchness* or *as-it-is-ness* of everything including the natural, the human, and the divine; *boundless openness* without any particular fixed center; *jinen* or the fundamental naturalness underlying both human beings and nature; the realization of not only the interdependence and interpenetration but also the mutual reversibility of everything in the universe; and most importantly, the two characteristics of wisdom and compassion.

With regard to the last point, Sunyata is wisdom in the light of which the suchness of everything is clearly realized in terms of its distinctiveness and sameness. This is because through the dynamic function of Sunyata — that is, through its self-emptying — Sunyata turns into wisdom in which everything without exception is realized in its suchness or as-it-is-ness. That is to say, everything is realized in its distinctiveness and yet in sameness, "sameness" in the sense that everything is *equally* and *respectively* realized in its distinctiveness. The dynamic realization of suchness includes the realization of the distinctiveness and sameness of everything. This is quite parallel to Tracy's statement about Eckhart:

The Godhead as One is indistinct and precisely as such is distinct from all reality (and vice versa). In more familiar dialectical terms, precisely the divine transcendence of all reality renders the divine reality immanent to all reality (and vice versa) (p. 148).

Tracy's subsequent statements are very provocative and suggestive:

This radically dialectical understanding of indistinction and distinction, of immanence and transcendence, allows Eckhart to interpret both the *bullitio* of the emergence of the divine relations of the Trinity and, in creation, the *ebullitio* of the birth of the Word in the soul (p. 149).

With this statement Tracy points out that a move to the self-manifestation of the Godhead in the distinct *bullitio* as the Trinity and the *ebullitio* of the creature is lacking in my interpretation of Sunyata. In this connection I should like to stress another aspect of Sunyata — that is, the aspect of compassion that is dynamically linked with the aspect of wisdom. As I stated in my essay:

> Sunyata is [also] compassion in the light of which the dominant-subordinate relationship among things in the ordinary and relative sense is freely turned over, and moral and ethical judgments ... are transcended in the ultimate dimension. Through compassion realized in Sunyata even an atrocious villain is ultimately saved, even evil passions are transformed into enlightenment (p. 32).

This compassionate aspect of Sunyata is somewhat parallel to, though not the same as, the self-manifestation of the Godhead. However, in order for Buddhists to respond to Tracy's critical comment and suggestion, they must develop the traditional *trikaya* (three-body) doctrine in relation to the contemporary human predicament. The *trikaya* doctrine—that is, the doctrine of *Dharmakaya* (dharma body, another term for Sunyata), *Sambhogakaya* (reward body or bliss body) and *Nirmanakaya* (transformation body)—is one of the most important doctrines of Mahayana Buddhism. The *trikaya* is the self-manifestation of Sunyata. It is wisdom and compassion that is working consistently through the whole process of the self-manifestation of Sunyata. Buddhists must develop the *trikaya* doctrine through East-West encounter in the contemporary world, particularly in the arena of Buddhist-Christian dialogue. This development requires, however, an extensive discussion that is beyond the scope of this essay, so I simply point out its necessity at this time.

GOD AND THE MEANING OF BUDDHISM FOR CHRISTIANITY

Expressing affinity with my understanding of the ground of ultimate reality, Schubert Ogden poses the following question:

> Given this assumption [of dependent co-origination], it clearly could make sense to talk about a self-emptying God; for then even God would be simply one individual among others faced with the same fundamental option between inauthentic self-affirmation and ignorance of emptiness, on the one hand, and authentic realization of emptiness and self-denial, on the other. But what reason does Abe give either for thinking that such talk could make sense on any other assumption or for supposing that this same assumption is somehow integral, if not to the beliefs expressed by Philippians 2:5–11, then to the necessary implications of Christian faith in God? (p. 129).

My answers to these questions can be summarized in the following three points:
1. It is clear that my argument for the "kenotic God" is inspired by

Buddhism, but this does not mean that I simply impose Buddhist beliefs on the Christian notion of God as kenotic God. Instead, I discovered the notion of kenotic God within Christianity. Without the self-emptying of God the Father, the self-emptying of the Son of God is inconceivable, and if God is truly the God of love, God must be a completely self-negating God. This understanding earns the agreement of Moltmann, Tracy, and Altizer.

2. If God is understood as the kenotic God, the notion of God is free from any duality and thereby fully indicates the unobjectifiable, all-embracing, ultimate reality. It also becomes compatible with the Buddhist notion of dependent co-origination.

3. If God is understood as a self-emptying God, why would God be one individual among others? Elsewhere Ogden states:

> In my judgment, anything like his [Abe's] notion of a self-emptying God, implying as it does that God is at best a particular individual who at least could be self-assertive instead, is not only not necessarily implied by Christian faith but also necessarily precluded by it. Because such faith is the unreserved trust and loyalty for which the ground of ultimate reality is the boundless love decisively represented through Jesus Christ ... from the standpoint of Christian faith any individual who could conceivably be the kenotic God could not really be God at all but only an idol in whom faith could believe only by ceasing to be itself (p. 129).

I am puzzled by this strongly negative statement about the notion of kenotic God when I contrast it with Altizer's equally strong but affirmative statement about kenotic God:

> If modern Christian visionaries have realized an opening to the kenosis of God, thereby they have realized an opening to absolute emptiness itself, an emptiness that is the very center of what the radical modern Christian has known as the crucifixion of God (p. 77).

Advancing the notion of the "kenotic God," I do not presuppose that God is self-assertive and must be emptied. Rather I claim that since God is unconditional love, the kenosis of the Son of God must originate in the kenosis of God the Father. This is why I highly appreciate Karl Rahner when he states: "The primary phenomenon given by faith is precisely the self-emptying of God" (*Foundations of Christian Faith*, p. 222).

In marked contrast to Schubert Ogden who rejects the application of certain Buddhist ideas in interpreting Christianity, Altizer rather boldly and straightforwardly tries to appropriate Buddhist notions into the Christian context. Regarding the Kyoto School of philosophy as an example of modern Buddhist thinking, Altizer takes the notion of "absolute self-negation" as the key term for both Buddhist and Christian understandings of ultimate reality. He writes: "If true deity 'is' in its 'is notness,' . . . then God is most truly God in the emptying and death of Godhead, in God's own full and final self-negation" (p. 71).

Then Altizer contrasts contemporary Buddhist thinkers with Christian theologians and suggests that "absolute self-negation" is essential to Buddhism and Christianity:

> It is truly remarkable that contemporary Buddhist thinkers are able to think critically and sensitively about the contemporary Christian problem of God, and not the least reason for this is that they themselves have been so deeply open to modern radical thinking. Moreover, they are Buddhist and modern at once, and there is no such parallel in any group or body of Christian thinkers. Christian theologians are now profoundly alienated and estranged from the actual consequences of their own Christian history, whereas Buddhist thinkers have been reborn . . . as Buddhist thinkers. Thereby Buddhist thinking has become Eastern and Western at once, and Christian and Buddhist at once, and above all so by way of their understanding of absolute self-negation (p. 71).

Although this overestimates contemporary Buddhist thinkers, it does indicate the basic intention of Kyoto School philosophers. Then, referring to the kenosis of the Godhead, Altizer warns his fellow theologians, "Historical Christianity has never envisioned the full or total ubiquity of God . . . and that is surely because historical Christianity has been so deeply bound to the pure transcendence of God, or to the transcendence of transcendence itself" (pp. 71–72).

Following Kitaro Nishida's characterization of Christianity and Buddhism, Altizer takes Christianity as representing the objective identity of transcendent transcendence and Buddhism as reflecting the absolute's subjectivity as immanent transcendence. In Altizer's own words, "Christianity encounters the absolute's own self-expression as an objective transcendence, and Buddhism encounters it as an immanent transcendence" (p. 70).

As quoted above, Altizer criticizes historical Christianity as deeply bound to the transcendence of transcendence — that is, the pure transcendence of God — and as thereby alienated from the historical and cultural world. On the other hand, according to Altizer, the pure transcendence of God has never truly been known in Buddhist history and thus Buddhism can grasp the contemporary theological problem of the disappearance or absence of God. Buddhist transcendence is transcendent in its own absolute self-negation, a self-negation realizing itself in consciousness and history alike; and in this case the absolute self-negation is the absolute presence of the absolute itself.

Altizer notes that immanent transcendence has been lacking in traditional Christianity while absolute objectivity has been lacking in Buddhism. I appreciate this interpretation by Altizer of Buddhism and his remarks about how the Kyoto School argues that the absolute is identical with itself especially in its own self-negation, and that self-abnegation is present in all consciousness and history as their deepest ground.

In this regard, Altizer raises an important question. "Can such an emptiness or self-negation of God [which is dialectically identical with the fullness of God] be present or manifest upon a historical horizon determined by the transcendence of transcendence?" He answers himself by arguing that this is possible only:

> ... if the transcendence of transcendence has disappeared in that horizon, and disappeared in the real and actual absence of God. Then Christian and Buddhist thinking would be homologous in their mutual ground in the absence of an objective or manifest transcendence, and each would be open to a wholly immanent transcendence, an immanent transcendence that Buddhism can know as the absolute's own subjectivity (p. 72).

For Buddhist-Christian dialogue, this is an extremely important statement. My reaction to it is ambivalent.

1. I agree with Altizer in that the emptiness of God dialectically identical with the fullness of God can be manifest upon a historical horizon only if the transcendence of God has disappeared.

2. In Christianity, however, the emptiness or kenosis of God manifests itself upon a historical horizon as the kenosis of Christ and Jesus' crucifixion and resurrection. This constitutes a type of immanent transcendence.

3. In order for a wholly immanent transcendence to be realized, however, the kenosis of God, as I emphasized before, must not be partial but total. The absolute self-negation of God must be realized.

4. On the other hand, in Buddhism the emptiness of the sacred, which is dialectally identical with the fullness of the sacred, is present in the historical dimension because of the absence of any transcendent God. This can be seen in such Mahayana Buddhist phrases as "Mountains, rivers, and the earth all disclose the Dharmakaya" and "All the trees, grasses, and lands attain Buddhahood."

5. Such Mahayana phrases should not be mistaken for nature mysticism, for nature mysticism lacks the realization of emptiness essential to Mahayana Buddhism. In historical Mahayana Buddhism, however, emptiness dialectically identical with fullness is scarcely manifest in the *historical* dimension.

Altizer himself is, of course, well aware of the event of Christ as a symbol of immanent transcendence. He writes: "Christianity has always known the absolute's own subjectivity as Christ, and from its very beginning Christianity has been initiated into Christ as the kenosis of God" (p. 72). At the same time Altizer never fails to point out that a modern critical and historical understanding of the New Testament was made possible in the wake of the disappearance of God in the contemporary world. On this basis he clarifies the crucial points of Buddhist-Christian dialogue as follows:

Thus only the absence of God opened Christianity itself to a critical understanding of its original ground, and so, too, it was only in this historical situation that Christianity became open to the challenge of Buddhism. What could Buddhism mean to a Christianity that truly and fully knows the transcendence of God? And could Buddhist thinkers absorb a Christianity that is fully and finally grounded in the transcendence of transcendence? (p. 72).

Altizer's questions will certainly provide a new starting point for Buddhist-Christian dialogue.

SUNYATA AND ETHICS

In addition to "kenotic God," "dynamic Sunyata" is a crucial issue in our present dialogue. Generally speaking, my treatment of Sunyata received a more negative response than my treatment of the "kenotic God," although several respondents recognized to some extent its positive meaning.

Schubert Ogden describes his difficulties with the Buddhist notion of Sunyata as centering on the distinction between the parts and the whole. After supporting my idea of translating the term "Sunyata" with the gerund "self-emptying" rather than the nominal "emptiness," Catherine Keller discusses the problematic connotations of "emptiness": stagnation, boredom, and dispersion. Such linguistic associations of "emptiness" are a hindrance to properly introducing the Buddhist concept of Sunyata to the West.

What is a more serious difficulty in this regard, however, is grasping the metaphysical or doctrinal connotations and practical or soteriological connotations of Sunyata. We can clearly see this difficulty in Ogden's statements concerning the possible disappearance of any real difference between things if everything is interpenetrating, and what this implies for differential thought and action and for the distinction between ignorance and enlightenment. Similar critical remarks appear in John Cobb's response:

In typical Buddhist fashion Abe concentrates attention on what characterizes every situation whatsoever. This is the place where Buddhism has made its greatest and most profound contribution. I hope I am not understood as belittling this. But when we have recognized how everything is bound up with everything else, so that nothing exists by itself or has any existence in itself, this need not lead us to suppose that everything plays an equal role in the constitution of everything else or that the discrimination of just what role is played by what and when is unimportant. ... Is Buddhism so committed to encouraging the realization of the universal condition of all things that it cannot give equal weight to what is particular to each thing? (pp. 94–95).

In order to properly respond to these questions and critical comments, I should like to explain my basic understanding of human existence, and clarify the notion of Sunyata, especially in connection with the problems of difference and equality, the particular and the universal, and ethical responsibility.

My understanding of human existence consists of two dimensions: horizontal and vertical. The horizontal dimension refers to the socio-historical aspect of human existence, conditioned by time and space, whereas the vertical dimension indicates the metaphysical or religious aspect of human existence, trans-spacial and trans-temporal. The former is the realm of immanence whereas the latter is the realm of transcendence. These two dimensions are essentially and qualitatively different from one another and yet are inseparably connected with one another in the living reality of human existence. We are a dialectical existence oriented both physically and metaphysically, both temporally and eternally, both culturally and religiously. We are always living at the intersection of the horizontal and the vertical dimensions. This can be properly understood not objectively from the outside but only existentially from within.

This means that each of us is identical with the intersection of temporality and eternity, particularity and universality, immanence and transcendence, distinction and nondistinction. Accordingly, each of these poles is necessary or indispensable for human existence. We must not forget, however, that the latter (eternity, universality, transcendence, nondistinction; that is, the religious dimension) is *more fundamental* than the former (temporality, particularity, immanence, distinction; that is, the socio-historical dimension). In other words, the religious dimension is indispensable as the *ground* or *source* of human existence while the socio-historical dimension is indispensable as the *condition* or *occasion* necessary for human existence. Without the religious dimension as the ground, the socio-historical dimension is groundless and rootless, whereas without the socio-historical dimension as a condition or occasion, the religious dimension does not manifest itself.

We should not confuse the "ground" with "condition," however, for there is an irreversibility between them. This is why I stated that the horizontal dimension and the vertical dimension are qualitatively different from each other and yet are inseparably connected with each other.

As a dialectical existence, each of us is identical with and living at the intersection of temporality and eternity, particularity and universality, immanence and transcendence. This is why in Christianity Jesus said, "The Kingdom of God is within you" (Luke 17:21) and "He [God] maketh his sun to rise on the evil and the good, and sendeth rain on the just and the unjust" (Matthew 5:45). Likewise, Buddhism emphasizes that "samsara as it is is nirvana, nirvana as it is is samsara," and "form itself is emptiness, emptiness itself is form." One may say that the intersection of the two dimensions is symbolized in Christianity by Jesus Christ who is the true human and the true God, and in Buddhism by Sunyata, in which emptiness and fullness are dynamically identical.

In the horizontal dimension—that is, the secular, socio-historical dimension—all things and persons are different from one another in their own distinctiveness. This world is a realm of distinction, as recognized by Christianity and Buddhism. That everything is distinctive, however, has a double meaning—positive and negative. It has a positive meaning because without distinction the world would be chaotic and relations among things and persons would be inconceivable. On the other hand, it has a negative meaning because once we reify or substantialize distinctions—an activity innate in human nature—the substantialized distinctions lead to opposition, struggle, and conflict.

In order to overcome such inevitable conflict and to attain eternal peace, we must transcend the horizontal, secular dimension and turn to the vertical, religious dimension. Here distinction is overcome and equality is realized. This appears in Christianity in the nondiscriminating love of God, who makes the sun rise on the evil and the good, and sends rain on the just and the unjust. In Buddhism it is emphasized that although everything and everyone has its own distinctiveness, we should not substantialize and become attached to it as if it were enduring but rather awaken to the reality that everything and everyone is equally nonsubstantial and empty. In these two traditions, once we move from the horizontal and immanent realm—in which distinctions are clearly realized—to the vertical and transcendent realm, equality without distinctions is realized. Ogden's concern about the disappearance of real difference is based, I am afraid, on confusion of the socio-historical dimension as the condition and the religious or metaphysical dimension as the ground. As Cobb writes, interdependence "need not lead us to suppose that everything plays an equal role in the constitution of everything else or that the discrimination of just what role is played by what and when is unimportant" (p. 94).

In the Buddhist worldview, interdependence is possible only when each and every thing has its own independent existence. How would *inter*dependence be possible if everything had no *in*dependent, *distinctive* existence? Buddhism insists that although everything in the horizontal, socio-historical dimension is, with its distinctiveness, different from every other thing, everything is interdependent precisely because, speaking from the vertical, religious dimension, everything has no unchangeable, enduring essence, and thus is nonsubstantial and "empty." Buddhism never says that distinctions are unreal or delusory in the socio-historical dimension, for it is only in the metaphysical or religious dimension that the equality of everything is realized.

Further, the socio-historical dimension and the metaphysical or religious dimension are inseparable from each other in Buddhism. Only by taking distinctions in the socio-historical dimension as a "condition" or "occasion" does Buddhism open up the religious dimension of equality as the ground of human existence. The latter dimension would be an abstraction if it did not take the former dimension as its condition or occasion. Again, Buddhism never supposes, as Cobb perhaps thinks it does, that "everything plays an equal role in the constitution of everything else" in the horizontal socio-historical dimension. Equality free from distinctions is realized in the vertical, religious dimension only by overcoming distinctions substantialized in the horizontal, socio-historical dimension, which is a moment or condition to be negated. Particularity in the socio-historical dimension is not trivial, for the universal ground of human existence cannot be realized apart from the particular "what" and "when" as the condition or occasion.

Accordingly, my answer to the two questions raised by Moltmann at the end of his response are both negative. His first question is, "Can Sunyata be interpreted 'dynamically' without paying heed to the uniqueness of each occurrence and the finality of the redeeming future?" Dynamic Sunyata can be properly realized not *without* but only *by* "paying heed to the uniqueness of each occurrence and the finality of the redeeming future" in the horizontal dimension.

His second question is, "Can Sunyata be understood 'dynamically' without expanding the naturalist categories through personalist categories?" Because Sunyata indicates the intersection of the socio-historical dimension and the metaphysical or religious dimension it can *not* "be understood 'dynamically' without expanding the naturalist categories through personalist categories." The metaphysical, trans-spatial and trans-temporal dimension and the personalist socio-historical dimension, though essentially different frrm one another, are inseparable in dynamic Sunyata.

I hope it is now clear that in Buddhism the realization of the particularity and distinction of everything is indispensable — as the condition for awakening to equality beyond distinctions. Buddhism tells us not to take the particularity or distinctiveness of things and the self as the ground or source of human life by substantializing and absolutizing it, for such a substantialization and absolutization of distinction is the basic cause of human suffering. However, once we awaken to the nondistinctive equality of everything as the ground of human life by realizing everything's distinctiveness as "condition" but not as "ground," then on the ground of equality, the distinctions of everything are realized as the "condition."

Expressed slightly differently, distinctions are *regrasped* and *reestablished* as the indispensable condition for human life on the basis of equality.

Ethical judgments and moral decisions are made in Buddhism on the basis of this renewed realization of distinction and particularity. Since this realization is free from the substantialization and absolutization of distinction, it is no longer the cause of suffering. In Buddhism, moral decisions and responsibility are established on this realization, which is not destructive but creative and constructive.

I hope the above explanation will sufficiently respond to the following critical comment by Ogden:

> What he [Abe] never makes clear, at least to me, is how the "universal compassion" that may indeed overcome attachment to self-interest can possibly provide the ground for the differential thought and action apart from which all our meliorative efforts are quite impossible (p. 133).

"Universal compassion" takes place not merely on the socio-historical dimension but essentially at the intersection between the socio-historical dimension and the religious, universal dimension discussed above.

CHRISTIAN CONTRIBUTIONS TO THE DEVELOPMENT OF BUDDHISM

Among the seven respondents, John Cobb is remarkable in offering suggestions about ways Buddhism can develop in the light of Christianity. He not only criticizes the weaknesses of Buddhism but also points out both its potential and the directions in which Buddhism should evolve in the future. This constitutes a highly creative contribution to interfaith dialogue, and my response is one of sincere appreciation.

In his response Cobb discusses a number of issues to be developed in Buddhism, such as the problem of compassion, the criteria of value judgment, the freedom of the will, spontaneity, and human reason. Due to restrictions, I will confine myself to discussion of compassion and the problem of value judgment.

While welcoming my concern over the ultimate criterion of value judgment in the context of Sunyata, Cobb criticizes as too narrow my interpretation of vow and act as the ultimate criterion because I argued that the criterion of judging a thing or action is whether it makes oneself and all others awakened. He writes:

> I would argue that Buddhist judgment is broader and richer than this. It judges positively the relief of suffering in some independence of its connection with awakening. Abe's presentation does not do justice to this characteristic of Buddhist compassion. It therefore does not connect Buddhist compassion successfully to ethics and history. Once again the failure seems to result from unwillingness to consider what

particular things and events are of primary importance in the dependent arising of a particular moment (p. 95).

This is a penetrating criticism, and Buddhists must heed it carefully. In it I detect at least the following three points: (1) Buddhist judgment and compassion should not be limited to the universal and unchanging feature of the world—namely, the continual presence of unawakened persons; (2) Buddhism should concern itself with particular things and events in the world today, and in this way Buddhists can connect their compassion more successfully to ethics and history; (3) Buddhists should not become attached to metaphysical doctrines of dependent co-origination and nondiscrimination. The Buddhist emphasis on nondiscrimination and pure spontaneity perhaps discourages particular concern about particular events, but the recognition of particular differences *is* compatible with the Buddhist teaching of interdependence.

I agree with Cobb's suggestion that we should interpret compassion in ways broader than helping others to awaken. At this point, however, I should like to call attention to my previous assertion that we are always working at the intersection of the horizontal, socio-historical dimension and the vertical, religious dimension, and that the former is the occasion or condition but the latter is the ground or source of human existence. I understood compassion primarily as helping others to awaken to reality because awakening is the ground or root-source of human life—not because Buddhism is concerned with the "universal" feature of the world and hence neglects the "particular." My emphasis on compassion primarily as helping others awaken is based on the realization of the "ground." Further, as I stated earlier, awakening as the ground is opened up through a particular event as "condition," and at the same time it also provides a particular event in the socio-historical dimension as an occasion for the awakening of self and others. Awakening as the ground is inseparable from the particular historical situation as the condition in the above double sense. This is why I stressed that we are always working at the intersection of the eternal religious dimension and the socio-historical dimension. The issue hence is not necessarily one of broadening the scope of our concern.

In her response Catherine Keller raises a question:

Does not the enlightened one work *outside* of the causal net of influence? "Vow and act" notwithstanding, or rather in the light of them, how can the one who is "enlightened" (and should we wait to attain this state before attempting "right action"? How long?) find the motivation to work in and through history, institutions, ongoing relationships? (p. 111).

The enlightened one does not work *outside* the causal net of influence, but in the causal net based on awakening as the ground or source of activity.

It is not that we should wait to attain enlightenment before attempting "right action," but that we should and can attain enlightenment in the midst of the causal net at any moment insofar as we become free from ego-centeredness. One can attain true enlightenment only through helping others to attain enlightenment "in and through history, institutions, ongoing relationships." This is the way of Bodhisattava as the model of a Buddhist.

Even so, there remains a problem. Recognizing that I acknowledge "a level at which ethical and historical considerations are relevant," Cobb makes the following critical remark:

> What I do object to is the speed with which that level is passed over in the quest for the ultimate one. For me as a Christian, also, it is important to relativize the ethical, as Abe knows. But the movement to the Christian level from the ethical one deepens the sense of concrete particularity and historical responsibility. The movement to the Buddhist level in Abe seems to leave all this behind (p. 94).

It is undeniable that the history of Buddhism proves that the Buddhist doctrines of nirvana, Sunyata, and nondiscrimination lead Buddhists to be detached from concrete historical involvement in the sense of responding to social injustice and historical evils.

To overcome such a tendency in Buddhism, I should like to stress the following points:

1. As I stated in my initial essay, Sunyata or nirvana should not be understood as a goal or end to be attained in Buddhist life, but as the ground or the point of departure from which Buddhist life and activity can properly begin. Sunyata as the goal or end of Buddhist life is Sunyata conceived outside one's self-existence, which is not true Sunyata. Sunyata is realized only in and through the self here and now, and is always the ground or the point of departure for Buddhist life.

2. Sunyata has two aspects: wisdom and compassion. They are inseparable and working together in the realization of Sunyata. Wisdom without compassion is not true wisdom; compassion without wisdom is not true compassion. In contrast to the Buddhist pair of "wisdom and compassion," the Christian pair is "love and justice." In Christianity the notion of love is closely linked with the notion of justice. The Bible tells of God's righteousness. God is holy and just. Accordingly, in Christianity, love without justice is not true love and justice without love is not true justice. They are working together in Christian life. The Buddhist equivalent to the Christian notion of love is the notion of compassion, but there is no Buddhist equivalent to the Christian notion of justice.

Overall, Buddhist history shows indifference to social evil. There are such exceptions as Nichiren's emphasis on justice as opposed to injustice, and Pure Land Buddhist revolts against feudal lords who attempted to extend political control over religious orders, but the general attitude of

Buddhism toward social injustice has been rather weak. This lack of a strong notion of justice leads Buddhists to be less active than Christians in their social and historical lives. It is important for Buddhists to grapple with the question of how to incorporate the notion of justice into the traditional context of wisdom and compassion.

3. If I am not mistaken, the Christian notion of justice has at least two aspects. The first is justice as a kind of balancing between human beings as they strive to actualize their potential for being.[1] The second is justice that entails judgment and punishment. The first aspect of justice is defined by Paul Tillich as "the form in which power of being actualizes itself in the encounter of power with power"[2] and as "the form of the reunion of the separated."[3] This aspect of justice is not antithetical to the Buddhist notion of wisdom and compassion. But it is hard for Buddhism to incorporate the second aspect of justice into itself, and in my opinion it is not necessary for it to do so. Justice in the second sense is a two-edged sword. On the one hand, it judges sharply what is right and what is wrong. On the other hand, judgment based on justice naturally calls forth a counter-judgment as a reaction from the side judged. Accordingly, we fall into an endless conflict and struggle between judge and judged. Gautama Buddha clearly realized this endless conflict as a result of the judgment inherent in the notion of justice. He said that to meet resentment with resentment is to give rise to endless conflict. Instead, the Buddha preached the interrelationality between things and the nonexistence of any fixed self-nature.

We must be careful in applying the Buddhist notion of interrelationality and compassion within the social level, however, because such an application may serve to mask social inequality and injustice. This is an important warning I received from liberation theology. Buddhists must develop "dynamic Sunyata" and create a new notion of justice on the basis of wisdom and compassion, which, while clearly realizing distinctions, can actualize and maintain the balance of power.

THE PROBLEM OF THE HOLOCAUST: THE RELATIONSHIP BETWEEN ETHICS AND RELIGION

In my initial essay I presented "A Buddhist View of the Holocaust" partly as a test case for discussing the problem of ethics and religion in Buddhism and Christianity, and partly to open up Jewish-Buddhist dialogue. Because the problem of the Holocaust during the Second World War is such a sensitive and subtle issue, I tried to understand it as deeply as possible from my Buddhist point of view. I waited anxiously for the Jewish and Christian reaction to my presentation. Now I find that although a few respondents expressed sympathy with my interpretation of Auschwitz in the context of collective karma, most respondents presented strong disagreements with my statement that while Auschwitz is an unpardonable absolute evil in the human, moral dimension, from the ultimate religious point of view it should be taken as a relative rather than an absolute evil. Because this disagreement clearly reflects characteristics of the Jewish and Christian ways of thinking, I should like to heed their voices carefully and reconsider my own Buddhist view of the Holocaust. At the same time I am afraid that my Buddhist interpretation is not sufficiently understood by my respondents, so I should like to clarify it further.

Moltmann expresses concern that my karmic interpretation might lead to a relativizing of the Holocaust. John Cobb calls for specificity:

Original sin and *avidya* have always been with us, but events like the Holocaust are fortunately not everyday occurrences. A specific event requires specific explanation. Awareness of interconnectedness aids in this explanation, but it does not take its place (p. 93).

The basic problems involved in this regard are that of how we should understand the relation between the historical, ethical dimension and the universal religious dimension of human existence, and how we are to understand the particularity and uniqueness of such a historical event as the Holocaust. In this section of my rejoinder I will clarify the relation between ethics and religion, and in the next section I will discuss the uniqueness of the Holocaust and a way to cope with this problem.

In my understanding, the ethical arena of human life is part of the horizontal, socio-historical dimension whereas religion involves the vertical, eternal dimension. I hold this view because ethics concerns human-human relationships whereas religion concerns the divine-human relationship. The former functions in this immanent realm whereas the latter pertains to the transcendent realm. They are thus essentially or qualitatively different from one another. This means that there is no continuous path from ethics to religion. In order to enter the realm of religion, human ethics must be overcome. Ethics must "die." In other words, however important ethics may be to human beings, ethics cannot stand alone, because when carried out as far as possible, ethical life falls into a dilemma and finally collapses. We can see this dilemma in St. Paul's painful confession: For the good which I would I do not; but the evil which I would not, that I practice — wretched man that I am! Who shall deliver me out of the body of this death? This is not peculiar to St. Paul but inevitable to all seriously reflective persons, including Buddhists. It is also stated in Exodus that God told Moses he could not see his face without dying. We can encounter God not directly but only through death — a spiritual death. In Buddhism the great death as the death of the ego is emphasized as the necessary moment for awakening. In this regard, religion is not an extension of ethics.

Accordingly, we must clearly realize that because the "death" of ethics is inevitable, there is no direct and continuous path from ethics to religion. We must also realize, however, that there is a path — directly in Christianity, but dialectically through negation in Buddhism — from religion to ethics, for ethics can be established anew by religion. Religion beyond rigid ethical judgment can provide a new basis for ethical judgment without falling into the existential dilemma concerning good and evil.

Up to this point of the discussion, there is no fundamental difference between Buddhism and Christianity. Going a step further, however, we see a significant difference between the two. This difference primarily comes from their different understandings of religious transcendence. Transcendence in Christianity indicates God and God's kingdom whereas transcendence in Buddhism refers to Buddha (an awakened one) and nirvana. This is not merely a verbal difference. In historical Christianity God is the God of love and justice, and God is the supreme good. Accordingly, even in the transcendent religious realm, nondistinction is not the final word. New distinctions based on divine providence must be established on the basis of nondiscriminative equality. Although God makes the sun rise on the evil and the good, they must undergo the last judgment. If I am not mistaken, Christian ethics and moral judgment are established on this new distinction based on divine providence and are eschatologically oriented.

In contrast, however important they may be, if Buddha and nirvana as the symbols of Buddhist transcendence are grasped as "transcendence" and substantialized or reified as if they were an unchangeable and supreme good, they fall short of being the ultimate reality. For transcendence (Buddha and nirvana) thus substantialized is not completely free from distinction. Although this transcendence indicates nondistinction as the negation of distinction, it is still involved in a form of distinction—that is, a distinction between distinction and nondistinction. In order to attain true equality, nondistinction as the negation of distinction must be overcome; transcendence as the negation of immanence must be negated or transcended. Such a double negation is necessary to attain true equality or true transcendence. This means that we must clearly realize not only the nonsubstantiality or emptiness of everything's distinctiveness in the socio-historical dimension but also the nonsubstantiality or emptiness of Buddha and nirvana in the religious dimension. The nonsubstantial emptiness of both the immanent, secular realm and the transcendent, sacred realm must be fully realized. Since this realization of emptiness that refers to both the secular and sacred realm is based on the double negation or the negation of negation, it is not a static state of emptiness but a dynamic function of *emptying* everything, including itself. This dynamic function of emptying is nothing but Sunyata in the Buddhist sense, and this is "transcendence," to use the term, in Buddhism.

We may therefore say that Christian transcendence is God as the supreme good whereas Buddhist transcendence is Sunyata which is neither good nor evil. This means that while the religious dimension in Christianity is realized by overcoming ethics and the good-evil distinction, it is oriented by God as the supreme good. Thus the relation between ethics and religion is not realized to be fully discontinuous but rather continuous, at least in the move from religion to ethics. In Buddhism, on the other hand, religious transcendence is not God as the supreme good but Sunyata, which is neither good nor evil; and the relation between ethics and religion is realized to be fully discontinuous, not only in the move from ethics to religion but also in the move from religion to ethics. This implies that in Buddhism, ethics is to be established in the religious dimension not directly — as God's commandment in the case of Christianity — but dialectically through the realization of Sunyata and dependent co-origination.

Reflecting on my statement, "while in a human moral dimension the Holocaust should be condemned as an unpardonable, absolute evil, from the ultimate religious point of view even it should not be taken as an absolute but a relative evil," Ogden raises a question:

> What could Abe mean by this if not that from the ultimate religious point of view, authorized by the emptiness and interdependence of all things, even "absolute" moral differences cease to make any difference? After all, any "relative" difference they could make would have to be a difference within the ethical dimension, not the religious one (p. 132).

Reading these statements, I get the impression that Ogden thinks that there is a continuous path from ethics to religion. Moral difference in the socio-historical dimension does not, however, translate *directly* to the religious, eternal dimension. This is the case even with the "absolute" moral difference insofar as it takes place in the horizontal socio-historical dimension. If one *absolutizes* moral difference on the socio-historical dimension, it will result in an endless conflict between "good" and "evil" and fall into a hopeless dilemma. Only through this collapse of moral difference on the socio-historical dimension can there emerge the eternal, religious dimension in which the difference and distinctiveness of everything is realized in the entirely new light of the divine.

Perhaps Ogden implies in the above statement that the absolute moral difference does not or should not cease to make a difference but should continue to be an "absolute difference" in light of divine providence and divine justice. This perhaps is the fundamental Christian understanding of the issue. However, is not divine providence and divine justice in the ultimate religious dimension opened up by overcoming the human ethical dimension? Because the discontinuity from ethics to religion and the collapse of ethics as the necessary moment for reaching the religious dimension are not clear in Ogden, "divine providence" and "divine justice" might be projections from his human ethical side. If divine providence and divine justice are not his projections, they must be realized through the negation of human ethics, including even "absolute" moral difference.

John Cobb also criticizes what he sees as the insufficiency of my interpretation of Buddhist compassion and suggests that I focus more on the particular historical situation. He also calls me to consider the various forms of suffering and possible responses to them.

I greatly appreciate his critical comments and advice, for there are many things Buddhists can learn from Christianity in this regard. It is my failure if my discussion of compassion gives the impression that the only task of an awakened one is to have others awaken. I emphasized the importance of awakening others as the essential function of compassion because awakening is the ground of human life. As I repeatedly mentioned before, however, the religious dimension and the socio-historical dimension are inseparable from one another in human existence and we are always working at the intersection of the two. Accordingly, if the compassionate work of awakening others takes place apart from the socio-historical context, it is abstract and unreal. Rather, it must be done out of connection with socio-historical events as the necessary conditions. On the other hand, compassionate work in the socio-historical dimension without a religious ground might be humanitarian or socialistic work, but not Buddhist work. Buddhists must work from the religious ground — that is, the realization of Sunyata and dependent co-origination in connection with even small events in the socio-historical dimension. And Buddhists can deepen their realization of Sunyata and dependent co-origination through such involvement in socio-historical events.

In historical Buddhism this involvement has been limited, focusing on culture — including the arts and literature — though not extending significantly to social, political, and economic issues. In order for Buddhism to be active in the contemporary world situation, it must be more theologically and practically involved in particular social-historical events from its religious ground. In this connection there are many things for Buddhism to learn from Christianity.

THE PROBLEM OF HOLOCAUST: ITS UNIQUENESS AND SOLUTION

In reading Eugene Borowitz's response, "Dynamic Sunyata and God whose Glory Fills the Universe," I was deeply moved by how horrible the Holocaust was, and still is, to Jewish people and how seriously they have been struggling for a new way of Jewish community after the Holocaust. Although in my initial essay I tried to understand the Holocaust as deeply as possible through Emil Fackenheim, I am left with the impression that the Jewish experience of the Holocaust is beyond the comprehension of any non-Jew. This impression does not, however, prevent me from an inquiry into the meaning of the Holocaust and participation in Jewish-Buddhist dialogue. For I am concerned with the problem of the Holocaust as a human being, and the significance of the Holocaust for religion is an inescapable issue for me as a Buddhist.

In his response, Borowitz says that the ultimate issue is not how we can now think, though that is important to *homo sapiens*. Rather, it is how we might now mend our covenant relationship with God "so that the essential *Tikkun*, the mending of human history, can take place." (p. 81). Further, emphasizing the importance of "creating various new-old ways to live in Covenant," Borowitz states that, "neither philosophy nor theology is the basis for identifying the critical Jewish response to the Holocaust. Instead, the surprisingly positive activity of the Jewish community in the post-Holocaust period finally forced Jewish thinkers to reflect on its meaning" (p. 81). This confirmed what I had sensed about contemporary Jewish people after the Holocaust.

In order to properly and sufficiently understand the above statement, it is necessary for me as a Buddhist to understand the basic standpoint of Judaism. As the key characteristics of Judaism, Borowitz emphasizes divine forgiveness, the responsibility and capability of all people to turn from evil, and the creation of holiness through righteous living. Learning this, I have realized that in Judaism the relation between ethics and religion is not understood to be discontinuous but distinctively continuous. Judaism is clearly different from Buddhism, a tradition in which there is no continuous path from ethics to religion or from religion to ethics, for in Buddhism ethics and religion are dialectically connected through mutual negation. It is also significantly different from Christianity in which there is a continuous path from religion to ethics (God's commandments constitute the basis of ethics) but there is no continuous path from ethics to religion (before God "there is none righteous, no, not one"). This characteristic of Judaism is all the more evident when Borowitz states that "because God is holy/good, Jews are to be holy/good" (p. 82). This means that in Judaism the realization of spiritual death ("the wages of sin is death") and great death (the complete death of the human ego) are absent.

It is thus quite natural for Borowitz to disagree with my idea that "all issues are properly and legitimately understood *ultimately* from the vantage point of the third dimension," which is different from the human ethical dimension and is "a transhuman, fundamental dimension represented by religious faith or awakening" (p. 46). And it is even more natural for him not to accept my statement, "while in a human, moral dimension the Holocaust should be condemned as an unpardonable, absolute evil, from the ultimate religious point of view even it should not be taken as an absolute but a relative evil" (p. 53).

At this point I must return to Jewish experience for clarification.

The Holocaust was not a case of genocide. . . . The genocides of modern history spring from motives, human, if evil, such as greed, hatred, or simply blind, xenophobic passion. This is true even when they masquerade under high-flown ideologies. The Nazi genocide of the Jewish people did not masquerade under an ideology. . . . The ideal was to rid the world of Jews as one rids oneself of lice. It was also, however, to punish the Jews for their "crime" and the crime in question was [Jews'] existence itself (Emil Fackenheim, Foreword, in Yehudah Bauer, *The Jewish Emergence from Powerlessness* [Ann Arbor, Mich.: Books on Demand, Univ. of Mich. Microfilms, 1979]).

In this context I understand Borowitz with deep sympathy when he states:

The caring Jewish community will overwhelmingly reject the suggestion that, for all the trauma connected with the Holocaust, we ought to understand that it *ultimately* has no significance; or, to put it more directly, that ultimately there is no utterly fundamental distinction between the Nazi death camp operators and their victims (p. 83).

Why, then, did I state, "from the ultimate religious point of view even it [the Holocaust] should not be taken as an absolute but a relative evil"? In order to answer this question I should like to elucidate my standpoint by emphasizing the following six points:

1. In my Buddhist understanding, all things in the universe are interdependent, co-arising, and co-ceasing—nothing exists by itself.

2. Each and every human deed is conditioned by the socio-historical situation in which it takes place and yet the person is thoroughly self-responsible because the act is determined ultimately by the individual's free will. In Buddhist terminology this volitional act is call karma.

3. Karma is individual as well as collective, deeply rooted in the fundamental ignorance (*avidya*) and blind will to live innate in human existence. In the individual aspect of karma we are responsible for everything caused by *our own avidya* realized in the innermost depth of our existence, while in the collective aspect of karma we are responsible for everything caused by *human avidya* universally rooted in human nature.

4. In our collective karma nothing happens in the universe entirely unrelated to us insofar as we realize that everything human is ultimately rooted in the fundamental ignorance (*avidya*) innate in human nature.

5. It is from the realization of this collective karma that in my initial article I stated that although I have no direct social or historical involvement in the Holocaust, "I am not free from responsibility for the Holocaust in Auschwitz. I must accept that 'Auschwitz is a problem of my own karma. In the deepest sense I myself participated as well in the Holocaust'" (p. 50).

6. Since the Holocaust is *ultimately* rooted in the fundamental ignorance and the endless blind thirst to live inherent in human existence, in which I am also deeply involved through my own individual karma, "I am sharing the blame of the Holocaust because at the depth of my existence I am participating in the fundamental ignorance together with the overt assailants in the Holocaust" (p. 51).

Does this realization of collective karma and sharing of responsibility at the *ultimate* level of human existence reduce the uniqueness of the Holocaust and obscure the particular evil and horrible acts of the Nazis? Should we reject such a realization at the ultimate level, move to the socio-historical level, and persistently blame the Holocaust as the absolute evil? If we do, how can we solve the problem of the Holocaust without falling into an endless dilemma of hatred and counter-hatred? Is not this realization the only legitimate basis on which we can solve the problem of the Holocaust and work creatively toward the future?

It is from this realization of collective karma and the sharing of responsibility at the ultimate level of our existence, not from the socio-historical, ethical dimension, that I suggested that "the Holocaust should not be taken as an absolute but a relative evil." The realization of collective karma and the sharing of responsibility do not make the uniqueness of the Holocaust insignificant. Rather, a clear realization of its uniqueness opens up a new spiritual horizon in which we can work cooperatively to build a better world in the future.

Accordingly, I greatly appreciate the Jewish response to the Holocaust described by Borowitz:

> The almost unanimous response of Jewish thinkers and lay people to the Holocaust has been to try to act to frustrate its goals and prevent its replication. Negatively, that means opposing evil wherever one sees it; positively, it means fostering goodness to the extent that one can. And this form of *Tikkun* has been the most important Jewish response to the Holocaust (p. 82).

Together with the appreciation of such a Jewish response to the Holocaust I cannot help but ask how Jewish people understand that the holy/good God ultimately allowed such a uniquely horrible event as the holocaust to occur and whether the Holocaust has a fixed, enduring, absolutely evil nature. At one point Borowitz writes: "insofar as the 'absolute' God is holy/good, the Holocaust is enduringly evil" (p. 84). This is perhaps the inevitable stance of Judaism. It is also emphasized by Fackenheim (with whom Borowitz seems to agree), however, that the Holocaust is a radical rupture in history in which the Jewish people's very Covenant with God is questioned. How *Tikkun*, the mending of human history, can be attained is the central task of post-Holocaust theology.

If I understand Borowitz correctly, he suggests two possible approaches in this regard. One is a return to the God of the Covenant through belief in the ultimate commanding power of living in holy goodness. The other is a shift in the direction of mysticism as suggested by Richard L. Rubenstien. Borowitz opts for the first, not the second. I myself support the second approach.

According to Borowitz, traditional Jewish believers hope the goodness of God day by day will set the context for their confrontation with evil. This hope is based on the classical Jewish understanding that "because God is holy/good, Jews are to be holy/good, which means to do holy/good deeds and create a holy/good human order, which ultimately embraces nature in its fulfillment, with God's help" (p. 82). I admire such faith and hope, but my personal existential experience does not allow me to accept this sort of faith and hope as realistic. In my personal experience the more seriously I tried to do good and to avoid evil, the more clearly I realized myself to be far away from good and to be involved in evil. The realization of the radical evil at the bottom of the struggle between good and evil, and the realization of my fundamental ignorance of ultimate truth were the outcome of my ethical life. In short, this realization in its ultimate form was nothing other than a realization of the death of the ego-self. Through this realization of the ego's death, however, the "holy" was opened up in me. It is not, however, God as the absolute good but God as the absolute nothingness that is neither good nor evil and yet both good and evil dynamically. To me, this realization of absolute nothingness is the basis of my life and the source of my activity. In this sense I find a great affinity with Rubenstein, to whom God is "the Holy Nothingness," and with Jewish mysticism in general.

To me, the realization of the spiritual death of the ego is essential for a new religious life. It is the radical realization of our finitude in both the ethical and the ontological senses. It is not a pessimistic but a highly realistic event, which provides us with a basis for a resurrected, creative life. From this point of view the Holocaust is not the responsibility of the holy/good God but our responsibility, to be realized through the death of the ego in the bottomless depths of our existence.

Let me now say several things in response to Professor Borowitz's letter. It is my interpretation that, with regard to Nietzsche's idea of the three stages of human history, the first stage "may be said" to correspond to the time of the Old Testament. Borowitz criticizes me by saying, "In this context 'the time of the Old Testament,' and thus the 'Old Testament' itself, and thus the Judaism derived from it are identified with *pre-moral* religion" (my emphasis). Borowitz also indicates that the charge that Judaism is "premoral" is part of traditional Christian anti-Semitism. (He carefully corrects this statement later and replaces it by a statement that the charge "is a creation of post-Enlightenment anti-Semitism—and a typical example of secularism" (pp. 88–89).

All these criticisms and comments, it seems to me, are based on Borowitz's view that in *Beyond Good and Evil* Nietzsche divides history into premoral, moral, and postmoral periods. This is certainly a possible interpretation, for in his writing Nietzsche himself attaches the label "the moral epoch of mankind" to the second stage. But he does not explicitly use the term "premoral" for the first stage and the term "postmoral" for the third stage. Moreover, a careful reading of the text leads us to understand that the main point of Nietzsche's scheme of three historical stages parallels three different ways of sacrifice and not necessarily three stages characterized as premoral, moral, and postmoral. Nietzsche speaks of the first stage as follows: "Once upon a time, man sacrificed human beings to their God and perhaps just those they loved the best." As for the second stage Nietzsche states, "They [humans] sacrificed to their God the strongest instincts they possessed, their 'nature!' " And about the third stage he asks himself, "Finally, what still remained to be sacrificed? Was it not necessary to sacrifice God himself?" He answers, "To sacrifice God for nothingness." As can be seen clearly, Nietzsche is concerned with historical transitions in modes of sacrifice that lead to the "advent of nihilism," in which, he insists, as active nihilists we must endure nihility without God. Accordingly, while his three stages of human history may be interpreted as premoral, moral, and postmoral, this is not his main concern in the text.

This understanding of the text is the basis of my interpretation of it. For this reason I state in my initial essay, "To the first stage of human history Nietzsche ascribes the sacrifice of all primitive religions and also the sacrifice of the Emperor Tiberius in the Mithra Grotto on the Island of Capri." Then, when I mentioned the time of the Old Testament in relation to the first stage I did not use the term "premoral" but stated, "It may be said that this first stage corresponds to the time of the Old Testament, which relates the stories of this kind of sacrifice in such cases as Abraham and Isaac."

Accordingly, if my identifying the first stage with the time of the Old Testament must be criticized, we must examine whether the time of the Old Testament can be properly identified with the time in which people sacrificed to their God those they loved the best. Since the story of Abraham and Isaac is so remarkable in the Old Testament I stated that the first stage "may be said" to correspond to the time of the Old Testament. Accordingly, I hope it is now clear that my intention was not to identify the time of the Old Testament with the premoral period or to say that Judaism—derived from the "Old Testament"—is a premoral religion.

At the end of his letter Borowitz writes, "What astonishes me is that the four academics [including two Jews] to whom you express gratitude for their suggestions did not call the offensiveness of this material to your attention." I understand, however, that they were not insensitive to "the offensiveness of this material" but understood my point properly as I have now clarified it again.

TIME AND HISTORY

In connection with the problem of ethics, the problem of time and history has been discussed in our Buddhist-Christian dialogue. In this section of my rejoinder I will focus on the reversibility of time, and the forward movement of time.

1. The Buddhist notion of the *reversibility of time* needs further clarification. It does not indicate the type of reversibility of time expounded by

natural scientists. Physicists, for instance, talk about the reversibility and repeatability of time in the laboratory. In this case the reversibility of time is demonstrated by experiment by abstracting all concrete material, natural and human, from the process of time. It is proved purely abstractly or mechanistically by removing all living realities from time. The Buddhist notion of the reversibility of time is also different from the type of reversibility exhibited when we reverse a movie. This sort of reversibility is realized technically, only in an artificial sense.

On the other hand, as Altizer rightly points out, the Buddhist notion of the reversibility of time is not to be confused with a mythical reversibility of time as found in the primordial myth of eternal return. The mythical notion of the reversibility of time is realized not by abstracting but rather by fully including the concrete living stuff of realities, natural, human, and divine. It is based on the cyclical view of time, which is divine work. It does, however, lack the realization of nonsubstantiality or emptiness of being and time, the realization essential to the Buddhist notion of the reversibility of time. The Buddhist notion of the reversibility of time is neither mechanistic nor mythological — it is entirely demythologized.

How is reversibility possible? Buddhism understands time without any creator or ruler of time who is beyond time. Time is grasped in terms of ever-changing processes, especially the process of living-dying. Buddhism does not regard life and death as two different entities, but as one indivisible reality that is "living-dying." When we grasp our life subjectively or existentially from within, we realize we are living and dying fully at each and every moment; in light of this inseparability, I said that we "are not moving from life to death, but in the process of living-dying" (p. 59).

In short, living and dying are two inseparable aspects of one and the same reality, and this process of living-dying is undirectional. However, we must also realize that this process of "living-dying" has no beginning and no end. The process extends beyond our present life both into the direction of the remote past and into the direction of the distant future. With no God as creator and ruler of the universe, Buddhism holds no notion of creation as the beginning of time and no notion of last judgment as the end of time. Instead, what is important is the clear realization of the beginninglessness and endlessness of time as well as the process of living-dying. For if one clearly and existentially realizes the beginninglessness and endlessness of the process of living-dying at *this moment*, the whole process of living-dying is concentrated *into this moment*. In other words, this moment embraces the whole process of living-dying by virtue of the clear realization of the beginninglessness and endlessness of the process of living-dying. One can thus transcend the beginningless and endless process of living-dying at this moment.

This implies at least the following three points:

(a) Through the clear realization of the beginninglessness and endlessness of the process of living-dying (samsara) at this moment in samsara, one transcends samsara into nirvana: nirvana is realized in the midst of samsara, not at the end of samsara.

(b) Through this realization at this moment in time one transcends time into eternity; eternity is realized in the midst of time, not at the end of time.

(c) This transcendence or "trans-descendence" is possible by cutting off the process of living-dying and opening up the bottomless depth of the trans-temporal, eternal dimension. This cutting off is possible not by our speculation but by our religious practice and the "death" of the ego-self (See Diagram 1).

Diagram 1

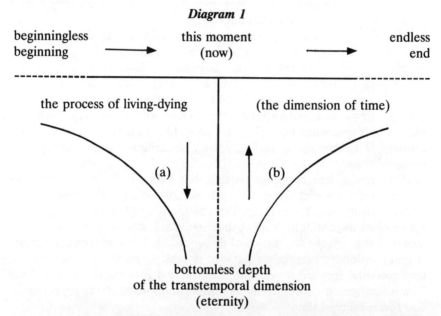

beginningless beginning ⟶ this moment (now) ⟶ endless end

the process of living-dying | (the dimension of time)

(a) | (b)

bottomless depth
of the transtemporal dimension
(eternity)

The cutting off of the beginningless and endless process of living-dying or time and the opening up of the bottomless depth of eternity have the following two meanings:

Through the cutting off and the opening up one goes down or transdescends into the bottomless depth of the transtemporal dimension and realizes eternity right "below" the present (a). This is the aspect of wisdom in which time is overcome. From this depth of eternity one can grasp or embrace the entire process of living-dying without beginning and without end, and thus can reverse the process. The unidirectionality of time is thus overcome and the reversibility of time is realized from this bottomless depth of eternity.

Through the cutting off of time and the opening up of eternity, one rises up from the bottomless depth to the dimension of temporality and moves forward toward the endless end along the process of living-dying (b). But now, coming from the bottomless depth of eternity, one is not confined by living-dying while one is working for others in the midst of living-dying. This is the aspect of compassion in which one tries endlessly to save others.

In the cutting off of the process of time and the opening up of the depth of eternity, the going down into and the coming up from the depth of eternity work together. This is the structure of this moment, the "now" — which is dynamically related to the bottomless depth of eternity — that is, nirvana. One's movement from this moment to the next moment always involves this dynamic structure.

Accordingly, we must say that time has two aspects: the aspect of continuity or forward movement and the aspect of discontinuity or "trans-descending" movement. And these two aspects are dynamically linked together at each and every moment.

The usual understanding of time as a continuity or a unidirectional forward movement represents only one aspect of time and is thus not sufficiently real. We must ask several questions to those who embrace this understanding. Where does one take one's stand when one understands time as a unidirectional continuity and a forward movement from the past, through the present, and into the future? Does not the person stand somewhat *outside* time when he or she talks about time in terms of unidirectional continuity? Is this understanding not an objectification and conceptualization of time?

If we grasp time not from outside, but existentially from within, we realize the discontinuity of time at each moment — that is, the depth of time rather than the expanse of time. The continuity of time without the realization of its discontinuity is an abstraction. Real continuity of time is realized only through the realization of discontinuity. Discontinuous continuity is real continuity. Passageless passage is real passage. An unrepeatable, unidirectional forward movement is not a real forward movement. Real forward movement must include its self-negation — that is, the repeatability and reversibility of time.

Christianity seems to realize this dialectical nature of time to some extent. In Christianity creation is not fixed at the beginning of time. Theologians talk about sustaining creation, directing creation (Tillich), and eternal creation. Again, the eschaton is not restricted to the end of history. Theologians speak of realized eschatology (C.H. Dodd) as well as future eschatology. In Christianity, however, the dialectical nature of time in terms of discontinuous continuity or repeatable forward movement is not fully realized. As a whole, Christianity is future-oriented. This is because Christianity does not grasp time as it is in its reality, but as a creation of God and something ruled by God who is essentially trans-temporal. If Christian eschatology is not a completely realized eschatology and Christians are believed to live in the *Zwischenzeit* — that is, the time between the first coming and the second coming of Christ — is there not an "optical illusion" in Christian eschatology?[4]

With this understanding of time and its reversibility in mind, I should like to comment on the responses by Keller and Altizer. In her response Keller writes:

> That difference which I make in the future of my world, my relationship, cannot be reversed. Our causal — ethical — responsibility is in this sense nonnegotiable. My effects on the world can be altered, negotiated, diminished or augmented, but what I become and do here and now cannot be retroactively annihilated. The intuition into the irreversible spiral of time may be essential not only to a feminist sensibility ... but also to any liberationist commitment to justice in history (p. 110).

It is undeniable that "what I become and do here and now cannot be retroactively annihilated" insofar as we remain in the dimension of time in which unidirectional continuity is predominant. However, if we cut through this process of time and open up the transtemporal, eternal depth through our religious practice — or, to use a more Christian way of expression, if we give up our will and be open to God's will by saying, "not as I will, but as thou wilt" (Matthew 21:39) — it is not necessarily impossible to alter the meaning of our past deed.

For instance, if we give up our will completely in our heartfelt repentance and accept God's will through prayer — if God so wills and forgives us — we may be redeemed from our past sinful deed. Of course, this does not mean that our past deed becomes undone. But the meaning of that past deed to our life at this present moment may be changed through our repentance and God's forgiveness.

At this point some may say that it is only a change of meaning, not a change of fact, that it is merely a cognitive change, not a real change. I must ask ourselves at this point, however, if there are any pure facts apart from meaning for us in this actual world. In our living reality every fact has a certain meaning for us. Meaning and fact are inseparable. A sheer fact devoid of meaning is an abstract idea, not a real fact. Accordingly, we can say with justification that through our repentance and God's forgiveness the meaning of our past deed to our life at this moment may be retroactively changed. Our past deed is now regrasped in light of God's forgiveness. Otherwise, such a religious practice as repentance or *metanoia* is either meaningless or a self-deception. Repentance is not a psychological change of consciousness but a turning away from a life of rebellion to God through the death of our ego. (This refers to the move [a] to the bottomless depth of eternity.) Repentance also includes responsiveness to the will of God, which is ongoing through the gift of grace. (This refers to the move [b] from the bottomless depth of eternity to the dimension of temporality.) Accordingly, the realization of the reversibility of time through the cutting off of the process of time and the opening up of the depth of eternity does not conflict with, but rather supports, the "intuition into the irreversible spiral of time" essential to the relational responsibility of the feminist or others working toward human liberation.

2. With regard to the *forward movement of time*, Altizer emphasizes the importance of a modern Christian's belief in the forward movement of history, which was the center of the political and social revolutions of the modern world. He warns us about forms of Christianity and Buddhism that stake their destiny upon the erasure and dissolution of the forward movement of time and history. He also takes Hegelianism and the Kyoto School as Christian and Buddhist models for a new way of thinking, which state the "absence of any objective manifestation of God or the absolute from our history and consciousness, an absence that is nevertheless a possible sign of the full or total presence of absolute Spirit or Sunyata" (p. 75). After suggesting that in Buddhism the pure simultaneity of time does not preclude the possibility of a truly forward historical movement, Altizer stresses that although there is a difference between Christian time and Buddhist time in that the Christian knows the incarnation as a once-and-for-all and final event, both the Christian apprehension of the incarnation and ancient Buddhism are radical instances of demythologizing. To this point of the discussion, I appreciate Altizer's understanding of Buddhism and have no fundamental disagreement.

Then Altizer raises a question and states:

Is it not rather that Buddhism divests time of all positive identity, therein and thereby negating every possible positive or definite image of time, including the images of past and future? Here is a demythologizing as radical or more radical than that of Christianity, and a demythologizing dissolving every possible image or sign. Consequently, it is not that Buddhism is closed to the possibility of a forward-moving and irreversible historical time, but rather that Buddhism transcends and negates every possible identity of history and time (p. 76).

My question in this regard is how Altizer thinks that Buddhism "divests time of all positive identity, therein and thereby negating every possible positive or definite image of time, including the images of past and future." Buddhism "divests time of all positive identity" not while remaining in the dimension of temporality, but, as I discussed earlier, from the transtemporal depth of eternity after cutting through the temporal dimension. And this trans-temporal depth of eternity is the root-source of temporality to which the descending movement from the dimension of temporality returns and from which the ascending movement to the dimension of temporality springs. Time dies and is reborn at each and every moment. Accordingly, Buddhism is not closed to the possibility of a forward-moving and irreversible historical time; further, it affirms anew every possible identity of history and time on the basis of the transtemporal depth of eternity.

To a Buddhist, in any moment of the beginningless and endless process of history, to move forward toward the future is nothing but to return to the source of time and history, and to return to the source of time and history is to move forward toward the future.

Accordingly, I do not agree with Altizer when he states that "the pure simultaneity of Buddhist time is a purely negative simultaneity ... because rather than conjoining present, past, and future, it knows a pure and empty time with no possible concrete temporal dimension or dimensions."

Toward the end of his response, referring to Buddhist emptiness and the crucifixion of God, Altizer writes:

> Christian theology itself will inevitably be partial and incomplete if it fails to realize for itself a Buddhist ground, and a Buddhist ground that is not only inseparable from a Christian ground, but a Buddhist ground that in this perspective will inevitably be known as a Christian ground. The Kyoto School discovered a Christianity that it could know as a Buddhist ground, and discovered it by way of the Christian symbol of the death or kenosis of God, a symbol it was able to understand as a symbol of an absolute and total self-emptying (p. 77).

This is a very important and insightful suggestion, with encouraging potential for future Buddhist-Christian dialogue.

FEMINIST CRITIQUE AND A BUDDHIST RESPONSE

I find Catherine Keller's response quite discerning and provocative. Her feminist criticism is a serious challenge to Buddhism in general and to me in particular. As Keller detected, I had "not even the faintest feminist concern" in my essay, although I tried to avoid gender-specific language as much as possible, deeming what I wrote to be relevant to all people, male and female. Keller's basic criticism of the present Buddhist-Christian dialogue is that it neglects "the most obvious common denominator of these two world religions: their patriarchalism." Upon this basic criticism Keller develops her discussion.

First, she asserts the need "to ask whether the kenosis doctrine as Abe interprets it helps or hinders the prophetic purposes of women." With regard to this question Keller writes:

> If Sunyata must be understood as a state of absolute selflessness, Abe's move will tend to reinforce the more patriarchal implications of the kenotic Christ idea. But inasmuch as his strategy serves to underscore the panrelational interdependence in the universe, then the implicit iconoclasm of dynamic Sunyata can support a feminist revision of kenosis (p. 104).

Later she argues that my "interpretation of the kenosis passage in Philippians brings us (inadvertently) to the very heart of women's disenchantment with traditional religious categories, but also of our hope for certain radical revisions" (p. 105).

Insofar as the political aspect of religion is concerned, we must recognize how the move to Sunyata might tend to reinforce the more patriarchal implications of traditional religion. But if we grasp the emphasis on Sunyata or kenosis existentially from within, the move to it, as Keller indicates, will open up "the panrelational interdependence in the universe." We must clearly discern these two aspects—the aspect of politics and that of inner existential realization—and their interrelationship. They correspond to what I discussed earlier as the horizontal, socio-historical dimension and the vertical, eternal-religious dimension. We must be aware that we are always standing at *the intersection* of these two dimensions. Yet most religious thinkers (up to this point in history usually male), including myself, have emphasized the ideal of selflessness in the vertical religious dimension, while failing to recognize its negative effect of reinforcing the oppression of women in the horizontal, socio-historical dimension. Now, however, feminist theologians are pointing out this negative political aspect and attacking the patriarchal approach as the source of the oppression of women. It is urgently necessary for us to eradicate this negative effect of the teaching of selflessness.

This should not, however, lead to an undermining of the ideal of selflessness. Rather, while correcting the negative effect of reinforcing the oppression of women in the political dimension, we should maintain the ideals of self-emptying and selflessness in the religious dimension. In taking this approach, we must fully realize the paradoxical inseparability of the two dimensions and work dynamically at their intersection.

Accordingly, although I understand the sentiment and background of Elizabeth Cady Stanton's words, "Self-development is a higher duty than self-sacrifice," I cannot completely agree with them, for the issue is not that of whether self-development or self-sacrifice is more important, but that of how we can confront the conflict between self-development and self-sacrifice and break beyond this dilemma to open up a deeper spiritual horizon in which self-sacrifice in a religious sense is self-development. The crucial issue in this regard is how to grasp one's own self, how to understand the problem of the self.

For this reason, I greatly appreciate Keller's statement: "Often one hears 'women need to have a self before they can sacrifice it.' Yet this sentiment falls short of what I take the more radical feminist project to be: the reconstruction of the very notion of self" (p. 106).

A new norm of selfhood calls for the transformation of women's profound relational sensitivity and affective vitality into an acknowledged strength. Thus Keller states:

We will not be able to return now or—I hope—in the foreseeable future, to embrace any ideals of self-sacrifice, self-denial, and self-lessness that have not first thoroughly struggled with the concrete contexts in which selfhood is *engendered* [p. 106].

Here I see that Keller is well aware of the conflict between self-denial and self-development, and is trying to go beyond the conflict. Immediately after the above statement, however, when Keller raises the following questions, I wonder if she perhaps misses the most crucial point:

In this way I fear that Masao Abe's coupling of Christian self-sacrifice with Buddhist *anatta* attenuates the problem. Will the Christian-Buddhist dialogue offer the worst of both worlds to women? How can the two patriarchies, with their common problem of the inflationary male ego and their common solution of selflessness, fail to redouble the oppressive irrelevance of the "world religions" for the liberation of women? Or indeed of any persons already suffering from their internalization of the role of the victim? (p. 106).

In her discussion I perceive the same sort of confusion evident in the discussion of Ogden and Cobb—that is, a confusion of the horizontal, socio-historical dimension as the "condition" with the vertical, religious dimension as the "ground." And I perceive a serious misunderstanding of the Buddhist notion of *anatta* or no-self.

1. Keller apparently regards the Buddhist notion of anatta (together with the Christian notion of self-sacrifice) as the main cause of the oppression of women and a main hindrance to the liberation of women. Of course, her discussion connects with a larger criticism of historical Buddhism (and Christianity) as reinforcing the subordination of women to men, and I do not deny this as a historical fact. In criticizing this subordination, however, Keller seems to take Buddhism (or Christianity) merely as a historical phe-nomenon in the horizontal socio-historical dimension without paying due attention to its eternal, religious aspect in the vertical dimension. Even when she mentions the Buddhist metaphysics of selflessness and relational interdependency, she apparently does not take it as the *ground* or *source* of human existence, which is essentially different from a historical event, which is the *condition* or *occasion*. Although it is an urgent task for us to eradicate the subordination of women as a possible negative effect of the Buddhist ideal of selflessness, this cannot become the *ground* or *source* of the liberation of women, for it is a historical event that is no more than the condition or occasion. In order to bring about the liberation of women in the horizontal, socio-historical dimension, we must appropriate its ground or source in the vertical, religious dimension, for the *real* ground or source of this liberation cannot be found merely within the socio-his-torical dimension. We must turn from the human-human relationship to

the divine-human relationship — that is, from the socio-historical dimension to the religious dimension.

Yet as I have emphasized repeatedly, although these two dimensions are essentially different from one another, they are, in living reality, inseparable. They are dialectically identical at their intersection, where we *are living* from moment to moment. The *real* ground of the *true* liberation of women cannot be realized merely in the secular, socio-historical dimension apart from the eternal, religious dimension, yet it can be realized there insofar as each point in the socio-historical dimension is grasped as an intersection of the two dimensions. The religious dimension as the ground is opened up only in and through a historical event as a condition. And we must go beyond the socio-historical dimension to the eternal religious dimension to find the *real* ground of liberation, for the socio-historical dimension is no more than a condition or occasion."

I do not see in Keller's discussion a clear realization of this dynamism between "that which is the condition or occasion" and "that which is the ground or source," between the socio-historical dimension and the religious dimension. Rather, I fear that these two dimensions are confused in her discussion and that everything is understood in the socio-historical dimension.

2. In order to properly understand the dialectical relationship between the horizontal, socio-historical dimension and the vertical, religious dimension, we must accurately understand the Buddhist notion of *anatta* or selflessness.

The Buddhist notion of *anatta* or "no-self" does not indicate a mere negation of the self or the absence of any self whatsoever. It is true that Buddhism negates the ego-self as the cause of human ignorance and suffering because the self-centered ego-self substantializes itself and discriminates others from itself. In order to realize equality without discrimination and the interrelatedness of all things, we must realize *anatta* by negating the ego-self. *Anatta* as a negation of the ego-self is still not free from discrimination, however, for it stands opposed to and thus discriminated from the ego-self. In order to attain true, nondiscriminative equality with others, even *anatta* must be negated. In this negation we realize true *anatta*, which is neither ego-self nor no-self and hence is both ego-self and no-self. It is the self freed from both attachment to the ego-self and attachment to nihilistic notions of no-self. This real *anatta* is the true self, which is the basis of equality and interrelatedness with others. Accordingly, in the awakening to the true self, the realization of one's own distinctiveness and the realization of the interrelatedness of all things are dynamically linked together. The dynamism at the intersection of the horizontal and vertical dimensions of human existence is realized in this awakening to the true self.

Next, concerning the "underlying metaphysical tension" between feminism and Buddhism, Keller states that she finds affinity with the Buddhist ontology, but "whereas for Buddhism this interdependency (*pratitya-samut-pada*) functions as a radically deconstructive analysis, for feminism it functions as our most radically constructive vision." In what sense does the Buddhist notion of interdependency function as a radically deconstructive analysis? Keller claims:

> Buddhism uses the analysis of interpenetration to stress the unreality of any kind of individual existent. To affirm the self, precisely as awakened to its "suchness and interpenetration," is impossible. For Buddhism this is just where we must extinguish the rhetoric of self. Is this just a semantic difference? Or is there not rather a fundamental move in Buddhism, including Abe's variety, toward the obliteration of all differentiation from the perspective of the absolute—that is, the realization of Sunyata? (p. 108).

Here again, I encounter both a confusion of the socio-historical dimension and the religious dimension, and a lack of any dialectical understanding of the two dimensions. As I stated earlier in this rejoinder, Buddhism never asserts that distinctions are unreal or delusory in the socio-historical dimension, for if they were unreal or delusory this world would be chaotic and the interdependency of everything would be inconceivable. Indeed, how would *inter*dependence be possible if everything had no *in*dependent, *distinctive* existence? Buddhism insists that we should not take this distinctiveness or differentiation of everything as something fixed, substantial, and enduring, for when we substantialize the distinctiveness of everything we create opposition and struggle—that is, human suffering.

In order to overcome suffering we must shift from the socio-historical dimension to the religious dimension in which the nonsubstantiality of everything is clearly realized. This means that "the unreality of any kind of individual existent" (Keller's words) is realized in Buddhism in the religious dimension, not in the socio-historical dimension. Further, once we awaken to the nonsubstantiality or emptiness of everything in the religious dimension, the distinctiveness and differentiation of everything in the socio-historical dimension is *regrasped* just as it is, for the religious dimension is the ground or source of the socio-historical dimension, which is the condition or occasion. The Buddhist notion of interdependency or dependent co-origination is realized on this basis as a way of emancipation from human suffering. This is my answer to Keller's question: "Is there not rather a fundamental move in Buddhism, including Abe's variety, toward the obliteration of all differentiation from the perspective of the absolute—that is, the realization of Sunyata?" (p. 108).

In her conclusion Keller mentions seven ways in which the Buddhist-Christian dialogue and my contribution to it may enhance the feminist project. Due to space restrictions, let me comment only on number five.

After emphasizing Buddhist meditative praxis as essential to enlightenment, Keller states:

> We may affirm a dynamic process of enlightening rather than a final, qualitatively removed product. Would not an evolving process of coming to wisdom and compassion, always exercising the "vow and act," best coordinate with Abe's dynamic Sunyata? (p. 113).

I agree with Keller that an evolving process of coming to wisdom and compassion coordinates with dynamic Sunyata. At the same time, however, we must realize that this evolving process is beginningless and endless, for it is always taking place in dynamic—not static—Sunyata. When *at this moment* we realize the beginninglessness and endlessness of the evolving process, the whole beginningless and endless process is concentrated *in this moment*. Otherwise stated, *this moment* embraces the whole evolving process within itself by virtue of the clear realization of the beginninglessness and endlessness of the process. This moment thus becomes a new starting point toward the endless end while it also has meaning as the end of the process stretching from the beginningless beginning to this moment.

Our Buddhist-Christian dialogue is also beginningless and endless. With a clear realization of the beginninglessness and endlessness of our dialogue we find ourselves at a new starting point for dialogue—not only at this moment, but also at each and every moment. In this way we are in an evolving process and yet always in the dynamic Sunyata-kenosis that is our home.

> Never leaving home:
>   right on the way.
> Having left home:
>   not on the way.[5]

NOTES

1. Christoper A. Ives, "A Zen Buddhist Social Ethic," unpublished, p. 258.
2. Paul Tillich, *Love, Power, and Justice* (New York: Oxford University Press, 1954), p. 67.
3. Ibid., p. 62.
4. Masao Abe, *Zen and Western Thought* (London: Macmillan, 1985), p. 183.
5. From the *Rinzai-roku (Lin-chi lu)*. This translation is taken from *A Zen Forest: Sayings of Masters*, translated with an introduction by Soika Shigematsu (New York, Tokyo: Weatherhill, 1981), p. 63.

PART IV

Masao Abe Bibliography

Masao Abe Bibliography

PUBLICATIONS IN EUROPEAN LANGUAGES

Books

Zen and Western Thought. William R. LaFleur, ed. London and New York: Macmillan; Honolulu: University of Hawaii Press, 1985 (paperback edition, 1989). Articles included in this volume are indicated below with an asterisk. This won the Book of Excellence award from the American Academy of Religion for 1987. A German translation is in preparation.

A Zen Life: D. T. Suzuki Remembered. Masao Abe, ed. Photographs by Francis Haar. Tokyo and New York: Weatherhill, 1986.

Chapters in Books

"The Idea of Purity in Mahayana Buddhism." In *Guilt or Pollution Rites of Purification.* Proceedings of the 11th international congress of the International Association for the History of Religions. Vol. 2, 1968, pp. 148–51.

"A Budhhism of Self-Awakening, not a Buddhism of Faith." In *Anjali. A Felicitation Volume Presented to Oliver Hector de Alwis Wijesekera on his Sixtieth Birthday.* J. Tilakasiri, ed. Peradeniya, Ceylon: University of Ceylon, 1970, pp. 33–39.

"The Buddhist View on Inter-Religious Dialogue." In *Report of the Consultation on Inter-Religious Dialogue with Special Reference to World Peace.* Kyoto: N.C.C. Center for the Study of Japanese Religions, 1970, pp. 32–35.

"Buddhist Nirvana: Its Significance in Contemporary Thought and Life." In *Living Faiths and Ultimate Goals.* S.J. Samartha, ed. Lausanne, Switzerland: World Council of Churches, 1974, pp. 12–22.

"Man and Nature in Christianity and Buddhism." In *Man and Nature.* George F. McLean, ed. Calcutta: Oxford University Press, 1978, pp. 165–72. And in *Person and Nature.* George F. McLean and Hugo Meynell, ed. Boston: Boston University Press of America, 1978, pp. 161–67.

"Religion and Science in the Global Age: Their Essential Character and Mutual Relationship." In *International Conference of Scientists and Religious Leaders.* Proceedings of the International Conference of Scientists and Religious Leaders on Shaping the Future of Mankind. Tokyo, 1978, pp. 24–29.

"Toward the Creative Dialogue between Zen and Christianity." In *A Zen-Christian Pilgrimage: The Fruits of Ten Annual Colloquia in Japan, 1967-1976.* Tokyo: Zen-Christian Colloquium, 1981, pp. 36–44.

204 Masao Abe Bibliography

"Zen and Nietzsche." In *Buddhist and Western Philosophy*. Nathan Katz, ed. New Delhi: Sterling Publishers, 1981, pp. 1–17.

"God, Emptiness, and the True Self." In *The Buddha Eye: An Anthology of the Kyoto School.* Frederick Franck, ed. New York: Crossroad, 1982, pp. 61–74.

"Man and Nature in Christianity and Buddhism." In *The Buddha Eye: An Anthology of the Kyoto School.* Frederick Franck, ed. New York: Crossroad, 1982, pp. 148–56.

"Emptiness is Suchness." In *The Buddha Eye: An Anthology of the Kyoto School.* Frederick Franck, ed. New York: Crossroad, 1982, pp. 203–8.

"Zen in Japan." In *Zen in China, Japan, and East Asian Arts*. H. Brinker, R. P. Kramers, and C. Ouwehand, ed. Schweizer Asiatische Studien/Etudes Asiatiques Suisses, Studienheft 8. Berne, Frankfurt am Main, and New York: Peter Lang, 1984, pp. 47–72.

"The Oneness of Practice and Attainment: Implications for the Relation between Means and Ends." In *Dogen Studies*. William R. LeFleur, ed. Honolulu: University of Hawaii Press, 1985, pp. 99–111.

"A Dynamic Unity in Religious Pluralism: A Proposal from the Buddhist Point of View." In *The Experience of Religious Diversity*. John Hick and Hasan Askari, eds. Gower, Vermont: 1985, pp. 163–90.

"The Problem of Evil in Christianity and Buddhism." In *Buddhist-Christian Dialogue, Mutual Renewal and Transformation*. Paul O. Ingram and Frederick J. Streng, eds. Honolulu: University of Hawaii Press, 1986, pp. 139–54.

"Religious Tolerance and Human Rights—A Buddhist Perspective." In *Religious Liberty and Human Rights in Nations and in Religions*. Leonard Swidler, ed. Philadelphia: Ecumenical Press, 1986, pp. 193–211.

"A Buddhist Response to Dr. Mohamed Talbi's Paper, 'Religious Liberty: A Muslim Persective.'" In *Religious Liberty and Human Rights in Nations and in Religions*. Leonard Swidler, ed. Philadelphia: Ecumenical Press, 1986, pp. 189–93.

"The Problem of Time in Heidegger and Dōgen." In *Being and Truth: Essays in Honour of John Macquarrie*. Alistair Kee and Eugene Thomas Long, eds. London: SCM Press, 1986, pp. 200–244.

"On Keiji Nishitani's *Religion and Nothingness.*" In *Encounter with Emptiness: Initial Responses to Nishitani's Religion and Nothingness*. Taitesu Unno, ed. Forthcoming, Albany: SUNY Press.

"Nishitani's Challege to Western Philosophy and Theology." In *Encounter with Emptiness: Initial Responses to Nishitani's Religion and Nothingness*. Taitesu Unno, ed. Forthcoming, Albany: SUNY Press.

"Will, Śūnyatā, and History: Nishitani's View of History and its Examination." In *Encounter with Emptiness: Initial Responses to Nishitani's Religion and Nothingness*. Taitetsu Unno, ed. Forthcoming, Albany: SUNY Press.

"Kenosis and Śūnyatā." In *Buddhist Emptiness and Christian Trinity: Essays and Explorations*. Roger Corless, ed. Forthcoming, Mahwah, N.J.: Paulist Press.

"The Self in Jung and Zen." In *Self and Liberation: A Sourcebook on Jung and Buddhism*. Robert L. Moore, ed. Forthcoming, Mahwah, N.J.: Paulist Press.

Articles

"A Living-Dying Life." *Pacific Philosophy Forum*, vol. 3, no. 4 (May 1965), pp. 9–102.

"Buddhism and Christianty as a Problem of Today," Part I. *Japanese Religions*, vol. 3, no. 2 (summer 1963), pp. 11–22; Part II, vol. 3, no. 3 (autumn 1963), pp. 8–31.

*"Review Article: Paul Tillich's Christianity and the Encounter of the World Religions." *The Eastern Buddhist*, n.s., vol. 1, n. 1 (September 1965), pp. 109–22. Reprinted in *Indian Philosophy and Culture*, vol. 19, no. 2 (June 1974), pp. 107–24.

"In Memory of Paul Tillich." *The Eastern Buddhist*, n.s., vol. 1, no. 2 (September 1966), pp. 128–31.

"Professor Abe's Reply to the Debate." *Japanese Religions*, vol. 4, no. 2 (March 1966), pp. 26–57.

"Zen and Buddhism." *Japan Studies*, no. 11, 1966, pp. 1–11.

*"The Idea of Purity in Mahayana Buddhism." *Numen*, vol. 13, fasc. 3 (October 29, 1966), pp. 183–89. Reprinted in *The Middle Way*, vol. 42, no. 4 (February 1968), pp. 158–62.

*"Zen and Compassion," *The Eastern Buddhist*, n.s., vol. 2, no. 1 (August 1967), pp. 54–68.

"Christianity and Buddhism: Centering around Science and Nihilism." *Japanese Religions*, vol. 5, no. 3 (July 1968), pp. 36–62.

" 'Life and Death' and 'Good and Evil' in Zen." *Criterion*, vol. 9, no. 1 (autumn 1969), pp. 7–11. Reprinted in *The Young Buddhist*, 1973, pp. 41–45.

"God, Emptiness, and the True Self." *The Eastern Buddhist*, n.s., vol. 2, no. 2 (November 1969), pp. 15–30. Reprinted in *The Buddha Eye*, Frederick Franck, ed., 1982.

*"Zen and Western Thought."*International Philosophical Quarterly*, vol. 10, no. 4 (December 1970), pp, 501–41.

"Man and Nature in Christianity and Buddhism." *Japanese Religions*, vol. 7, no, 1 (July 1971), pp. 1–10. Reprinted in *The Young Buddhist*, 1972, pp. 37–40; *Man and Nature*, George F. McLean, ed., 1978; and *The Buddha Eye*, Frederick Franck, ed., 1982.

*"Dōgen on Buddha Nature." *The Eastern Buddhist*, n.s, vol. 4, no. 1 (May 1971), pp. 28–71.

*"Zen and Nietzsche." *The Eastern Buddhist*, n.s., vol. 6, no. 2 (October 1973), pp. 14–32. Reprinted in *Buddhist and Western Philosophy*, Nathan Katz, ed., 1981.

*"Buddhist *Nirvana:* Its Significance in Contemporary Thought and Life." *The Ecumenical Review*, vol. 25, no. 2 (April 1973), pp. 158–68. Reprinted in *Dialogue*, no. 20–21 (June 1970), pp. 8–10.

*"Religion Challenged by Modern Thought." *Japanese Religions*, vol. 8, no. 2 (November 1974), pp. 2–14.

*"Zen as Self-Awakening." *Japanese Religions*, vol. 8, no. 3 (April 1975), pp. 25–45. Reprinted in *The Young Buddhist*, no. 30 (1980), pp. 99–105.

*"Non-Being and *Mu:* The Metaphysical Nature of Negativity in the East and in the West." *Religious Studies*, vol. 11, no. 2 (June 1975), pp. 181–92.

*"Mahayana Buddhism and Whitehead: A View by a Lay Student of Whitehead's Philosophy," *Philosophy East and West*, vol. 25, no. 4 (October 1975), pp. 415–28.

"The Crucial Points: An Introduction to the Symposium on Christianity and Buddhism." *Japanese Religions*, vol. 8, no. 4 (October 1975), pp. 2–9.

"Zen and Buddhism." *Journal of Chinese Philosophy*, vol. 3, no. 3 (June 1976), pp. 64–70.

"Education in Zen." *The Eastern Buddhist,* n.s., vol. 9, no. 2 (October 1976), pp. 235–52.

*"Zen is not a Philosophy, but. . . ." *Theologische Zeitschrift,* Jahrgang 33, Heft 5 (September/October 1977), pp. 251–68.

"Le Zen n'est pas une philosophie, mais. . . ." *La Falaise Verte,* n.s., no. 5 (1979), pp. 25–29 [translator unknown].

*"Emptiness is Suchness." *The Eastern Buddhist,* n.s., vol. 10, no. 2 (October 1973), pp. 132–36. Reprinted in *The Young Buddhist,* 1979, pp. 35–37.

"The End of World Religion." *The Eastern Buddhist,* n.s., vol. 13, no. 1 (spring 1980), pp. 31–45. Reprinted in *World Faiths Insight,* n.s., vol. 8, pp. 1–34.

"Substance, Process, and Emptiness." *Japanese Religions,* vol. 11, nos. 2 and 3 (September 1980), pp. 1–34.

"Buddhism is not Monistic, but Non-dualistic." *Scottish Journal of Religious Studies,* vol. 1, no. 2 (fall 1980), pp. 97–100. Reprinted in *The Young Buddhist,* 1981, pp. 87–88.

*"Sovereignty Rests with Mankind." *World Faiths Insight,* vol. 1 (autumn 1980), pp. 31–36.

"Hisamatsu's Philosophy of Awakening." *The Eastern Buddhist,* n.s., vol. 14, no. 1 (spring 1981), pp. 26–42.

"Hisamatsu Shin'ichi, 1889–1980." *The Eastern Buddhist,* n.s., vol. 14, no. 1 (spring 1981), pp. 142–49.

"Buddhist-Christian Dialogue: Past, Present, and Future." Masao Abe and John Cobb with Bruce Long. *Buddhist-Christian Studies,* vol. 1 (1981), pp. 13–29.

"Comments on 'Christian and Buddhist Personal Transformation.' " *Buddhist-Christian Studies,* vol. 2 (1982), pp. 45–49.

"God, Emptiness, and Ethics." *Buddhist-Christian Studies,* vol. 3 (1983), pp. 53–60.

"A History of the FAS Zen Society." *FAS Newsletter* (autumn 1984), pp. 1–12.

"The Self in Jung and Zen." *The Eastern Buddhist,* n.s., vol. 18, no. 1 (spring 1985), pp. 57–70.

"John Cobb's *Beyond Dialogue.*" *The Eastern Buddhist,* n.s., vol. 18, no. 1 (spring 1985), pp. 131–37.

"Responses to Langdon Gilkey." *Buddhist-Christian Studies,* vol. 4 (1985), pp. 67–92.

"The Japanese View of Truth." *Japanese Religions,* vol. 14 no. 3 (December 1986), pp. 1–6.

"The Problem of Death in East and West—Immortality, Eternal life, and Unbornness." *The Eastern Buddhist,* n.s., vol. 19, no. 2 (autumn 1986), pp. 30–61.

"Shin'ichi Hisamatsu's Notion of FAS." *FAS Society Journal* (winter 1986–87), pp. 21–23.

"Shinto and Buddhism: The Two Major Religions in Japan." *The Scottish Journal of Religious Studies,* vol. 8, no. 1 (spring 1987), pp. 53–63.

"Philosophy, Religion, and Aesthetics in Nishida and Whitehead." *The Eastern Buddhist,* n.s., vol. 20, no. 2 (autumn 1987), pp. 53–62.

"Transformation in Buddhism." *Buddhist-Christian Studies,* vol. 7 (1987), pp. 5–24.

"Umgestaltung im Verständnis des Buddhismus im Vergleich mit platonischen und christlichen Auffassungen." *Concilium,* 24, Jahrgang, Heft 2 (April 1988), pp. 110–22.

"Nishida's Philosophy of 'Place.' " *International Philosophical Quarterly*, vol. 28 (December 1988), pp. 355–71. Appended: "Kitaro Nishida Bibliography" compiled by Masao Abe and Lydia Brüll.

"The Problem of Self-Centeredness as the Root-source of Human Suffering." To be published in *Japanese Religions*, vol. 15, no. 4 (1989).

"There is No Common Denominator for World Religions—The Positive Meaning of this Negative Statement." To be published by *The Journal of Ecumenical Studies* (winter 1989).

Unpublished Papers

"The Core of Zen—The Ordinary Mind is Tao." 1985.

"Religion and Social Transformation in Contemporary Japanese Zen Buddhism: Shin'ichi Hisamatu's Notion of FAS." 1985.

"The Buddhist View of Human Salvation: With Special Reference to Shin'ichi Hisamatu's Notion of FAS." 1985.

"Buddhist-Christian Dialogue: Its Significance and Future Task." 1986.

"The Philosophy of Absolute Nothingness: A Modern Japanese Philosophy of Religion." 1986.

"A Buddhist View of Monotheism: Monotheistic Oneness and Nondualistic Oneness." 1986.

"Thomas J. J. Altizer's Kenotic Christology and Buddhism." 1987.

"God and Absolute Nothingness." 1987.

"A Response to Professor Langdon Gilkey's Paper, 'Tillich and the Kyoto School,' " 1987.

"The Impact of Dialogue with Christianity on My Self-Understanding as a Buddhist." 1987.

"A Buddhist View of Paul Tillich's 'The Significance of the History of Religions for the Systematic Theologian.' " 1988.

Miscellaneous

"Conversation between Professor Masao Abe and Don Aelred Graham in Kyoto, August 26, 1967." In Don A. Graham, *Conversations*, "Geleitwort" in *Sonne, Wolken, Staatsvisite* by Werner Utter. Tübingen and Basel: Horst Erdmann Verlag, 1969.

"As Zen Comes to the West." In *Blind Donkey*, vol. 8, no. 1 (1983), pp. 15–20.

"Shintō and Buddhism in Japan." In *The Hawaii Herald*, vol. 5, no. 23 (December 1, 1984), p. 14; vol. 5, no. 24 (December 14, 1984), p. 14; and vol. 6, no. 1 (January 1, 1985), p. 30.

"An Interview with Masao Abe." In *FAS Society Journal*, winter 1985–86, pp. 6–13.

PUBLICATIONS IN JAPANESE: A SELECTED LIST
(TITLES GIVEN IN ENGLISH)

Chapters in Books

"Buddhism and Marxism." In *Gendai Shūkyō Kōza* (Lectures on modern religions), vol. 2, 1954, pp. 155–78.

"Nenbutsu and Zen." In *Shinran Zenshū* (A collection of studies on Shinran). Ko Yaekashi, ed. Vol. 7, 1959, pp. 182–95.

"Buddhist Faith and Human Reason." In *Bukkyō ni okeru Shin no Mondai* (The problem of faith in Buddhism). The Nippon Buddhist Research Association, ed. 1963, pp. 21–45.

"The Unborn and the Rebirth in Pure Land." In *Zen no Honshitsu to Ningen no Shinri* (The essence of Zen and the truth of man). Shin'ichi Hisamatsu and Keiji Nishitani, eds. 1969, pp. 643–93.

"D. T. Suzuki's Influence on the West." In *Suzuki Daisetsu—Hito to Shisō* (Suzuki Daisetz—man and thought). Shin'ichi Hisamatsu, Susumu Yamaguchi, and Shōkin Furuta, ed. 1971 pp. 3–9.

"Personality—A Dialogue with Christianity." In *Shūkyō no Taiwa* (Dialogue of religions). Kakichi Kadowaki and Hideharu Inoue, eds. 1973, pp. 119–37.

"Non-Buddha, Non-Devil." In *Bukkyō no Hikakushisōronteki-Kenkyū* (A study of Buddhism from the viewpoint of contemporary philosophy). Kōshirō Tamaki, ed. 1979, pp. 635–711.

"Dōgen on Time and Space." In *Kōza Dōgen* (Lectures on Dōgen). Genryū Kagamishima and Kōshirō Tamaki, ed. Vol. 4 (1980), pp. 164–90.

"What is Comparative Philosophy?—From the Existential Point of View." In *Hikakushisō no Susume* (Toward a comparative philosophy). Hideo Iineshima et al., eds. 1979, pp. 122–77.

"The Philosphy of Self-Awakening in Shin'ichi Hisamatsu." In *Hisamatsu Shin'ichi no Shūkyō to Shisō* (The religion and thought of Hisamatsu Shin'ichi). Jikai Fujiyoshi, ed. 1983, pp. 77–102.

"Introduction to 'Religious Experience and Language' " and "Comment on Professor Kadowaki's Presentation." In *Religious Experience and Language. A Dialogue between Buddhism and Christianity*. Nanzan Institute for Religion and Culture, ed. Tokyo: Kinokuniya, 1983, pp. 9–14, 230–38.

"A Stone Sheds Light of Breaking Heaven." In *Shinnin Hisamatsu Shin'ichi* (True man, Hisamatsu Shin'ichi). Jikai Fujiyoshi, ed. 1985, pp. 170–78.

Articles

" 'Kritik' and 'Metaphysik' in Kant." *Shūkyō kenkyū* (Journal of religious studies), vol. 32, no. 2 (December 1958), pp. 44–62.

"The Ultimate Task of Kant's Critique of Pure Reason." *Tetsugaku kenkyū* (Journal of philosophical studies), vol. 39, no. 12 (December 1958), pp. 31–53; vol. 40, no. 6 (October 1959), pp. 28–49; vol. 40, no. 7 (November 1959), pp. 60–81.

"The Fundamental Standpoint of Kant's Practical Philosophy." *Nara Gakugei Daigaku Kiyō* (The journal of Nara Gakugei University), vol. 4, no. 3 (March 1955), pp. 1–16.

"How are Practical Synthetic a priori Judgements Possible?" *Nara Gakugei Daigaku Kiyō* (The journal of Nara Gakugei University), vol. 8, no. 1 (February 1959), pp. 29–36.

"Marx and Shinran." *Toho* (The east), no. 10 (June 1949), pp. 18–29.

"Karl Marx's View of History." *Nara Gakugei Daigaku Kiyō* (The journal of Nara Gakugei University), vol. 10, n. 2 (November 1962), pp. 18–29.

"Immortality. Eternal Life, and the Unborn—The Issue of Death in the East and the West." *Zengaku kenkyū* (Studies in Zen Buddhism), vol. 51 (February 1961), pp. 88–112.

"Realization of Death in Dōgen and Shinran." *Risō* (Ideal), no. 366 (November 1963), pp. 75–87.

"Original Sin and History in Kierkegaard." *Shūkyō kenkyū* (Journal of religious studies), vol. 36, no. 4 (March 1965), pp. 1–24.

"Falsehood and the Devil—On the Problem of Religion and Nihilism." *Risō* (Ideal), no. 443 (April 1970), pp. 29–40.

"Zen and Nationalism." *Risō* (Ideal), no. 501 (February 1975), pp. 18–28.

"On the Establishment of a Self-Awakened Cosmology," *Postmodernist*, no. 4/5 (October 1976), pp. 29–58.

"Creation and Dependent-origination." *Risō* (Ideal), no. 531 (August 1977), pp. 151–68; no. 533 (October 1977), pp. 171–95.

"The Notion of 'Place' in Nihida's Philosophy." *Risō* (Ideal), no. 537 (February 1978), pp. 119–38.

"The Problem of 'Inverse Correspondence' in Nishida's Philosphy—For its Critical Understanding." *Risō* (Ideal), no. 562 (March 1980), pp. 109–26; no. 565 (June 1980), pp. 108–22.

"Inverse Correspondence in Nishida's Philosophy—Around its Formation." *Daijōzen*, n. 694 (April 1981), pp. 3–18.

"Buddhism and Pure Reason." *Risō* (Ideal), no. 583 (December 1981), pp. 65–83; no. 584 (January 1982), pp. 111–27.

"To Awaken to the Formless Self." *Buddhist*, no. 32 (1988), pp. 16–29.

"God and Absolute Nothingness—A Point of Contact between Christianity and Buddhism." *Deai* (Encounter), vol. 9, no. 4 (1988), pp. 1–20.

Contributions to Dictionaries

"Space," "Time," and "Nothingness." *Shūkyōgaku-jiten* (Dictionary of religious studies). Iichi Oguchi and Ichirō Hori, ed. Tokyo University Press, 1973.

"Dōgen." *The Encyclopedia of Religion*. Mircea Eliade, ed. New York: Macmillan, vol. 4 (1986), pp. 388–89.

WORKS TRANSLATED FROM JAPANESE INTO ENGLISH

Nichida Kitarō. "The Problem of Japanese Culture" (excerpts; joint translation with Richard DeMartino). In *Sources of Japanese Tradition*. (New York: Columbia University Press, 1958, pp. 857–72. Paperback edition, vol. 2 (1958), pp. 35–65.

Hisamatsu Shin'ichi. "The Characteristics of Oriental Nothingness" (joint translation with Richard DeMartino). In *Philosophical Studies of Japan*, vol. 2 (1960), p. 65-97.

Dōgen's *Bendōwa*. In *The Eastern Buddhist*, n.s., vol. 4, no. 1 (May 1971), pp. 124–57.

Dōgen's *Shōbōgenzō Ikkamyōju*. In *The Eastern Buddhist*, n.s., vol. 4, no. 2 (October 1971), pp. 108–18.

Dōgen's *Shōbōgenzō Zenki* and *Shoji*. In *The Eastern Buddhist*, n.s., vol. 5, no. 1 (May 1972), pp. 70–80.

Dōgen's *Shōbōgenzō Genjōkōan*. In *The Eastern Buddhist*, n.s., vol. 5, no. 2 (October 1972) pp. 129–40.

Dōgen's *Shōbōgenzō Zazengi* and *Furkanzazengi*. In *The Eastern Buddhist*, n.s., vol. 6, no. 2 (October 1973), pp. 115–28.

Dōgen's *Shōbōgenzō Sammai-ō-Zammai*. In *The Eastern Buddhist*, n.s., vol. 7, no. 1 (May 1974), pp. 116–23.

Dōgens *Shōbōgenzō Buddha-nature*, part I. In *The Eastern Buddhist*, n.s., vol. 8, no. 2 (October 1975), pp. 94–112; part II, vol. 9, no. 1 (May 1976), pp. 87–105; part III, vol. 9, no. 2 (October 1976), pp. 71–87.

(All translations of Dōgen's Shōbōgenzō were done with Norman Waddell)

An Inquiry into the Good. A joint translation with Christopher A. Ives of Kitarō Nishida's *Zen no kenkyū*, including an introduction by Masao Abe. New Haven: Yale University Press, 1990.

BOOK-LENGTH MANUSCRIPTS IN THE FINAL STAGES OF PREPARATION

Searching for Common Ground: Buddhism and Christianity Challenged by Irreligion. A collection of the following papers: (1) the basic article, Masao Abe, "Buddhism and Christianity as a Problem of Today," from *Japanese Religions*, vol. 3, nos, 2 and 3; (2) comments and criticisms on this article by Paul Wienpahl, Charles Hartshorne, Winston King, Neles Ferre, I. T. Ramsey, Hans Waldenfels, and others, in *Japanese Religions*, vol. 4, nos. 2 and 3; (3) Abe's rejoinder, including his papers, "Christianity and Buddhism: Centering around Science and Nihilism," and "Man and Nature in Christianity and Buddhism" in *Japanese Religions*, vol. 3, no. 3; vol. 5, no. 3; vol. 7, no. 1; (4) further comments and criticisms by Ernst Benz, Paul Wienpahl, Winston King, Thomas J. J. Altizer, Fritz Buri, Horst Burkle, and Hans Waldenfels; (5) Abe's second rejoinder. Hakan Eilert and Roald E. Kristiansen, ed. Forthcoming, Albany: SUNY Press.

Zen as the Religion of Self-Awakening. A revised and enlarged manuscript of a series of six lectures on Zen Buddhism delivered at the Divinity School of the University of Chicago for the spring quarter, 1969.

Dōgen, A Realizer of the Dharma. A collection of joint translations with Norman Waddell of the major *Shōbōgenzō* chapters published in *The Eastern Buddhist*.

A Study of Dōgen: His Philosophy and Religion. A collection of papers on Dōgen, including "The Oneness of Practice and Attainment," "Dōgen on Buddha Nature," "Dōgen's View of Space and Time," "The Problem of Time in Heidegger and Dōgen," "The Problem of Death in Dōgen and Shinran," and "Dōgen's View of Ethics." Steven Heine, ed. Forthcoming, Albany: SUNY Press.

Index of Names

Augustine, Saint, 14, 74, 119, 123, 137-38
Baeck, Leon, 80, 82-83
Barth, Karl, 13, 19-20, 54, 143-44, 148, 151
Bernard of Clairvaux, Saint, 145-7
Blake, William, 77
Böhme, Jakob, 24, 120, 162
Bradley, F.H., 84
Buber, Martin, 80
Bultmann, Rudolf, 54
Burrell, David, 137
Colledge, 147
Copleston, Frederick, 137
Cusanus, 141, 144
Cyril of Jerusalem, Saint, 19
Dante, Alighieri, 71, 74
Deleuze, 142
Derrida, Jacques, 142
Descartes, René, 81, 138
Dilworth, David A., 69
Dodd, C.H., 192
Dogen, 35
Dostoevsky, Feodor, 77, 143
Eckhart, Meister, 24, 73, 120, 136-37, 141-44, 146-49, 150-54, 162, 164, 166-69
Eriugena, John Scotus, 141, 144, 146
Ezekiel, 81-82, 87
Fabro, Cornelio, 137
Fackenheim, Emil, 53-55, 80-81, 83-84, 123, 184, 186
Frei, Hans, 143
Gilson, Etienne, 137
Greenberg, Irving, 52-53
Gregory of Nyssa, Saint, 145
Gutiérrez, Gustavo, 138
Hartshorne, Charles, 130, 137, 139
Hauerwas, Stanley, 143

Hegel, Georg, 22, 34-35, 69, 73-75, 77, 100, 140, 144, 146, 150
Heidegger, Martin, 7, 27, 54, 144, 146-47
Herman, N., 118
Himmelfarb, Milton, 89
Irenaeus, Saint, 145
Joachim of Flora, 74
John the Evangelist, Saint, 9-10, 101, 119, 121, 145-46, 153
John of the Cross, Saint, 145, 147, 153-54
Jüngel, Eberhard, 153-54
Kant, Immanuel, 34-37, 57, 100, 117
Kierkegaard, Søren, 73, 77,- 123, 137, 143
Kuhn, Thomas S., 4
Küng, Hans, 4-6, 14, 25-26, 120
Kushner, Harold, 85
Lin-chi I-Hsuan, 41-42, 56
Lindbeck, George, 143
Longeran, Bernard, 138
Luke, Saint, 121, 145, 175
Luria, Isaac, 87
Luther, Martin, 13, 30-31, 74, 123, 143, 153-54
McGinn, Bernard, 147-48
MacQuarrie, John, 140, 150
Maggid of Mezerith, 87
Marechal, Joseph, 138
Maritain, Jacques, 137
Martin, Marianne M., 116
Mark, Saint, 145
Matthew, Saint, 145
Merton, Thomas, 143, 150
Metz, Johann, 138
Nagarjuna, 27, 111, 142, 147
Niebuhr, Reinhold, 133
Nietzsche, Friedrich, 3-4, 16-17, 27, 31,